FOOD LAW:
POLICY & ETHICS

Cavendish
Publishing
Limited

London • Sydney

FOOD LAW:
POLICY & ETHICS

Dominique Lauterburg, BA, LLB, LLM
Senior Lecturer in Law, LLB Programme Leader
University of Sunderland

Cavendish
Publishing
Limited

London • Sydney

First published in Great Britain 2001 by Cavendish Publishing Limited, The Glass House, Wharton Street, London WC1X 9PX, United Kingdom

Telephone: + 44 (0)20 7278 8000   Facsimile:+ 44 (0)20 7278 8080

Email: info@cavendishpublishing.com

Website: www.cavendishpublishing.com

British Library Cataloguing in Publication Data

Lauterburg, Dominique
Food law: policy & ethics
1 Food law and legislation – Great Britain
I Title
344.4'1'04232

1 85941 524 5

Printed and bound in Great Britain

This book is dedicated to the following people with heartfelt thanks for their help, support and encouragement:

Robert

My parents, Kim and Gwyn Lauterburg

Mark and Clare

Gotte Lisgi

Ted Roose

Fred

PREFACE

The aim of this book is to provide an overview of the different areas of law relating to food. In the first three chapters I examine the international, European and UK contexts of the law relating to food. In later chapters, specific areas of food law are examined, covering many of the most topical and challenging issues of the present time. The book is not intended to be a practitioner text, nor is it intended in any way to be a definitive text on all the law relating to food. My intention has been to draw the attention of readers to the main areas of law governing the food we eat. Consumers are becoming increasingly concerned about the safety of the food they consume and are demanding more detailed information about exactly what is in the food we eat. I have also tried to highlight some of the moral and ethical concerns that arise in the context of food production and distribution. In an age where there is an excess of food in some developed nations, but where nearly 800 million people in the developing world do not have enough to eat, there are serious issues not only about the safety of food, but also about its availability.

I should like to express my thanks to Rhona Rowland, Lorraine Barton and Lyndsey Thomas for their hard work, efficiency and initiative in helping me to gather materials for this book.

I should also like to thank John Bowis MEP for taking the time to meet me in Brussels to discuss the proposals for the new European Food Safety Authority.

Finally, I am very grateful to my colleagues at the University of Sunderland for their encouragement and enthusiasm for my research.

Dominique Lauterburg
June 2001

CONTENTS

TABLE OF CASES

TABLE OF STATUTES

TABLE OF STATUTORY INSTRUMENTS

TABLE OF ABBREVIATIONS

ACAF	Advisory Committee on Animal Feeding Stuffs
ACMSF	Advisory Committee on the Microbiological Safety of Food
ACMSF	Advisory Committee on the Microbiological Safety of Food
ACNFP	Advisory Committee on Novel Foods and Processes
ADI	Acceptable daily intake
AIA	Advanced information agreement
APA	Association of Public Analysts
APEC	Asia Pacific Economic Co-operation (agreement between 18 countries in Asia and the Pacific
ASNFP	Advisory Committee on Novel Foods and Processes
BAB	Born after the ban
BSE	Bovine Spongiform encephalopathy
BST	Bovine Somtatotrophin
CAC	Codex Alimentarius Commission
CBD	Convention on Biological Diversity
CCFL	Codex Committee on Food Labelling
CCGP	Codex Committee on General Principles
CCMAS	Codex Committee on Method of Analysis and Sampling
CEN	European Committee for Standardisation
CFI	Court of First Instance
CJD	Creutzfeldt-Jacob disease
CMO	Chief Medical Officer
CoC	Committee on Carcinogenicity in Food, Consumer Products and the Environment
CoM	Committee on Mutagenicity of Chemicals in Food, Consumer Products and the Environment
COREPER	Committee of Permanent Representatives
COT	Committee on Toxity of Chemicals in Food, Consumer Products and the Environment
CPHL	Central Public Health Laboratory
CSC	Certificate of specific character
CSL	Central Science Laboratory
CVL	Central Veterinary Laboratory
CVO	Chief Veterinary Officer

DETR	Department of the Environment, Transport and the Regions
DG	Directorate General
DoH	Department of Health
DSU	Dispute Settlement Understanding
EAEC	European Atomic Energy Community (Euratom)
ECSC	European Coal and Steel Community
EFA	European Food Authority
EFSA	European Food Safety Authority
EHOs	Environmental health officers
EP	European Parliament
ESC	Economic and Social Commission (European)
EUFA	European Food Authority
EVM	Expert Group on Vitamins and Minerals
FAC	Food Advisory Committee
FAO	Food and Agriculture Organisation
FAO	Food and Agriculture Organisation
FAPAS	Food Analysis Performance Assessment Scheme
FSA	Food Standards Agency
FSE	Feline Spongiform encephalopathy
GATS	General Agreement on Trade in Services
GATT	General Agreement on Trade and Tariffs
GM	Genetically modified (foods)
GMOs	Genetically modified organisms
HACCP	Hazard Analysis Critical Point Control
HSE	Health and Safety Executive
HVP	Hydrolysed vegetable protein
IAEA	International Atomic Energy Agency
IBEA	Intervention Board Executive Agency
IFST	Institute of Food and Science Technology
IPCC	Intergovernmental Panel on Climate Change

JCAMS	Joint Sub-committee on Antimicrobial Substances
JECFA	Joint Expert Committee on Food Additives
JFSSG	Joint Food Safety and Standards Group
LACOTS	Local Authorities Co-ordinating Body on Food and Trading Standards
LMOs	Living modified organisms
MAFF	Ministry of Agriculture, Fisheries and Food
MBM	Meat and bone meal
MERCOSUR	Treaty of Asunción (Argentina, Brazil, Paraguay, Uruguay)
MHIs	Meat hygiene inspectors
MHS	Meat Hygiene Service
MRLs	Maximum residue levels
MTs	Meat technicians
NAFTA	North American Free Trade Agreement (Canada, US, Mexico)
NATO	North Atlantic Treaty Organisation
OA	Ochnadioxin
OECD	Organisation for Economic Co-operation and Development
OEEC	Organisation for European Economic Co-operation
OTMS	Over Thirty Months Slaughter scheme
OVS	Official Veterinary Surgeon
PARNUTS	Foods for particular nutritional purposes
PCBs	Polychlorinatedbiphenyls
PDO	Protected designations of origin
PGI	Protected geographical indicators
PHLS	Public Health Laboratory Service
PIAS	Poultry inspection assistants
QUID	Quantitative ingredient declarations
RCF	Regenerated cellulose film
RDA	Recommended daily allowance
RSU	Radiological Safety Unit

SBO	Specified bovine offals
SBS	Sanitary and Phytosanitary Agreement
SCAHAW	Scientific Committee on Animal Health and Animal Welfare
SCF	Scientific Committee on Food
SCF	Standing Committee on Foodstuffs
SCVPH	Scientific Committee of Veterinary Measures Relating to Public Health
SEA	Single European Act
SEAC	Spongiform Encephalopathy Advisory Committee
SMEs	Small and medium enterprises
SOFI	*State of Food Insecurity in the World*
SPS	Sanitary and phytosanitary
SRM	Specified risk material
SVS	State Veterinary Service
TBT	Technical barriers to trade
TBT	Technical Barriers to Trade Agreement
TEU	Treaty on European Union
TRIPS	Trade Related Aspects of Intellectual Property
TSOs	Trading standards officers
UKROFS	United Kingdom Register of Organic Food Standards
vCJD	Variant of CJD
VCM	Vinyl chloride monomer
VFS	Veterinary Field Service
VMD	Veterinary Medicines Directorate
VPC	Veterinary Products Committee
WHO	World Health Organisation
WTO	World Trade Organisation

CHAPTER 1

THE INTERNATIONAL CONTEXT

There are a number of major international organisations which are involved in various aspects of food production and distribution. The World Trade Organisation (WTO) is the body which regulates international trade. Two of the United Nations bodies are also concerned with food issues, namely, the Food and Agriculture Organisation (FAO) and the World Health Organisation (WHO). These two bodies provide the secretariat for the Codex Alimentarius Commission (CAC), which is an intergovernmental body with 165 member countries. It protects consumer health, ensures fair practices in food trade and promotes the co-ordination of food standards. The Organisation for Economic Co-operation and Development (OECD) is also an important player on the international scene as far as food is concerned, and is particularly active in the field of biotechnology and food.

WORLD TRADE ORGANISATION

The WTO is an intergovernmental organisation and is the only international organisation overseeing the rules of international trade between nations. Its overriding objective is to help trade flow as freely as possible in a system based on specific rules. It achieves this through administering trade agreements, reviewing national trade policies, organising trade negotiations, co-operating with other international organisations and, importantly, settling trade disputes between governments. It also assists developing countries in trade policy matters.

The WTO was established in 1995 at the Uruguay round of the General Agreement on Tariffs and Trade (GATT), which preceded it. This began in September 1986, in Uruguay, and concluded in April 1994, in Marrakesh. The 'Final Act'[1] is 550 pages long and contains the texts of the agreements entered into, and also the texts of ministerial declarations; these further clarify certain provisions of some of the agreements, which are lengthy and complex because they are legal documents.

The creation of the WTO marked the most significant reform of international trade since the end of the Second World War. The GATT was established in 1947 and was, in fact, two separate things. It was an international organisation and also an international agreement setting out the

---

1   Final Act Embodying the Results of the Uruguay Round of Multilateral Trade Negotiations, 1994.

rules for international trade. It had developed from a failed attempt to establish an International Trade Organisation in 1948. The GATT established a strong, prosperous, multilateral trading system, through a series of trade negotiation rounds. It had provided the rules for much of world trade, but it had always been intended as an *ad hoc*, provisional measure. By the 1980s, however, there was a need for a reorganisation and refocusing of the whole system.

The WTO is based on the fundamental principle of non-discrimination. This means that a country should not discriminate between its trading partners, who are all granted 'most favoured nation' status, and it should not discriminate between its own and foreign products, services or nationals, all of which should be given 'national treatment'. It is also based on the fundamental principle that the trading system should be free, predictable, more competitive and more beneficial for less developed nations.

'Most favoured nation' status sounds like a contradiction. It seems to indicate that one country is treated more favourably than others, but under the WTO it actually means that virtually all countries are treated equally. All members of the WTO treat all other members as 'most favoured' trading partners. It is such an important principle that it is the first article of the General Agreement on Tariffs and Trade, which governs trade in goods. It is also a priority in the General Agreement on Trade in Services (GATS) (Art 2) and in the Agreement on Trade Related Aspects of Intellectual Property (TRIPS) (Art 4), although the principle is handled slightly differently in each agreement and there are certain exceptions to this principle.

The WTO has 130 members, accounting for more than 90% of world trade. Decisions are made by the entire membership, usually by consensus. There is provision for majority voting, but this has never been used in the WTO and was rarely used in the GATT. The rules have to be ratified by the parliaments of all the Member States.

The top level decision making body is the Ministerial Council, which meets at least once every two years. Below that is the General Council, which usually comprises ambassadors or heads of delegations in Geneva, but sometimes representatives are sent from Member States. This body meets several times a year. It also meets as the Trade Policy Review Body and as the Dispute Settlement Body. Below the General Council are the three other specific councils (goods, services and intellectual property) as well as working groups and specialised committees.

At the heart of the WTO are the agreements negotiated and signed by most of the trading nations of the world. They are essentially contracts which bind governments and ensure that their trade policies are kept within agreed limits. They form the legal basis for international commerce.

The main legal document is the Final Act Embodying the Results of the Uruguay Round of Multilateral Trade Negotiations. Its main text is the Marrakesh Agreement Establishing the World Trade Organisation, together with its annexes.

Annex 1 contains the agreements for the three main areas dealt with by the WTO, namely, goods, services and intellectual property. The GATT is the umbrella agreement relating to trade in goods. It has annexes which deal with specific sectors such as agriculture; the GATS deals with services such as banking and insurance; and the TRIPS contains rules regarding trade and investments, ideas and inventions. Annex 2 contains the Understanding on Rules and Procedures Governing the Settlement of Disputes.

Annex 3 contains the Trade Policy Review mechanism and Annex 4 contains plurilateral agreements – agreements signed by a number of States, but not all, together with ministerial decisions and declarations and individual countries' commitments.

With regard to food, the relevant agreements which are of most relevance are the Agreement on Agriculture, the Agreement on Trade Related Aspects of Intellectual Property, the Agreement on Sanitary and Phytosanitary Measures (the SPS Agreement) and the Agreement on Technical Barriers to Trade (the TBT Agreement).

Under the Agriculture Agreement, WTO members have to reduce their subsidised exports. Some countries, however, have been very dependent on cheap, subsidised food imported from the major industrialised nations. These include some of the poorest and least developed countries and, although their farming sectors might well benefit from higher prices for farm products, they might need temporary assistance to make the necessary adjustments to cope with higher priced imports and eventually to export their products. A special ministerial decision[2] lays down objectives and certain measures for the provision of food aid, the provision of basic foodstuffs in full grant form, and aid for agricultural development. It also refers to the possibility of assistance from the International Monetary Fund and the World Bank to finance commercial food imports.

The two agreements which are of most importance with regard to food are the SPS and the TBT Agreements.

Both these agreements have had a considerable impact on EC food law. The purpose of these agreements is to avoid any unjustified barriers to trade which might flow from technical legislation intended to provide protection to the consumer or to public health.

---

2   Decision on Measures Concerning the Possible Negative Effects of the Reform Programme on Least Developed and Net Food-Importing Developing Countries, 1994.

As the EC is a party to these agreements, they are binding within the EC and in the individual Member States.

This raises the question, of course, as to what constitute 'unjustified' barriers to trade. This is at the heart of the debate about free trade and free movement of goods versus the protection of the environment, human and animal health and protection of the consumer.

Sanitary and Phytosanitary (SPS) Agreement

This agreement concerns the application of sanitary and phytosanitary measures. It covers food safety and animal and plant health standards. The agreement recognises that national governments have the right to introduce sanitary and phytosanitary measures, but that they should be applied only to the extent necessary to protect human, animal or plant life or health and should not arbitrarily or unjustifiably discriminate between members where identical or similar conditions apply.

In order to harmonise sanitary and phytosanitary measures, members are encouraged to apply international standards, guidelines and recommendations where they exist, although they are allowed to introduce higher standards if there is scientific justification or as a consequence of consistent risk decisions based on an appropriate risk assessment.

The agreement includes provisions on control, inspections and approval procedures. Governments must provide advance notice of new or revised sanitary or phytosanitary measures and establish a national inquiry point to provide information. The agreement complements the TBT Agreement.

Annex A to the Agreement include the following definitions. 'Sanitary or phytosanitary measures' are defined as:

> Any measure applied ... to protect human or animal life or health within the territory of the Member from risks arising from additives, contaminants, toxins or disease-causing organisms in food, beverages or feedstuffs ... Sanitary or phytosanitary measures include all relevant laws, decrees, regulations, requirements and procedures including, *inter alia*, end product criteria; processes and production methods; testing, inspection, certification and approval procedures; quarantine treatments including relevant requirements associated with the transport of animals or plants, or with the materials necessary for their survival during transport; provisions on relevant statistical methods, sampling procedures and methods of risk assessment; and packaging and labelling requirements directly related to food safety.

'International standards or phytosanitary measures' are:

> Food for safety, the standards, guidelines and recommendations established by the Codex Alimentarius Commission relating to food additives, veterinary drug and pesticide residues, contaminants, methods of analysis and sampling, and codes and guidelines of hygienic practice.

The SPS Agreement applies to all sanitary and phytosanitary measures 'which could directly or indirectly affect international trade'.

Member countries are encouraged to use international standards, guidelines and recommendations where they exist. They can introduce measures which result in higher standards if there is scientific justification, or on the appropriate assessment of risk, as long as the standard is consistent and not arbitrary.

If an exporting country can demonstrate that the measures it applies on its exports achieve the same level of health protection as in the importing country, the importing country is expected to accept the exporting country's standards and methods.

Some of the provisions of the SPS are quoted below.

Article 2 – Basic Rights and Obligations

2.1 Members have the right to take sanitary and phytosanitary measures necessary for the protection of human, animal or plant life or health, provided that such measures are not inconsistent with the provisions of this Agreement.

2.2 Members shall ensure that any sanitary or phytosanitary measure is applied only to the extent necessary to protect human, animal or plant life or health, is based on scientific principles and is not maintained without sufficient scientific evidence, except as provided for in para 7 of Art 5.

Article 3 – Harmonization

3.1 To harmonize sanitary and phytosanitary measures on as wide a basis as possible, Members shall base their sanitary or phytosanitary measures on international standards, guidelines or recommendations, where they exist, except as otherwise provided for in this Agreement, and in particular in para 3.

3.2 Sanitary or phytosanitary measures which conform to international standards, guidelines or recommendations shall be deemed to be necessary to protect human, animal or plant life or health, and presumed to be consistent with the relevant provisions of this Agreement and of GATT 1994.

3.3 Members may introduce or maintain sanitary or phytosanitary measures which result in a higher level of sanitary or phytosanitary protection than would be achieved by measures based on the relevant international standards, guidelines or recommendations, if there is a scientific justification, or as a consequence of the level of sanitary or phytosanitary protection a Member determines to be appropriate in accordance with the relevant provisions of paras 1 through 8 of Art 5. Notwithstanding the above, all measures which result in a level of sanitary or phytosanitary protection different from that which would be achieved by measures based on international standards, guidelines or recommendations shall not be inconsistent with any other provision of this Agreement.

Article 4 – Equivalence

4.1 Members shall accept the sanitary or phytosanitary measures of other Members as equivalent, even if these measures differ from their own or from those used by other Members trading in the same product, if the exporting Member objectively demonstrates to the importing Member that its measures achieve the importing Member's appropriate level of sanitary or phytosanitary protection. For this purpose, reasonable access shall be given, upon request, to the importing Member for inspection, testing and other relevant procedures.

4.2 Members shall, upon request, enter into consultations with the aim of achieving bilateral and multilateral agreements on recognition of the equivalence of specified sanitary or phytosanitary measures.

Article 5 – Assessment of Risk and Determination of the Appropriate Level of Sanitary or Phytosanitary Protection

5.1 Members shall ensure that their sanitary or phytosanitary measures are based on an assessment, as appropriate to the circumstances, of the risk to human, animal or plant life and health, taking into account risk assessment techniques developed by the relevant international organizations.

5.2 In the assessment of risks, Members shall take into account available scientific evidence; relevant processes and production methods; relevant inspection, sampling and testing methods; prevalence of specific diseases or pests; existence of pest- or disease-free areas; relevant ecological and environmental conditions; and quarantine or other treatment.

5.3 In assessing the risk to animal or plant life or health and determining the measure to be applied for achieving the appropriate level of sanitary or phytosanitary protection from such risk, Members shall take into account as relevant economic factors: the potential damage in terms of loss of production or sales in the event of the entry, establishment or spread of a pest or disease; the costs of control or eradication in the territory of the importing Member; and the relative cost-effectiveness of alternative approaches to limiting risks.

5.4 Members should, when determining the appropriate level of sanitary or phytosanitary protection, take into account the objective of minimizing negative trade effects.

Under Art 3(1) of the Agreement, member countries should base their food safety standards on the standards of the CAC. However, under Art 3(3), a 'higher level of sanitary or phytosanitary protection' can be specified 'if there is a scientific justification, or as a consequence of the level of sanitary or phytosanitary protection a Member determines to be appropriate' under the provisions of Art 5.

Art 5 requires the use of 'risk assessment techniques developed by the relevant international organisations' and the use of 'scientific evidence'. Where controls are adopted, however, they must 'take into account the objective of minimising negative trade effects'.

Technical Barriers to Trade (TBT) Agreement

This agreement aims to ensure that technical negotiations and standards, as well as testing and certification procedures, do not create unnecessary barriers to trade. It recognises that countries have the right to adopt protection measures they consider appropriate, for example, relating to human, animal or plant life or health or protection of the environment, and to take the necessary steps to ensure that the levels of protection are met. The agreement therefore encourages countries to adopt international standards where they exist, but it does not require them to change their levels of protection as a result.

The Agreement covers all types of products, including industrial, agricultural and food products. It sets out a code of good practice for the preparation, adoption and application of standards by central government bodies. It also includes provisions detailing how local government and non-governmental bodies should apply their own regulations.

The procedures used to determine whether products conform with national standards should be fair and equitable and should not give domestic products an advantage over imports. Countries are encouraged to recognise each other's testing procedures – like the principle of mutual recognition in the EC. WTO member governments must make information available at national inquiry points so that manufacturers and exporters can check the latest relevant standards.

The Annex of the Agreement contains definitions, including the following. 'Technical regulation' is defined as:

> [A] document which lays down product characteristics or their related processes and production methods, including the applicable administrative provisions with which compliance is mandatory. It may also include or deal exclusively with terminology, symbols, packaging, marking or labelling requirements as they apply to a product, process or production method.

'International body or system' is defined as a 'Body or system whose membership is open to the relevant bodies of at least all members'.

The general provisions of the TBT are stated in Art 1:

1.3 All products, including industrial and agricultural products shall be subject to this agreement.

1.5 The provisions of this agreement do not apply to sanitary and phytosanitary measures as defined in Annex A of the Agreement on the Application of Sanitary and Phytosanitary Measures.

Article 2 deals with Preparation, Adoption and Application of Technical Regulations by Central Government Bodies:

2.2 Members shall ensure that technical regulations are not prepared adopted or applied with a view to or with the effect of creating unnecessary obstacles to international trade. For this purpose technical regulations shall not be more trade restrictive than necessary to fulfil a legitimate objective, taking account of the risks non-fulfilment would create. Such legitimate objectives are, *inter alia*, national security requirements, the prevention of deceptive practices, protection of human health or safety, animal or plant life or health, or the environment. In assessing such risks, relevant elements of consideration are, *inter alia*, available scientific and technical information, relevant processing technology or intended end-use of products.

2.3 Technical regulations shall not be maintained if the circumstances or objectives giving rise to their adoption no longer exist, or if the changed circumstances or objectives can be addressed in a less trade-restrictive manner. Where technical regulations are required and relevant international standards exist or their completion is imminent, Members shall use them, or the relevant parts of them, as a basis for their technical regulations except when such international standards or relevant parts would be an ineffective or inappropriate means for the fulfilment of the legitimate objectives pursued, for instance because of fundamental climate or geographical factors or fundamental technological problems.

Dispute settlement

The requirements of the SPS and TBT Agreements are part of the rules of the WTO and must, therefore, be complied with. In establishing rules, there are also provisions contained within a Dispute Settlement Understanding (DSU), which lays down the way in which disputes arising from the various agreements will be settled. The DSU contains provisions for negotiation to resolve disputes but, if necessary, there is a detailed procedure for the establishment of a Panel to investigate the matter and come to a decision in a *Panel Report*, which is published. There is also an appeals system where one party believes the Panel has interpreted the provisions of the agreements incorrectly and there are procedures for implementing the final report. Failure to implement the decision can result in any aggrieved member country being permitted to take action against the country which has failed to implement the report findings. All of these processes are meant to happen within a relatively short time.

FOOD AND AGRICULTURE ORGANISATION OF THE UNITED NATIONS

The FAO was founded in October 1945 with a mandate to raise levels of nutrition and standards of living, improve agricultural productivity and to better the condition of rural populations.

The FAO is the largest autonomous organisation within the United Nations and has 180 member nations. The European Community is also a member in its own right.

WORLD HEALTH ORGANISATION

The WHO is defined by its constitution as the directing and co-ordinating authority on international health work. Its aim is 'the attainment by all peoples of the highest possible level of health'. The WHO has defined health as: 'A state of complete physical, mental and social well-being and not merely the absence of illness or infirmity.'

CODEX ALIMENTARIUS

Codex Alimentarius means 'food code'. It is the compilation of all the standards, codes of practice, guidelines and recommendations of the CAC. This is the main international body responsible for developing international food standards. It was established in 1962 by the FAO and the WHO, both of which bodies jointly fund the CAC. The FAO funds 75% and the WHO 25%. The CAC is an intergovernmental organisation and any country which is a member of the FAO or WHO can become a member of the CAC. Membership does not impose any obligations on a country, but gives it the opportunity to participate in the setting of standards and the opportunity to have its views considered. There are currently 165 member nations, representing 98% of the world's population. The statutes of the CAC can be found in the *Procedural Manual*.[3]

The General Principles of the Codex state:

> The publication of the Codex Alimentarius is intended to guide and promote the elaboration and establishment of definitions and requirements for foods to assist in their harmonisation and in doing so to facilitate international trade.

One of the main concerns of national governments is to ensure that products imported into their territory are safe and do not pose a threat to human, animal or plant health. National governments, therefore, have their own mandatory standards and regulations governing food in order to avoid such a threat. These national measures, of course, can be seen as, and sometimes are, barriers to free trade in food.

The SPS and TBT Agreements both acknowledge the importance of harmonising standards internationally to prevent sanitary, phytosanitary or

---

3   Statutes of the CAC, *Procedural Manual*, 11th edn, 2000, FAO/WHO.

any other technical barriers becoming barriers to trade. In determining standards with regard to food, the SPS Agreement has identified and chosen the standards, guidelines and recommendations established by the CAC for food additives, veterinary drug and pesticide residues, contaminants, methods of analysis and sampling and codes and guidelines on hygiene practice. This means that the Codex standards are recognised as scientifically justified and accepted as the standards against which national measures can be evaluated. Specific recognition is given to Codex guidelines, standards and recommendations in the SPS and TBT Agreements. The adoption of the Codex standards as scientifically justified norms means that they have become an integral part of the legal framework within which international trade is being conducted.

As well as setting standards, guidelines and recommendations to facilitate trade in food, the CAC also encourages food traders to adopt voluntary ethical practices. The Commission has published a *Code of Ethics for International Trade in Food*.

On of the main objectives of the *Code of Ethics* is to stop exporting countries and exporters from dumping poor quality and unsafe food on the international market. It contains certain general principles:

4.1 International trade in food should be conducted on the principle that all consumers are entitled to safe, sound and wholesome food and to protection from unfair trade practices.

4.2 No food should be in international trade which:

(a) has in it or upon it any substance in an amount which renders it poisonous, harmful or otherwise injurious to health; or

(b) consists in whole or in part of any filthy, putrid, rotten, decomposed or diseased substance or foreign matter, or is otherwise unfit for human consumption; or

(c) is adulterated; or

(d) is labelled or presented in a manner that is false, misleading or is deceptive; or

(e) is sold, prepared, packaged, stored or transported for sale under insanitary conditions.

Codex and regional agreements and arrangements

The Uruguay Round Agreement provides for groups of member countries to enter into trade agreements amongst themselves. Probably the best known of these agreements is the North American Free Trade Agreement between Canada, the US and Mexico (NAFTA). Argentina, Brazil, Paraguay and Uruguay have signed the Treaty of Asunción, establishing the Southern Common Market (MERCOSUR), and in Asia and the Pacific 18 countries have formalised arrangements for economic co-operation under the title Asia

Pacific Economic Co-operation (APEC). All these organisations have adopted measures consistent with the Uruguay Round Agreements and with Codex standards.

NAFTA includes two ancillary agreements dealing with sanitary and phytosanitary measures and technical barriers to trade. In the SPS Agreement, Codex standards are cited as the basic requirements to be met by the three member countries with regard to the health and safety aspects of foodstuffs.

MERCOSUR's Food Commission has recommended a range of Codex standards for adoption by member countries and uses other Codex standards as points of reference for ongoing discussions. APEC has drafted a Mutual Recognition Arrangement on Conformity Assessment of Foods and Food Products which calls for consistency with the SPS and TBT Agreements and with Codex standards, including the recommendations of the Codex Committee in Food Import and Export Certification Systems.

EU Directives also often refer to the Codex Alimentarius as the basis for their rules.

The role of Codex

The importance of the role of the CAC can be seen by the fact that other international organisations make reference to it. Guidelines on consumer protection policies have been issued by the United Nations under Resolution 1985, which advises that 'Governments should take into account the need of all consumers for food security and should support and, as far as possible, adopt standards from the ... Codex Alimentarius'.

The importance of its role is also recognised in the WTO Agreements on SPS Measures and in TBT, which accept the standards set by the Codex as providing countries with the necessary protection with regard to food standards. Countries are permitted to introduce higher standards, but must be able to justify this on the basis of sound science and they must be based on appropriate risk assessment methods.

The full Commission meets every two years, but in between sessions, the Executive Committee is able to take decisions on behalf of the Commission. Most of the detailed preparatory work is undertaken in various 'subsidiary bodies'. There are three main groups of subsidiary bodies: World Wide General Subject Committees, World Wide Commodity Committees, and Regional Co-ordinating Committees.

One of the main functions of Codex is the preparation of food standards. International recommended standards, guidelines and codes of practice are adopted by the CAC after detailed consideration by all members.

There are currently over 200 standards. There are general standards or recommendations on food labelling; food additives; contaminants; standards of analysis and sampling; inspection and certification systems; residues of veterinary drugs in foods; and pesticide residues in foods. In addition, the Codex has developed an international code of practice on food hygiene.

The Codex Commission also encourages countries to adopt ethical practices and follow its Code of Ethics for International Trade in Food.

The Joint FAO/WHO Expert Committee on Food Additives (JECFA) advises the Codex Commission on food additives, contaminants and residues of veterinary drugs. JECFA establishes the amount of a particular additive that can be ingested on a daily basis, even for a lifetime, without significant risk. JECFA is independent of the Codex Commission. Its members come from the scientific community and must be impartial, working as individuals, not as representative of their government or their institution.

The Joint FAO/WHO Meeting on Pesticide Residues advises the Codex Commission on pesticide residues.

There is a specified procedure for the adoption of standards which is laid down in the rules of procedure. The procedure can take up to five to eight years to complete, although there is provision for an accelerated procedure if a matter is considered to be urgent. This could be in the event of, for example, 'new scientific information; new technology(ies); urgent problems related to trade or public health; the revision or updating of existing standards'.[4] The accelerated procedure, which omits steps 6, 7 and 8 may only be used if there is a two-thirds majority of votes cast.

Once a standard has been adopted, it is offered to the member countries for acceptance. There are three types of acceptance:

(a) full acceptance – the country will apply the standard to all products and will not restrict the distribution of products which comply with that standard;

(b) acceptance with specified deviations – the standards are accepted except for certain specific aspects of them;

(c) free distribution – a country may retain its own national standard, but will allow the import and free distribution of products which comply with the Codex standard. This is very similar to the concept of 'mutual recognition' in that they both allow imports of products which may not comply with the strict legal requirements of the importing country, but which meet the requirements of the Codex standard or another EU Member State.

It is important to note, however, that the Codex acceptance procedures have now become almost irrelevant. As noted above, members of the WTO (that is, most countries of Codex) are obliged to consider Codex standards as the basis for their national controls. The use of 'free distribution' would seem to be the

---

4   *Op cit*, CAC, fn 3, p 22.

most acceptable means of demonstrating compliance with the requirements of the WTO.

The adoption of the SPS Agreement has raised the profile of the Codex Alimentarius very significantly. Whereas, in the past, there was a feeling that its meetings were an opportunity to have discussions, but ultimately their recommendations could be ignored, its standards are now recognised as the basic standard upon which national measures will be judged. It is accepted that 'higher standards' may be deemed appropriate, but there are restrictions based on them and they must be developed using risk assessment techniques.

Since 1995, the Codex Alimentarius has recognised that the enhanced status given to it by the World Trade Organisation must be met by improved procedures and by the greater use of science and risk assessment techniques. Both of these are specifically required under the SPS Agreement.

Decision making in Codex

Decision making in the Codex Commission is governed by 'Statements of Principle' which are contained in the *Procedural Manual*.[5] At its 21st meeting, in 1995, the CAC adopted Statements of Principle Concerning the Role of Science in the Codex Decision Making Process and the Extent to which Other Factors are Taken into Account. The principles state:

(1) The food standards, guidelines and other recommendations of Codex Alimentarius shall be based on the principle of sound scientific analysis and evidence, involving a thorough review of all relevant information, in order that standards assure the quality and safety of the food supply.

(2) When elaborating and deciding upon food standards Codex Alimentarius will have regard, where appropriate, to other legitimate factors relevant for the health protection of consumers and for the promotion of fair practices in food trade.

(3) In this regard it is noted that food labelling plays an important role in furthering both of these objectives.

This second statement of principle means that science is not the only factor to be taken into account.

At the 22nd Session in 1997, the Commission adopted a Statement of Principle Relating to the Role of Food Safety Risk Assessment, which states:

(1) Health and safety aspects of Codex decisions and recommendations should be based on a risk assessment, as appropriate to the circumstances.

(2) Food safety risk assessment should be soundly based on science, should incorporate the four steps of the risk assessment process and should be documented in a transparent manner.

---

5   *Op cit*, fn 3, Appendix: General Decisions of the Commission.

(3) There should be a functional separation of risk assessment and risk management, while recognising that some interactions are essential for a pragmatic approach.

Joint FAO/WHO Consultation on Risk Management and Food Safety[6]

This Consultation recommended that the Commission should clarify the application of the Second Statement of Principle. They indicated that: '... in particular this clarification should include explicit description of the factors which may be considered, the extent to which these factors should be taken into account and the procedure to be used in this regard.'

The primary concerns of the joint FAO/WHO Food Standards Programme and the CAC are the protection of consumers and fair practices in food trade. It was felt that if all countries harmonised their food laws and adopted internationally agreed standards, these issues would be resolved and that there would be fewer barriers to trade and free movement of food products between countries, which would be to the benefit of producers, including farmers. The volume of food trade is estimated at between US $399 billion and US $400 billion.

The Joint FAO/WHO Consultation on Risk Management and Food Safety recommended that the Commission should clarify the application of the Second Statement of Principle. They indicated that 'in particular this clarification should include explicit description of the factors which may be considered, the extent to which these factors should be taken into account and the procedure to be used in this regard'.

In its 14th session in 1999, the Codex Committee on General Principles (CCGP) considered the role of science and the application of 'other factors' generally, and specifically in the case of Bovine Somatotropin.[7]

Joint FAO/WHO Codex Alimentarius Ad Hoc Intergovernmental Task Force on Foods Derived from Biotechnologies

The Task Force will develop standards, guidelines or recommendations for food derived by biotechnology or which contains traits introduced into it by biotechnological methods.

---

6   FAO Food and Nutrition Paper No 65.
7   CCGP, 14th Session, 19–23 April 1999.

ORGANISATION FOR EUROPEAN CO-OPERATION AND DEVELOPMENT

The OECD came into existence in 1961. It evolved out of the Organisation for European Economic Co-operation (OEEC), which had been established in 1948 to administer the financial aid provided by the US and Canada under the Marshall Plan for the reconstruction of Europe following World War II.

The OECD has 29 member countries. It provides a forum within which member governments can discuss and develop economic and social policy. They are able to exchange information and seek to find common solutions to shared problems. Sometimes, discussions will result in formal agreements, but more often they simply lead to better informed work within each member country. The OECD members are wealthy countries, committed to an open market economy and to pluralistic democracy and respect for human rights. Countries seeking membership also agree to participate in 'peer review'.

The OECD's 'vocation' is 'to build strong economies in its member countries, improve efficiency, hone market systems, expand free trade and contribute to development in industrialised as well as developing countries'.[8]

The OECD's interests, however, extend beyond those of its own member countries and it engages in dialogue with other countries. It considers policy areas within each member country, and also how various policies interact with each other across national borders and even beyond the borders of the OECD itself.

Amongst the wide range of activities undertaken by the OECD is its interest in biotechnology and food safety. A Task Force for the Safety of Novel Foods and Feeds is held under the auspices of the Environment Directorate. The OECD also held a Conference on the Scientific and Health Aspects of Genetically Modified Foods in Edinburgh in 1999 (see below, Chapter 6).

THE STATE OF FOOD INSECURITY IN THE WORLD

The FAO published its report on Food Insecurity (SOFI) in December 1999. According to the most recent estimates (1995–97), there are 790 million people in the developing world who do not have enough to eat. This is 40 million fewer than in 1990–92. At the World Food Summit in 1996, world leaders pledged to reduce this number to 400 million by 2015. At the present rate of reduction, this target will not be met.

According to *State of Food Insecurity in the World 1999*, the current reduction does not indicate uniform progress throughout the world. The data shows

---

8   'About OECD – OECD's origins', available at www.oecd.org.

that in the first half of the 1990s, only 37 countries achieved a reduction in the number of undernourished people, totalling 100 million, while in the rest of the developing world the number of undernourished people rose by almost 60 million. SOFI also makes clear that it is not only in the developing countries that people go hungry. It assesses the number of undernourished people in the developed world at eight million in industrialised countries and 26 million in countries in transition. In order to combat hunger in the world, it is necessary for specific action to be taken at local, regional and national level.

Combating hunger in the world is one of the issues which those who support the increased development and production of genetically modified foods use as an illustration of the benefits of this new technology. It is argued that genetically modified (GM) foods will help to solve food shortages in certain parts of the world. Opponents of GM foods argue that traditional sustainable farming methods would achieve the alleviation of hunger if they were properly supported.

In May 2000, Vandana Shiva delivered one of the BBC's Reith Lectures. She was very critical of the globalisation of trade in food and the effect that the increasing dominance of multi-national companies is having on small farms and local and regional food producers, particularly in India.

GLOBALISATION

One of the most contentious issues currently being debated in relation to international trade law is that of globalisation.

Those who are in favour of globalisation argue that introducing global rules for international trade and thereby theoretically creating a 'level playing field' will result in free trade and in greater prosperity for developing nations. Those who are opposed to globalisation argue that it leads to domination by multi-national companies from the developed world while developing nations are forced to adapt their production methods in order to comply with international trade rules. They argue that it threatens sustainable development.

Of particular concern in relation to international trade in food is the growing political and financial power of the multi-national biotechnology companies. It is argued by those who support globalisation and genetic engineering that biotechnology in the form of genetic modification of seeds will help to produce crops which are drought and pest resistant and therefore a vital contribution to defeating hunger in the world. Their opponents argue that genetically modified crops result in a loss of bio-diversity and that this threatens sustainability. There is also concern about genetically modified seeds which have a so called 'terminator gene' in them, which means that they die completely after one season and cannot be used again. This means that farmers have to buy new seeds every year and that they have no control over the cost.

In her Reith Lecture 2000 on BBC Radio 4, Professor Vandana Shiva said:

What a world need to feed a growing population sustainably is bio-diversity intensification, not the chemical intensification or the intensification of genetic engineering. ...

She went on to say:

The devaluation and invisibility of sustainable, regenerative production is most glaring in the area of food. While patriarchal division of labour has assigned women the role of feeding their families and communities patriarchal economics and patriarchal views of science and technology magically make women's work in providing food disappear. 'Feeding the World' becomes disassociated from the women who actually do it and is projected as dependent on global agribusiness and biotechnology corporations.

However, industrialisation and genetic engineering of food and globalisation of trade in agriculture are recipes for creating hunger, not for feeding the poor.

...

Economic globalisation is leading to a concentration of the seed industry, increased use of pesticides and finally increased debt.

She observes that farmers are having to pay ever more towards the cost of producing their crops and yet are receiving a fraction of what they received on the same commodity a decade ago, while consumers are paying more for their food. She highlights the problems of global rules on packaging which have resulted in extra costs for producers of edible oils in India and also in the environmental problem of extra waste.

The globalisation of the food system is destroying local food cultures and food economies.

She argues that the global free trade economy has become a threat to sustainability and that Economic Globalisation has become a war against the poor and against nature.

The views expressed by Professor Shiva and many others like her are obviously only one side of the debate. As already indicated there are supporters of global free trade in food who believe that it is the only way to combat world hunger. It is, however, an issue of great importance and the ongoing discussions at the WTO on food and agriculture will be keenly observed by those on both sides of the ideological divide.

CHAPTER 2

FOOD LAW IN THE EUROPEAN UNION

UK food law is now determined largely at European Union (EU) EU level. In order to appreciate the importance of the relationship between the EU and Member States and the way in which EU law operates within the UK, it is necessary to examine briefly the history and development of the European Community (EC) and European Union (EU), the institutions, the legislative processes and the types of legislation which can be made under them, and the fundamental principle of free movement of goods.

HISTORY AND DEVELOPMENT OF THE EC AND EU

Following the Second World War, Western Europe was in a state of physical and psychological chaos. The inability of individual nation States to protect themselves in the face of an aggressor had been demonstrated all too clearly. There was a desire in the immediate post war period for the nations of Europe to come together and work to restore their shattered economies. One of the driving forces behind this was the Marshall Plan, under which the US and Canada gave financial assistance for the reconstruction of Europe on the understanding that the European States would work together. At the same time, other initiatives were also going on in the areas of military and political co-operation with the establishment of the North American Treaty Organisation (NATO) and the Council of Europe.

In 1952, the Treaty of Paris was signed, establishing the European Coal and Steel Community (ECSC), based on a proposal put forward by the French Foreign Minister Robert Schumann, following an idea of Jean Monnet, a committed federalist. The ECSC followed the successful Benelux Union, which had created a 'common market' between the three Benelux countries, Belgium, The Netherlands and Luxembourg. The idea behind the ECSC was that control of the two essential industries of coal and steel should be taken out of the hands of national governments and put into the hands of a 'supranational' authority. This was because, at the time, coal and steel were the essential 'factors of production' for waging war. It was believed that if control of these products was removed from individual nation States, then no State would be able to wage war on its own again. Six countries joined the ECSC (France, Germany, Italy and the three Benelux countries). This Community proved so successful that, in 1957, following a proposal from a committee chaired by the Belgian Prime Minister, Paul-Henri Spaak, two Treaties of

Rome were signed, establishing two further Communities: the European Atomic Energy Community (EAEC or Euratom), and the European Economic Community (EEC). The same six countries were members. Britain declined to join for a number of reasons, including the nature of its relationship with the Commonwealth. The three Communities shared a court and an Assembly, but all had separate Councils of Ministers and High Authority.

Following the Merger Treaty of 1965, all three Communities shared all four institutions: the Court of Justice; the Parliament (Assembly); Council of Ministers; and a Commission (formerly the High Authority).

Attempts by the UK to join the three Communities during the 1960s were vetoed by the French until, in 1973, the UK, Eire and Denmark joined the three Communities. Norway almost joined, but following a referendum in which its population voted against joining, it had to withdraw. Greece joined in 1980, followed by Spain and Portugal in 1986.

In 1986, the Single European Act (SEA) was signed by the Member States of the Communities. Amongst other things, the SEA helped to direct and speed up the move towards the completion of the single market, as well as increasing the role of the European Parliament in the legislative process.

In 1992, the Treaty on European Union (TEU) was signed at Maastricht, creating a European Union. It did not, however, replace the three Communities. They are now part of a wider entity which is the European Union. The TEU also renamed the EEC, and it is now the EC (European Community). The word 'Economic' has been dropped from its title, reflecting the fact that its remit is far wider than simply dealing with economic issues. The European Union is often depicted in the form of three pillars: one pillar representing the three original Communities, and the two others representing Police and Judicial Co-operation (formerly called Justice and Home Affairs) and Common Foreign and Security Policy.

In 1995, Austria, Finland and Sweden became members of the EU.

Following the signing and ratification of the Treaty of Amsterdam in 1996, the EC Treaty was renumbered. In this book, the new numbering will be given, with the old numbering in brackets.

The EC is the Community with which most people are familiar and is the relevant Community for the purposes of this book. The EC is a 'common market'. This means that there is a 'customs union' between the Member States, where there are no fiscal or other barriers to trade, and a common customs tariff in relation to third countries (countries outside the Community). It is based on the 'four freedoms' – the fundamental principles of free movement of goods, person, services and capital in order to facilitate the smooth running of the internal market.

The objectives and purposes of the EC are set down in Art 2 and the activities necessary to achieve them are outlined in Art 3:

Article 2 (ex Art 2)

The Community shall have as its task, by establishing a common market and an economic and monetary union and by implementing common policies or activities referred to in Arts 3 and 4, to promote throughout the Community a harmonious, balanced and sustainable development of economic activities, a high level of employment and of social protection, equality between men and women, sustainable and noninflationary growth, a high degree of competitiveness and convergence of economic performance, a high level of protection and improvement of the quality of the environment, the raising of the standard of living and quality of life, and economic and social cohesion and solidarity among Member States.

Article 3 (ex Art 3)

For the purposes set out in Art 2, the activities of the Community shall include, as provided in this Treaty and in accordance with the timetable set out therein:

(a) the prohibition, as between Member States, of customs duties and quantitative restrictions on the import and export of goods, and of all other measures having equivalent effect;

(b) a common commercial policy;

(c) an internal market characterised by the abolition, as between Member States, of obstacles to the free movement of goods, persons, services and capital;

(d) measures concerning the entry and movement of persons as provided for in Title IV;

(e) a common policy in the sphere of agriculture and fisheries;

(f) a common policy in the sphere of transport;

(g) a system ensuring that competition in the internal market is not distorted;

(h) the approximation of the laws of Member States to the extent required for the functioning of the common market;

(i) the promotion of co-ordination between employment policies of the Member States with a view to enhancing their effectiveness by developing a co-ordinated strategy for employment;

(j) a policy in the social sphere comprising a European Social Fund;

(k) the strengthening of economic and social cohesion;

(l) a policy in the sphere of the environment;

(m) the strengthening of the competitiveness of Community industry;

(n) the promotion of research and technological development;

(o) encouragement for the establishment and development of trans-European networks;

(p) a contribution to the attainment of a high level of health protection;

(q) a contribution to education and training of quality and to the flowering of the cultures of the Member States;

(r) a policy in the sphere of development co-operation;

(s) the association of the overseas countries and territories in order to increase trade and promote jointly economic and social development;

(t) a contribution to the strengthening of consumer protection;

(u) measures in the spheres of energy, civil protection and tourism.

THE INSTITUTIONS

Article 7 (ex Art 4) provides that the tasks entrusted to the Community shall be carried out by a Council, a Commission, a Court of Justice, a Parliament and a Court of Auditors. The institutions must act within the limits of the powers conferred upon them by the Treaty.

In addition to the 'official' institutions, there are other bodies which carry out important functions within the EC/EU, such as the Social and Economic Committee and the Committee of the Regions, which act in an advisory capacity and advise the Council and the Commission, and the Court of First Instance, which now undertakes some of the tasks previously carried out by the European Court of Justice.

European Parliament

The European Parliament (EP) is the only democratically elected institution of the EC/EU. It is the body which represents the citizens of the European Union. Members of the European Parliament (MEPs) are elected every five years. They sit in groups according to their political allegiance, and are not bound by instructions or mandates from their national governments.

The EP has considerable powers in respect of the budget, including the power to reject the whole budget. One of its most important functions, like that of the UK Parliament, is to scrutinise the exercise of executive power. It exercises political control over the Commission by scrutinising its activities, asking questions, and it ultimately has the power to censure the whole Commission.

The EP's role was originally limited to being largely advisory and supervisory. It had very little say in the formulation of EC law as its role in the original legislative procedure was limited to a right only to be consulted. The Single European Act, the Treaty on European Union and the Treaty of Amsterdam all contain provisions which have significantly enhanced the EP's role in the legislative process (see below).

The TEU also increased the role of the EP in the following ways:

- It gave the EP a new power of initiative, which means that, where the EP considers that a Community act is necessary in order to implement the objectives of the Treaty, it can request the Commission to submit appropriate proposals. It provided that the 'European Parliament may, acting by a majority of its members, request the Commission to submit any appropriate proposals on matters which it considers that a Community act is required for the purpose of implementing this Treaty' (Art 138b). This went some way to meeting the EP's long standing desire to be given power of legislative initiative.

- The EP can now receive petitions from natural or legal persons who live or have a registered office in a Member State, on a matter within the sphere of competence of the Community and which affects that natural/legal person directly.

- Article 193 (ex 138c) provided formal recognition of the EP's right to set up temporary committees of inquiry to investigate alleged contraventions or maladministration in the implementation of Community law, except where the issue is already the subject of legal proceedings. These new powers have been used twice: first, to examine the problems of the Community transit system, and secondly, to examine the Commission's handling of the BSE crisis. In the latter case, there was also a follow-up committee to examine the implementation of the EP's original recommendations.

- The EP is also required to appoint an Ombudsman to receive and investigate complaints of maladministration on the part of EC institutions and other bodies (except the European Court of Justice and the Court of First Instance acting in their judicial capacity).

Council (Council of the European Union)[1]

The Council has all the characteristics of a traditional intergovernmental organisation. It is the body which represents the political interests of the Member States. Its membership comprises representatives of the national governments and its composition will change according to the topic under discussion. If agriculture is on the agenda, it will be the agriculture ministers who meet; if it is transport, the transport minister will attend, and so on.

The Council is the ultimate decision maker of the EC and is the institution which, usually together with the EP, adopts EC legislation. The Council reaches its decisions either by a majority or by unanimity. The Treaty will specify which is required.

Article 205 (ex Art 148) of the EC Treaty

1   Save as otherwise provided in this Treaty, the Council shall act by a majority of its members.

2   Where the Council is required to act by a qualified majority, the votes of its members shall be weighted as follows:

---

1   Formerly called the Council of Ministers.

Belgium 5; Denmark 3; Germany 10; Greece 5; Spain 8; France 10; Ireland 3; Italy 10; Luxembourg 2; Netherlands 5; Austria 4; Portugal 5; Finland 3; Sweden 4; United Kingdom 10.

For their adoption, acts of the Council shall require at least:

62 votes in favour where this Treaty requires them to be adopted on a proposal from the Commission; 62 votes in favour, cast by at least 10 members, in other cases.

Because the Council is composed of members of national governments who have responsibilities back in their own country and the membership changes according to the topic under discussion, the membership is not permanent and, therefore, the day to day work of the Council is undertaken by the Committee of Permanent Representatives (known by its French acronym, COREPER).

COREPER is composed of diplomats and civil servants. Its members have been described as 'the men who really run Europe';[2] the Council is not, however, merely a 'rubber stamp', and it retains overall political control.

European Council

This is the name given to the meetings of Heads of State or Government of the Member States ('Summit' meetings).

This institution was developed by the political will of the Member States and was not provided for in the original Treaty. It is at the meetings of the European Council which take place every six months that major policy issues are discussed at the highest political level.

European Commission

The Commission is the institution which represents the interests of the Community. The Commission comprises 20 Commissioners, two each from France, Germany, Italy, Spain and the UK, and one from each of the other Member States. They are chosen on the basis of their ability, and are expected to act completely independently of their national governments in the interests of the Community. There is a President assisted by two Vice Presidents. The President of the Commission holds a position of great power and importance, as it is the President who determines the general direction and focus of the Commission's policies and who liaises with the Council and the EP. The Commission is a collegiate body and acts collectively. Every Commissioner has responsibility for certain Community policies and is in charge of at least one 'Directorate General' (DG), which could be likened to a government

2   'COREPER: Europe's managing board' (1998) *The Economist*, 8 August.

department. The DGs of most importance as far as food is concerned are DG III (Industry), DG VI (Agriculture) and, particularly, DG XXIV (Health and Consumer Protection).

In a broader sense, when people refer to the 'Commission', they often mean the whole bureaucratic edifice which is the 'civil service' of the Community.

The Commission has a number of important functions:

- to initiate proposals for legislation;
- to act as the 'guardian of the Treaties', which means that it must ensure that EC law is being properly implemented, and in this capacity it has the power to take Member States before the European Court of Justice if it believes that they are in breach of EC law;
- it is also the manager and executor of Union policies and of international trade relations.

The Commission has been the subject of much criticism in recent years, and the whole Commission resigned on 15 March 1999 following the publication of a highly critical report on fraud, mismanagement and nepotism within the Commission.[3] This highlighted the need for a redefinition of the Commission's role, although there had been calls for reforms for many years.

The EP has the right to be consulted on the proposed Council nomination for Commission President, since the Maastricht Treaty, and to formally approve the nomination Art 214 EC (ex Art 158). The EP does not have the right, however, to veto individual commissioners.

Art 214(2) reads:

The governments of the Member States shall nominate by common accord the person they intend to appoint as President of the Commission; the nomination shall be approved by the European Parliament.

The governments of the Member States shall, by common accord with the nominee for President, nominate the other persons whom they intend to appoint as members of the Commission.

European Court of Justice (ECJ) and the Court of First Instance (CFI)

The role of the ECJ is 'to ensure that in the interpretation and application of this Treaty the law is observed'.

There are 15 judges, assisted by nine Advocates General. The role of the Advocate General is something with which the British legal system is

---

3   Committee of Independent Experts, First Report on Allegations regarding Fraud, Mismanagement and Nepotism in the European Commission, 15 March 1999, Brussels.

unfamiliar. The Advocates General assist the court by delivering an opinion containing a detailed and impartial analysis of the facts and the law before a case is heard by the ECJ, and their role is to clarify the legal position of the parties and the legal issues in the case. They are completely impartial. The case is then heard by the Court, and usually, although not always, the Court will follow the opinion of the Advocate General.

The ECJ has a very wide jurisdiction.

Preliminary rulings

Article 234 (ex Art 177) gives the Court the power to give preliminary rulings on the interpretation of the Treaties and secondary legislation and on the validity/legality of acts of the institutions. Any court or tribunal in a Member State may, where a provision of EC law is at issue in the case before it and where, if it believes that a ruling on that point of EC law is necessary for them to be able to make a decision in the case, request a preliminary ruling. Although Art 234 states that, where a provision of EC law arises in a case against whose decision there is no further legal remedy, that court or tribunal 'shall' refer the matter to the ECJ, in practice courts do not have to refer where:

- there has already been a previous ruling on that provision of EC law; or
- the meaning of the provision is so obvious, having regard to the particular nature of EC law and the overall aims and objectives of the Treaty, that no interpretation is required; or
- the provision of EC law in question is irrelevant to the case.

Actions against Member States

Under Arts 226 and 227 (ex Arts 169 and 170), the ECJ can hear actions against Member States for breaches of EC law, brought either by the Commission (Art 226) or by another Member State (Art 229).

Judicial review – actions against the Community institutions

Under Arts 230 and 232 (ex Arts 173 and 175), the ECJ can hear challenges to the legality of acts of the institutions brought either by another institution or by a Member State (Art 230) and challenges to an institution's failure to act when it was legally obliged to do so (Art 232). The ECJ can also hear indirect challenges under Art 241.

Non-contractual liability

Under Art 288 (ex Art 215), the ECJ can hear actions for damages brought by Member States against Community institutions.

Court of First Instance (CFI)

The CFI was established by the Single European Act and began hearing proceedings on 11 September 1999. Its jurisdiction comprises:

* staff cases where members of staff bring actions against one of the institutions as their employer;
* actions brought by undertakings against the institutions concerning levies, production, prices and agreements under the Coal and Steel Community Treaty;
* actions against the Community institutions brought by natural or legal persons.

Court of Auditors

This is the taxpayers' representative, responsible for checking that the European Union spends its money according to its budgetary rules and regulations and for the purposes for which it is intended.

Economic and Social Committee

In accordance with the Treaties, this Committee advises the Commission, the Council and the European Parliament. The opinions which it delivers, either in response to a referral or on its own initiative, are drawn up by representatives of the various categories of economic and social activity in the European Union.

The members of the Committee, who are divided into three groups (workers, employers and various interests), draw up opinions on draft Community legislation and the main issues affecting society. They represent the different sectors of civil society.

Committee of the Regions

This is the European Union's youngest institution, whose establishment reflects Member States' strong desire not only to respect regional and local identities and prerogatives, but also to involve them in the development and implementation of EU policies.

For the first time in the history of the European Union, there is now a legal obligation to consult the representatives of local and regional authorities on a variety of matters that concern them directly.

EC LEGISLATION

The primary source of EC law is the Treaty of Rome (establishing the European Community), as amended. The Treaty itself contains provisions for the making of secondary legislation. There is, however, no single institution that can be called the Community 'legislature', nor is there one single procedure for making secondary legislation. There are a number of legislative procedures in which three of the institutions, the Council, the Commission and the EP all play a role. In addition, the Treaty often requires the institutions to consult other bodies, usually the Economic and Social Committee and/or the Committee of the Regions, before making legislation. The Commission is the initiator of legislation and the legislative procedure will usually begin with a proposal from the Commission, although the Council's role in taking the political initiative has increased. The Commission will usually have consulted widely before making a proposal and will often have produced Green and White Papers for consultation in advance of issuing a formal proposal. Originally, there was only one legislative process – the consultation procedure in which the Parliament had very little part to play. It had the right to be consulted, but its opinion could be disregarded by the Council, which had the sole power to decide whether or not to accept, amend and ultimately adopt the measure proposed by he Commission.

The Single European Act introduced the co-operation procedure which increased the role of the Parliament in the legislative process in certain areas of EC law by giving it the opportunity for a second reading of a measure and to put down proposals for amendments. The amendments could, however, be overturned by the Council. The TEU introduced a new co-decision procedure, which significantly increased the role of the Parliament in a number of key policy areas – in particular, concerning the internal market. The co-decision procedure results, as its name would suggest, in a decision being reached jointly by the Council and the Parliament as to whether or not to adopt a particular legislative measure. There must be agreement between the Council and the Parliament. There is provision for convening a Conciliation Committee to try to reach agreement between the Council and the Parliament on a joint text where no agreement has been reached after the Parliament's second reading of draft legislation. For the first time, the Parliament has the right to veto legislation with which it does not agree, although in fact there have been only two rejections since the TEU came into force, but it did give the Parliament greater bargaining power.

Following the ratification of the Amsterdam Treaty, the number of decision making procedures for Community legislation was reduced to three: co-decision, assent and consultation. The old co-operation procedure remains for decisions in relation to Economic and Monetary Policy, although it is unlikely to remain for long. The co-decision procedure (Art 251 (ex Art 189b)) has been considerably simplified. There is no longer a third reading in Council, and the whole procedure may now be concluded in the event of agreement or rejection by the Parliament at first reading. In practice, the procedures which have been removed were only used in exceptional political cases anyway, but as the Parliament has said: '... they do change the institutional symbolism and hence the institutional balance.'

The co-decision procedure has also been extended to 24 new areas. The procedure is set out in Art 251 (ex Art 189b):

1   Where reference is made in this Treaty to this Article for the adoption of an act, the following procedure shall apply.

2   The Commission shall submit a proposal to the European Parliament and the Council. The Council, acting by a qualified majority after obtaining the opinion of the European Parliament ... if it approves all the amendments contained in the European Parliament's opinion, may adopt the proposed act thus amended; ... if the European Parliament does not propose any amendments, may adopt the proposed act; shall otherwise adopt a common position and communicate it to the European Parliament.

    The Council shall inform the European Parliament fully of the reasons which led it to adopt its common position. The Commission shall inform the European Parliament fully of its position.

    If, within three months of such communication, the European Parliament: (a) approves the common position or has not taken a decision, the act in question shall be deemed to have been adopted in accordance with that common position; (b) rejects, by an absolute majority of its component members, the common position, the proposed act shall be deemed not to have been adopted; (c) proposes amendments to the common position by an absolute majority of its component members, the amended text shall be forwarded to the Council and to the Commission, which shall deliver an opinion on those amendments.

3   If, within three months of the matter being referred, the Council, acting by a qualified majority, approves all the amendments of the European Parliament, the act in question shall be deemed to have been adopted in the form of the common position thus amended; however, the Council shall act unanimously on the amendments on which the Commission has delivered negative opinion. If the Council does not approve all the amendments, the President of the Council, in agreement with the President of the European Parliament, shall within six weeks convene a meeting of the Conciliation Committee.

4   The Conciliation Committee, which shall be composed of the members of the Council or their representatives and an equal number of representatives of the European Parliament, shall have the task of reaching agreement on a joint text, by a qualified majority of the members of the Council or their representatives and by a majority of the representatives of the European Parliament. The Commission shall take part in the Conciliation Committee's proceedings and shall take all the necessary initiatives with a view to reconciling the positions of the European Parliament and the Council. In

> fulfilling this task, the Conciliation Committee shall address the common position on the basis of the amendments proposed by the European Parliament.

5 If, within six weeks of its being convened, the Conciliation Committee approves a joint text, the European Parliament, acting by an absolute majority of the votes cast, and the Council, acting by a qualified majority, shall each have a period of six weeks from that approval in which to adopt the act in question in accordance with the joint text. If either of the two institutions fails to approve the proposed act within that period, it shall be deemed not to have been adopted.

6 Where the Conciliation Committee does not approve a joint text, the proposed act shall be deemed not to have been adopted.

7 The periods of three months and six weeks referred to in this Article shall be extended by a maximum of one month and two weeks respectively at the initiative of the European Parliament or the Council.

There are five different types of measure which can be made using one of the legislative procedures described in Art 249 (ex Art 189):

> In order to carry out their task and in accordance with the provisions of this Treaty, the European Parliament acting jointly with the Council, the Council and the Commission shall make regulations and issued directives, take decisions, make recommendations or deliver opinions.
>
> A regulation shall have general application. It shall be binding in its entirety and directly applicable in all Member States.
>
> A directive shall be binding as to the result to be achieved upon each Member State to which it is addressed, but shall leave to the national authorities the choice of form and methods.
>
> A decision shall be binding in its entirety upon those to whom it is addressed.
>
> Recommendations and opinions shall have no binding force.

Regulations are directly applicable and binding in their entirety. This means that they become law in all the Member States as soon as they are enacted without the need for any implementation.

A directive is 'binding as to the result to be achieved', but leaves it up to the governments of the Member States to determine how the directive is to be implemented. Directives will give a date by which Member States are required to implement them. In the UK, directives can be implemented by secondary legislation – they do not necessarily require an Act of Parliament.

Natural and legal persons may rely on provisions of EC law in their national courts where those provisions are deemed to be 'directly effective'. This means that the measure must be sufficiently clear and precise, unconditional and leave no discretion to the Member State. The doctrine of direct effect is not contained in the Treaty and has been developed by the ECJ during the course of giving preliminary rulings under Art 177, now Art 234. Questions as to whether particular provisions can be directly effective will be determined by the ECJ. Treaty Articles, regulations, directives and decisions have all been held to be capable of direct effect. Treaty Articles and regulations have been held to be capable of both 'vertical' and 'horizontal' direct effect. Vertical direct effect means that a natural or legal person may use the provision in question in an action against the State or a public authority ('emanation of the State'). Horizontal direct effect means that the provision may be used in an action against another natural or legal person (that is, against another private party). Directives, however, can only have vertical direct effect. This means that they cannot be used in an action against a private party.

If a Member State fails to implement a directive in time, it may be liable in damages to anyone who suffers loss as a result of the State's failure to implement.

FREE MOVEMENT OF GOODS

The free movement of goods requires that there should be no barriers to trade. The principle of free movement is based on the rule that there should be no discrimination between goods from any Member State. All goods from all Member State must be allowed to move freely throughout the EU.

Article 23 (ex Article 9) of the Treaty provides that the Community is to be based on a customs union covering all trade in goods:

> The Community shall be based upon a customs union which shall cover all trade in goods and which shall involve the prohibition between Member States of customs duties on imports and exports and of all charges having equivalent effect, and the adoption of a common customs tariff in their relations with third countries.

Articles 25, 26 and 27 deal with the establishment of the customs union and Arts 28–31 deal with the prohibition on what are known as 'quantitative restrictions' and measures having an equivalent effect:

> Article 28 (ex Art 30)
>
> Quantitative restrictions on imports and all measures having equivalent effect shall be prohibited between Member States.
>
> Article 29 (ex Art 34)
>
> Quantitative restrictions on exports, and all measures having equivalent effect, shall be prohibited between Member States.
>
> Article 30 (ex Art 36)
>
> The provisions of Arts 28 and 29 shall not preclude prohibitions or restrictions on imports, exports or goods in transit justified on grounds of public morality, public policy or public security; the protection of health and life of humans, animals or plants; the protection of national treasures possessing artistic, historic or archaeological values; or the protection of industrial and commercial property.

Such prohibitions or restrictions shall not, however, constitute a means of arbitrary discrimination or a disguised restriction on trade between Member States.

Under Art 28, quantitative restrictions or measures having equivalent effect are prohibited in relation to imports. 'Quantitative restrictions' means quotas, that is, imposing a restriction on the quantity or amount of a product that can be imported into a Member State, or an outright ban on a particular product. 'Measures having equivalent effect' have been defined in the following way:

> All trading rules enacted by Member States which are capable of hindering directly or indirectly, actually or potentially intra-Community trade are to be considered as measures having an effect equivalent to quantitative restrictions.[4]

The *Cassis de Dijon* case[5] is the classic case in which the ECJ emphasised the importance of the free movement of goods, while determining that consumers could be protected by adequate labelling.

Cassis is a French blackcurrant liqueur with an alcohol content of 15–20%. The German requirement at the time was that fruit liqueurs should have a minimum of 25% alcohol. The measure was not discriminatory in that it applied to all liqueurs, regardless of where they came from, but it was indirectly discriminatory in that it had the effect of excluding the French product from the German market. A challenge was brought in the German national court which made a reference to the ECJ for a preliminary ruling under Art 177 (now Art 234). The ECJ held that, in the absence of any specific EC rules concerning a particular product, Member States were entitled to regulate the production and marketing of alcoholic drinks. The Court reiterated the *Dassonville* formula, but added a new element:

> Obstacles to movement within the Community resulting from disparities between the national laws relating to the marketing of the product in question must be accepted insofar as those provisions may be recognised as being necessary in order to satisfy mandatory requirements relating in particular to the effectiveness of fiscal supervision, the protection of public health, the fairness of commercial transactions and the defence of the consumer.

In other words, if a measure is necessary to comply with a *mandatory* requirement relating to any of the issues mentioned, including consumer protection, then any resulting obstacle to free movement of goods must be accepted. This was the first principle to emerge from the case. Note, however, the word 'necessary'. If there is any other way to fulfil the mandatory requirement, then that way must be taken.

---

4   The '*Dassonville* formula': *Procureur du Roi v Dassonville* Case 8/74 [1974] ECR 837.
5   *Rewe-Zentral v Bundesmonopolverwaltung für Branntwein* Case 120/78 [1979] ECR 649.

The German authorities argued that the requirement for the higher alcohol content was necessary to protect consumers so that they could be sure of what they were buying and to discourage alcoholism. The Court rejected that argument, and held that the requirement was disproportionate and, although mandatory, it was not *necessary*, as consumers could easily be protected by the use of clear labelling.

In terms of free movement of goods generally, this first principle was important, and also in terms of food law in particular, as it emphasises the importance of consumer protection and the fact that consumers can be protected by the use of detailed labelling.

The second principle to come out of the case was the principle of mutual recognition, which means that goods which are lawfully produced and marketed in one of the Member States should be allowed to enter and circulate freely in all the other Member States. This principle has been developed by the ECJ and by the Commission and, in 1990, the Commission issued a Communication on the principle of mutual recognition. In 1999, the Commission issued another Communication on the subject, which examines ways of facilitating and improving the application of the principle of mutual recognition in the single market. The Communication, which was published at the request of the Member States and economic operators, was provided for in the Single Market Action Plan of June 1997, which indicated that this field required particular attention. Under the principle of mutual recognition, each Member State is required to accept on its territory products which are legally produced and/or marketed and services which are legally provided in other Member States. The Member States may only challenge the application of the principle in certain limited cases, for example, where public safety, health, or the protection of the environment are at stake, and the measures which they take must be compatible with the principles of necessity and proportionality. The Communication provides for a series of actions to improve the monitoring of mutual recognition, and to make citizens, economic operators and the competent authorities at all levels in the Member States more aware of it, establish and improve contacts between national authorities and improve the way in which the Commission deals with individual complaints.

The principle of mutual recognition plays a key part in opening the single market in all the sectors which have not been the subject of harmonisation measures at Community level or which are covered by minimal or optional harmonisation measures. Under the principle, a producer or service provider who has complied with the requirements of his country of origin basically has the right to sell his products or provide his services in all the other Member States. Mutual recognition is, therefore, a powerful factor in economic integration which respects the principle of subsidiarity. It allows goods and services to move freely within the single market, while respecting the diversity of practices, customs and regulations in the various Member States and avoiding excessive harmonisation at Community level.

It was noted in the Communication that, although mutual recognition has already achieved favourable results, the Commission, the Member States and the economic operators were aware of certain practical difficulties associated with its application.

The Communication provided for targeted measures designed to ensure the effectiveness of the principle of mutual recognition. The thrust of these actions is fourfold:

1 *Better monitoring of the application of mutual recognition*

The Member States will be required to draw up succinct, regular (annual) reports on the difficulties which they have encountered in applying mutual recognition and the possible improvements. Decision No 3052/95 of the European Parliament and of the Council already requires the Member States systematically to notify the Commission of any derogations from mutual recognition (see IP/97/3). The Commission, for its part, has decided to draw up an evaluation report for the Council and the Parliament every two years, setting out the tangible results achieved by applying the principle of mutual recognition to products and services. This report will highlight the sectors which are causing problems and suggest corrective measures. The first of these reports is annexed to the Communication.

2 *Making citizens and economic operators more aware of the principle*

As part of the Dialogue with Citizens and Businesses the Commission has decided to launch an information campaign featuring a general 'Guide' and sectoral guides. The Commission also intends to publish an explanatory brochure, intended for a broad public (economic operators, professional associations, etc), on the application of Decision 3052/95 on national measures derogating from the principle of the free movement of goods. Lastly, the Commission intends to hold sectoral round tables on mutual recognition.

3 *Improving the application of the principle by the national authorities*

It is the Member States who are responsible, in the first instance, for the proper application of the principle of mutual recognition. In the past, there have been shortcomings in this respect. The Commission, therefore, wants every Member State to take steps to ensure that all the authorities involved (at national, regional and local levels) are aware of their responsibilities in this area. The authorities in all the Member States, at all levels, must therefore co-operate more effectively with each other so that the principle of mutual recognition is applied more effectively.

4   *Improved case management by the Commission departments*

The Commission will systematically examine the extent to which the Member States are fulfilling their obligations concerning the proper application of Community law on mutual recognition and will subsequently improve its handling of cases of infringement. It will also endeavour to develop a modern method of managing mutual recognition which will allow rapid identification of the extent of the problem and make it possible to find a pragmatic, effective solution for the economic operators.

In cases of infringement of the principle of mutual recognition, the sectors most commonly affected are given below. As is clear, the foodstuffs sector accounts for the greatest number of infringement cases.

(1996–98)

Sector	Number of cases	% of total
Foodstuffs	61	26%
Electrical engineering	58	25%
Motor vehicles	57	25%
Precious metals	18	7%
Construction	17	7%
Chemicals	7	3%
Other	27	11%

The Commission has the power to take infringement actions against Member States. Infringement proceedings are provided for in Art 226 of the Treaty (ex Art 169). In 1999, the Commission pursued a number of infringement proceedings against the trade practices in a number of Member States.

HARMONISATION, OR THE APPROXIMATION OF LAWS

The Treaty recognised that, in order to help the Member States develop in a unified manner, the legislation in individual countries needed to be harmonised. The word used in the Treaty is approximated. The original power for this was contained in Art 100 (now Art 94). Additional Articles were subsequently added to extend the power:

Article 94 (ex Art 100)

The Council shall, acting unanimously on a proposal from the Commission and after consulting the European Parliament and the Economic and Social Committee, issue directives for the approximation of such laws, regulations or administrative provisions of the Member States as directly affect the establishment or functioning of the common market.

Art 95 (ex Art 100a)

1   By way of derogation from Art 94 and save where otherwise provided in this Treaty, the following provisions shall apply for the achievement of the objectives set out in Art 14. The Council shall, acting in accordance with the procedure referred to in Art 251 and after consulting the Economic and Social Committee, adopt the measures for the approximation of the provisions laid down by law, regulation or administrative action in Member States which have as their object the establishment and functioning of the internal market.

2   Paragraph 1 shall not apply to fiscal provisions, to those relating to the free movement of persons nor to those relating to the rights and interests of employed persons.

3   The Commission, in its proposals envisaged in para 1 concerning health, safety, environmental protection and consumer protection, will take as a base a high level of protection, taking account in particular of any new development based on scientific facts. Within their respective powers, the European Parliament and the Council will also seek to achieve this objective.

THE DEVELOPMENT OF EC FOOD LAW

EC food law was initially developed mainly through the use of Art 100, and the main purpose was to ensure the free movement of food within the internal market. Concerns about consumer protection and public health were very much secondary issues.

In 1985, the Commission issued a Communication entitled 'Completion of the Internal Market: Community Legislation on Foodstuffs'.[6] It stated that Community legislation on food should only be introduced if it could be justified by the need to:

• protect public health;

• provide consumers with information and protection in matters other than health and ensure fair trading;

• provide for adequate and necessary official control of foodstuffs.

In 1989, in response to the *Cassis de Dijon* case, the Commission published another Communication on the Free Movement of Foodstuffs within the

---

6   1985 COM(85) 603.

Community. The emphasis was still very much on free trade and free movement of goods.

Official control of foodstuffs

In seeking to remove national frontier controls on goods, it was recognised that Member States had concerns over the way in which food law was enforced in other Member States. In the UK, for example, the control system was largely based on inspection at the 'point of sale', whereas most other Member States concentrated inspection at the point of production. The Official Control of Foodstuffs Directive[7] was therefore promulgated to ensure that certain minimum controls were applied throughout the EC. The directive, agreed in June 1989, therefore specified certain minimum standards. It provides details on when and where inspections should be carried out, and the way in which they should be undertaken.

In agreeing the directive, there was considerable pressure for more specific controls to be applied relating to general hygiene. There were a number of hygiene controls in place relating to specific foods, but there was no general hygiene requirement covering all foods and food premises.

Although not listed in the original internal market proposals, the Commission agreed to the concept following pressure from the European Parliament and eventually, in June 1993, the Hygiene Directive was agreed (see Chapter 9).

A further development extending the official control directive was agreed in October 1993, and is known as the 'Additional Measures Directive'.[8] It introduced four main aspects:

(a) minimum qualifications for inspectors;

(b) inspection visits to Member States and reports to Commission;

(c) use of laboratories that meet EN45000 for official samples;

(d) co-operation on investigations between Member States.

The most interesting of these is the second point. Although this did not establish a 'European inspection' scheme, it has now become possible to read the actual reports submitted to the Commission by the various inspectors who have undertaken the visits. These are normally invited inspectors from other Member States.

Following the outbreak of BSE and the enormous consumer concern generated by this disease, the Commission agreed to review and reform its processes for the proposal of food legislation.

---

7   Directive 89/397/EEC (OJ L186, 30.6.89), p 23.
8   Directive 93/99/EEC (OJ L290, 24.11.93), p 14.

In 1997, the Commission issued a Communication on Consumer Health and Food. Two important elements were the reinforcement of risk analysis as the basis for legislation and a new approach to inspections and control. Probably the most important element of the Communication was the reinforcement of the role of the Scientific Committees in relation to providing advice on matters of consumer health.

1997 Green Paper on food law

It was generally accepted that EC food law had been developed on a somewhat *ad hoc* basis and with no overall structure, so the Commission engaged in discussions with many interested parties on how to develop food law in a coherent and comprehensive way in future. The discussions led to the publication, in 1997, of a Green Paper entitled *The General Principles of Food Law in the European Union*.

WHITE PAPER ON FOOD SAFETY

On 12 January 2000, the Commission adopted a White Paper on Food Safety and set out a 'farm to table' legislative action programme. The main aim of the European Commission is to achieve the highest possible level of health protection for the consumers of Europe's food. The White Paper sets out a plan for a major programme of legislative reform which is proposed to complete the EU's 'farm to table' approach as well as the establishment of a new European Food Authority. Achieving the highest standards of food safety in the EU is a key policy priority for the European Commission. The emphasis throughout the White Paper is that food safety policy must be based on a comprehensive, integrated approach. The White Paper was presented by David Byrne, the Health and Consumer Protection Commissioner, and Erkki Liikanen, the Enterprise and Information Society Commissioner. It represented the culmination of three months' extensive work by the Commission following its appointment in September 1999, and builds on the consultation arising from the Commission's Green Paper on Food Law published in 1997. Commenting on the launch of the White Paper, David Byrne said:

> This is a major initiative designed to promote the health of Europe's consumers by the establishment of world class food safety standards and systems. The proposals in the White Paper on Food Safety are the most radical and far-reaching ever presented in the area of food safety. They are, I believe, an essential prerequisite for Europe to have the highest possible standards in respect of food safety. Consumer confidence has been badly affected by the various food alerts and crises of recent years and months. I believe that our proposals in the White Paper should fundamentally address consumers'

legitimate concerns in this regard with a view to restoring and maintaining confidence in food safety.

Erkki Liikanen said:

> Today's initiative is aimed at achieving a double objective. By restoring and maintaining the confidence of European consumers in the safety of food in the EU, the programme launched by this White Paper will not only effectively increase the quality of the everyday lives of Europeans, it will also boost the competitiveness of the European food industry.

The main White Paper proposals

European Food Authority

The White Paper envisages the establishment of a European Food Authority based on the principles of the highest levels of independence, of scientific excellence and of transparency in its operations. Great emphasis is placed on the fact that the Authority must be guided by the best science, be independent of industrial and political interests, be open to rigorous public scrutiny, be scientifically authoritative and work closely with national scientific bodies.

The White Paper clearly identifies many weaknesses in the present system which it is hoped would be addressed in the context of establishing a European Food Authority. Among the weaknesses identified are: lack of scientific support for the system of scientific advice; inadequacies in monitoring and surveillance of food safety; gaps in the rapid alert system; and lack of co-ordination of scientific co-operation and analytical support.

The tasks of the Authority will essentially concentrate on risk assessment and risk communication. Risk management, including legislation and control, should remain the responsibility of the European institutions which are accountable to the European public, although future extension of the competencies of the Authority may occur. It is envisaged that the tasks of the Authority will comprise the following.

Establishment of risk assessments through scientific advice

The range of issues will include all matters having a direct or indirect impact on consumer health and safety arising from the consumption of food. Thus, it will cover primary food production (agricultural and veterinary aspects), industrial processes, storage, distribution and retailing. Its remit will encompass both risk and nutritional issues. The Authority will also cover animal health and welfare issues, and will take into consideration risk assessments in other areas, notably the environmental and chemical sectors, where these overlap with risk assessment in relation to food. The work currently carried out by the five Scientific Committees concerned with food safety will be a core part of the new Authority. However, the current system of the organisation of the EU's Scientific Committees will be reviewed in the light of decisions taken about the structure of the Authority after consultations and detailed feasibility studies.

Information gathering and analysis

It was acknowledged that there was a pressing need to identify and use the information currently available throughout both the Community and worldwide on food safety issues. The Authority will be expected to take a proactive role in developing and operating food safety monitoring and surveillance programmes. It will need to establish a network of contacts with similar agencies, laboratories and consumer groups across the European Union and in third countries.

Communication

The Authority will need to make special provision for informing all interested parties of its findings, not only in respect of the scientific opinions, but also in relation to the results of its monitoring and surveillance programmes. The Authority must become the automatic first port of call when scientific information on food safety and nutritional issues is sought or problems have been identified. A highly visible Authority with strong proactive presence on food safety matters will be a key element in restoring and maintaining confidence among European consumers.

Rapid alert

The White Paper foresees that the Authority would operate the rapid alert system. The rapid alert system will be significantly strengthened as part of this process and will include rapid alert for animal feed problems.

Food safety legislation

The White Paper proposes an action plan with a wide range of measures to improve and bring coherence to the Community's legislation covering all aspects of food products from 'farm to table'. It sets out over 80 separate actions that are envisaged over the period ahead and intends to close identified loopholes in current legislation. The new legal framework will cover animal feed, animal health and welfare, hygiene, contaminants and residues, novel food, additives, flavourings, packaging and irradiation. It will include a proposal on general food law which will embody the principles of food safety such as:

(a) responsibility of feed manufacturers, farmers and food operators;

(b) traceability of feed, food and its ingredients;

(c) proper risk analysis through:

- risk assessment (scientific advice and information analysis);
- risk management (regulation and control);
- risk communication; and

(d) the application of the precautionary principle if appropriate.

Control of implementation of legislation

A comprehensive piece of legislation is proposed in order to recast the different control requirements. This will take into account the general principle that all parts of the food production chain must be subject to official controls. There is a clear need for a Community framework of national control systems, which will improve the quality of controls at Community level, and consequently raise food safety standards across the European Union. The operation of such control systems would remain a national responsibility. This Community framework would have three core elements:

(a) operational criteria set up at Community level;

(b) Community control guidelines;

(c) enhanced administrative co-operation in the development and operation of control.

Development of this overall Community framework for national control systems would clearly be a task for the Commission and the Member States working together. It is envisaged that the experience of the EU's Food and Veterinary Office (Dublin), which exercises the control functions at Community level, will be an essential element in its development.

Consumer information

The proposal acknowledged that if consumers are to be satisfied that the action proposed in the White Paper is leading to a genuine improvement in food safety standards, they must be kept well informed. The Commission, together with the new European Food Authority, will promote a dialogue with consumers to encourage their involvement in the new food safety policy. At the same time, consumers need to be kept better informed of emerging food safety concerns, and of risks to certain groups from particular foods. Proposals on the labelling of foods, building on existing rules, will be introduced.

International dimension

The Community is the world's largest importer/exporter of food products. The Commission acknowledged that the actions proposed in the White Paper will need to be effectively presented and explained to our trading partners. An active role for the Community in international bodies will be an important element in explaining European developments in food safety.

The Commission has made it clear that the success of the measures proposed in this White Paper is intrinsically linked to the support of the European Parliament and the Council and that their implementation will depend on the commitment of the Member States.

The emphasis throughout the White Paper is on greater transparency at all stages of food safety policy in order to increase consumer confidence.

Economic and Social Committee's opinion

In its opinion adopted on 24 May 2000 in response to the European Commission's White Paper on Food Safety, the Economic and Social Committee (ESC) supports much of the content of the European Commission's White Paper. The opinion deals in depth with the central question of how best to guarantee food safety for Europe's consumers. The ESC particularly welcomed: the Commission's integrated approach to issues relating to the food chain; the strengthening of the EU's operational capacity and the creation of a new body – the planned European Food Authority (EFA) – which is to be responsible for risk assessment and communication; and the modernising and simplification of existing food legislation, to create more coherence and enable new measures to be launched where needed.

The ESC did, however, identify a number of shortcomings in the Commission's plans and their future implementation:

(a) The rapid alert system: experience has shown up to now that this system is not sufficiently rapid and efficient. The Commission should become fully accountable for the system's overall performance. The structure of the system needs to be established in such a way that responsibilities are properly assigned to the Member States and other parties involved.

(b) Social aspects: the ESC points out that the White Paper does not mention the importance of working conditions for ensuring that procedures are carried out properly. It thus calls for clear, understandable rules which workers will find easy to apply.

(c) Nutritional aspects: EU food policy must focus not just on safety, but on nutrition and diet as well. Health promotion should play a major role in any discussion of food safety, taking into consideration traditions in national diets.

On the crucial matter of the planned EFA, the ESC made a number of detailed recommendations. In addition to the tasks assigned in the White Paper, the ESC believes that the EFA should: be the only body responsible for defining and implementing suitable risk assessment models that enable evaluation of food safety risks; play a key role in ensuring that consumers are formally involved in stimulating further fields of action if deemed appropriate; be confined to questions of food safety and should not extend to environmental issues, if food safety is not involved; give scientific advice for the approval of novel foods, novel ingredients or novel production methods to the Commission; have responsibility for assessing the risks of new additives and flavourings; evaluate the safety of pesticide residues, animal medicine residues and contaminants in food; establish a Community-based system of collection of nutritional and food consumption data, including the establishment of a surveillance system of diet-related illnesses; ensure that health-related claims are assessed effectively; and provide impartial and objective scientific assistance to the European institutions on food safety issues that affect the obligations of the European Union under international trade treaties, including any issues arising from the WTO disputes settlement procedure.

The ESC also noted that the White Paper does not make it clear whether food from the sea (for example, fish, crab, shellfish, etc) and aquaculture products are included in its scope. A coherent food policy should cover all, or the vast majority of foodstuffs involved in all links of the food chain, from fisheries to agricultural products. The ESC also noted that no reference is made to the inclusion of drinking water in the scope of food safety legislation and urges the Commission to trigger the necessary procedures to remedy this.

UK Government's response

On 1 June 2000, the UK Government published its formal response to the EC White Paper on Food Safety. In its response, the Government supports the establishment of a European Union Food Authority (EUFA) in light of the need to adopt a more coherent and effective approach to food safety policy and decision making at EU level.

The response, however, indicates concern that the proposals for a EUFA as set out in the White Paper do not fully address the need to integrate the processes of risk assessment, risk management, and risk communication.

The response states:

> The key attributes of such a body must be scientific excellence, openness, independence of commercial interests, and a determination to act in the interests of consumers. The responsibilities and resources assigned to it must enable it to command the respect of consumers, industry, and national authorities.

The UK Government's response also suggests that:

The closest possible linkage must be established between risk assessment, risk management (identification of appropriate regulatory action), and risk communication. The EUFA should be responsible for communicating a single, coherent message on both risk assessment and risk management.

An obligation should be placed on the European Commission to respond in a timely way to any recommendations of the EUFA. A consultative committee of the heads of national agencies should be established to help the EUFA in its work.

More consideration needs to be given to effective arrangements for crisis management. The response also comments on the scope and remit of the proposed authority, and says that the UK Government awaits more detailed Commission proposals on its status and accountability. It suggests that the new authority should report annually to the Council of Ministers, the Commission and the European Parliament, as well as making such reports publicly available.

Sir John Krebs, Chairman of the UK Food Standards Agency, said:

I welcomed the EC White Paper when it was published, coincidentally on the day of my appointment as Chairman of the UK Agency, and I am pleased to do so again. Any refinement or harmonisation of food safety and standards within the European Union is to be welcomed, particularly in light of the large volume of food which is exported from this country and imported into it.

The EUFA will need to work constructively with national food agencies and authorities, at the same time ensuring that there is no unnecessary overlap of national and pan-European responsibilities.

European Parliament's resolution

In October 2000, the European Parliament adopted a resolution on the Commission's White Paper on Food Safety by 461:12, with 9 abstentions, thereby expressing its support for the establishment of a European Food Safety Authority (EFSA) to provide high quality scientific information to be used as a point of reference for the EU and the Member States.

Parliament's view is that the EFSA's remit should first be to assess risks in the field of food safety and to give scientific advice. It should also provide information to the public about its scientific conclusions and recommendations, although the Commission would remain responsible for explaining risk management decisions. The EFSA should play a key role in the existing rapid alert system, which should be improved and extended to cover all areas of food safety, including animal feed. The Director of the EFSA should be appointed by the Commission after a public hearing before the relevant Parliament committee. The EFSA, which should work in close co-operation with national food safety agencies, must be given powers to require

Member States to provide such information, statistics and research reports in their possession as the EFSA Board may consider necessary to assess a particular risk.

Parliament wants traditional preparations for local foods, which have been proven not to be a health hazard, to be allowed to continue through a licensing system. National agencies should co-ordinate a network of excellence for food safety with the aim of ensuring consistent monitoring of food quality throughout the food chain.[9]

In the debate, John Bowis MEP[10] delivered a report on the Commission proposals to establish a European Food Safety Agency (EFSA). He recognised that there had been many problems in this area in the past and that risk could not be completely eliminated. Nevertheless, it should be reduced as much as possible and, in order to achieve this, he welcomed proposals to establish the EFSA. The new body should be independent and transparent, he stressed. Parliament should have the powers to scrutinise its work and should receive an annual report from the new body. He also believed that the EFSA needs to play a key role in the existing rapid alert system, which should be improved and extended to cover all areas of food safety. The EFSA should have the role of assessing risk, while the Commission managed and controlled the risk. The EFSA should also work in close co-operation with national and international food safety organisations. Mr Bowis concluded by stressing that these proposals were workable and he commended them to the House. There was broad support from most speakers for the proposed establishment of the EFSA and for Mr Bowis's report.

European Commission's formal proposal

On 8 November 2000, the European Commission adopted a proposal for a Regulation of the Parliament and Council, to be adopted by co-decision, laying down fundamental principles and requirements of food law and establishing a European Food Authority (EFA).[11] The proposal is the centrepiece of the Commission's strategy for a proactive food policy covering the entire food chain. Its primary objective is to provide the basis for the assurance of a high level of protection of human life whilst ensuring the effective functioning of the internal market. It is hoped that the package will not only contribute to a high level of consumer health protection in the area of food safety, but also to the restoration and maintenance of consumer confidence in food. The Commission decided that the necessary staffing and resources would have to be devoted to the EFA to ensure its success. Within

9   EP Daily Notebook, 25 October 2000.

10   EPP-ED, London.

11   Details were also given in a Press Release from DG24, Health and Consumer Protection.

three years it is expected to have about 250 staff and a budget of some 40 million euros. A review of ultimate staffing and budgetary requirements will be made at this time so as to ensure that the Authority has the resources necessary for its full operation. The Commission will subsequently present a proposal for the location of the EFA.

The proposal for a regulation sets out the basic principles and requirements for the marketing of food and feed, to assure a safe food supply, and sets up the Food Authority as the key instrument in achieving the new food law objectives. The regulation establishes crisis management procedures, expands the rapid alert system, puts in place procedures to prevent the marketing of unsafe foods and places responsibility on businesses to put only safe food and feed on the market. The regulation is intended to establish an integrated and comprehensive approach to food safety.

The proposal lays down common overarching principles and requirements for EU food law which are intended to harmonise the approaches taken at European and at national level.

The main provisions of the law are:

- Definition of the term 'food':

  Food means any substance or product intended to be, or expected to be ingested by humans.

- Establishments of general principles:

  Food law shall pursue the protection of human life, taking into account the precautionary principle, the protection of the consumers' interest, the traceability of food and feed and clearly establish responsibilities for food and feed business operators and public authorities.

- Requirements of food and feed safety:

  Only safe food may be placed on the market and food shall be considered unsafe if it is potentially injurious to health or unfit for human consumption or contaminated. Similarly, no feed shall be placed on the market or fed to any food-producing animal unless it satisfies the feed safety requirements.

  Food and feed business operators shall ensure that at all stages of production and distribution under their control this principle is respected.

The establishment of the EFA will give effect to the general principles and requirements of food law and will have a key role in improving human health protection and consumer confidence. The Authority will be a separate legal entity from the Community institutions. Its mandate is broad, so that it can take a comprehensive view of the food chain and provide a coherent scientific basis for policy and legislation.

Therefore, the EFA will cover all issues having a direct or indirect impact of the safety of food, as well as animal health and welfare and plant health and nutrition. It will also provide scientific opinions on any issue related to genetically modified organisms.

The EFA will have six main functions:

(a) it will deliver independent scientific opinions (at the request of the Commission, Member States, national food bodies or the European Parliament);

(b) it will provide advice on technical food issues to underpin policy and legislation in the areas of food safety and nutrition, as well as animal health and welfare, and plant health;

(c) it will be responsible for the collection and analysis of data on dietary patterns, exposure and risks for monitoring food safety in the EU;

(d) it will identify emerging risks;

(e) it will be responsible for the day to day operation of the rapid alert system covering both food and feed;

(f) it will have a clear communication role to inform the public on all matters within its mandate.

The main focus of the EFA will be to provide excellent, independent scientific advice and establish a network of close co-operation with similar bodies in Member States. It will have a key function in assessing risks related to all food and feed operations.

It is intended that the Authority will be fully independent, will operate in a transparent way and will be accountable to democratic institutions.

Its Management Board will comprise:

• four representatives appointed by the Council of Ministers;

• four representatives appointed by the Commission;

• four representatives appointed by the European Parliament;

• four representatives of consumers and industry designated by the Commission.

On the basis of a proposal by the Commission, the Board will appoint the Executive Director for a period of five years.

The EFA will be assisted by an Advisory Forum, composed of 15 representatives from competent bodies in the Member States.

Seven scientific panels will be established, replacing the current Scientific Steering Committee and five sectoral Scientific Committees. The membership of panels will be drawn from independent scientific experts following a call for expressions of interest and will be appointed by the Management Board. The following panels will be established:

• the panel on food additives, flavourings, processing aids and materials in contact with food;

- the panel on additives and products or substances used in animal feed;
- the panel on plant protection products and their residues;
- the panel on genetically modified organisms;
- the panel on dietetic products, nutrition and allergies;
- the panel on biological hazards;
- the panel on contaminants in the food chain;
- the panel on animal health and welfare.

A Scientific Committee will be responsible for the general co-ordination necessary to ensure the consistency of the scientific opinion procedure. This Committee will be composed of the chairpersons of the scientific panels and six independent experts who do not belong to any of the panels.

The EFA will be funded from the Community budget and, when fully operational could, in the light of the review, employ about 330 staff, including internal scientific experts. Its resource needs will be reviewed within three to four years after it becomes operational.

The Authority will be mandated to exercise vigilance in order to ensure that any potential conflicts between its scientific opinions and the scientific opinions issued by other bodies carrying out similar tasks are identified early. Scientific networks will be established to help in the early identification of potential conflict. If a potential source of conflict is identified, the EFA will ensure that all relevant scientific information is shared. Where the conflict involves a national scientific body, the EFA and this body will be obliged to co-operate, in consultation with the advisory forum, with a view to either resolving the conflict or presenting a joint document clarifying the contentious scientific issues.

If this provision works effectively, it should ensure that the public is made aware of all the available scientific advice, even where there is no consensus between the scientists. This might not be particularly comfortable for some, who might be concerned at the lack of agreement, but it will ensure greater transparency and less likelihood of controversial scientific advice being withheld.

Members of the Management Board, the advisory forum and scientists on the panels will be required to act independently. For this purpose, they will make a declaration of commitment and a declaration of interests annually in writing. At every meeting, they will be required to declare any special interest which might be considered prejudicial to their independence in relation to the items on the agenda.

In order to restore consumer confidence, the Authority will have a proactive role in collecting and analysing scientific and other relevant data. This should enable any emerging risks in the food chain to be identified and handled at an early stage. The EFA will co-ordinate the collection of exposure data from a variety of monitoring programmes. The EFA will collaborate with scientific institutions in the Member States and the Joint Research Centre of the Commission to make the best possible use of available expertise. The Authority will be expected to set up fully integrated networks with authorities, universities and research institutes in the Member States. It will be able to commission short term scientific activities when necessary and to outsource certain of its tasks.

The Authority will be expected to communicate actively with the public about its work, providing objective, reliable and easily understandable information.

The EFA will make public the opinions of the Scientific Committee and the scientific panels. Minority opinions must always be included, together with the annual declarations of interest and the declarations of interest made in relation to items on the agendas of meetings and the results of scientific work. The Management Board may hold some of its meetings in public and may invite consumer representatives to observe some of the EFA's activities. It shall also ensure wide access to documents it possesses.

The Commission remains responsible for risk management measures, and for emergency measures such as marketing bans or imposing specific conditions for marketing. The emergency provisions that currently exist in the veterinary sector are to be extended to cover food, on the basis of which the Commission can adopt a ban, on its own initiative or at the request of a Member State, in case of serious risk to human health. Within fewer than 10 working days, such measures should be reviewed by a newly created Committee on Food Safety and Animal Health. This Committee will be established through the merger of four existing standing Committees. It is proposed that the EFA will be responsible for the day to day operation of a broadened rapid alert system for food and feedstuffs involving the Member States, the Commission and the EFA. The new rapid alert system will apply to the entire food chain, notably adding feed to its scope. The system is based on the obligation for the members of a network to notify to the EFA any information relating to the existence of a serious direct or indirect risk to human health deriving from food or feed. Food and feed businesses shall also immediately inform their national competent authorities if they establish that a product poses a serious direct or indirect risk to health. Member States must forward any such information to the EFA and also notify all measures taken to restrict the marketing of a product, whether of EU origin or imported. The EFA will evaluate if the product in question poses a serious risk to health and, if so, immediately transmit such information to other authorities in the rapid alert network. The expertise of the Authority will bring the necessary scientific and technical expertise to assess the notifications received through this system on their health impact and urgency. The Authority will also assist as necessary in crisis management. The Commission will, together with the EFA and the Member States, draw up a plan for food and feed crisis management. In case of a crisis, the Commission would set up immediately a crisis unit, involving the Authority for necessary scientific and technical advice. The crisis unit would collect and evaluate all relevant information and identify options to prevent, reduce or eliminate the risk effectively and rapidly. The crisis unit would equally be in charge of measures to inform the public in times of crises.

EC SCIENTIFIC COMMITTEES

High quality scientific advice for the drafting and amendment of Community rules regarding consumer protection in general and consumer health in particular is of utmost importance. This was also underlined in the April 1997 Commission Communication on Consumer Health and Safety.[12] 'Consumer health' is here defined as including matters on consumer health in its strictest sense, animal health and welfare, plant health and environmental health.

Many issues relating to consumer health are of a multidisciplinary nature and require input from various scientific disciplines. As announced in the above Communication, the entire system of scientific advice was reformed in the period from June to October 1997. A Scientific Steering Committee and eight new Scientific Committees have been established, respectively by Commission Decision No 97/404/EC of 10 June 1997[13] and Commission Decision 97/579/EC.[14] They replace, and have an updated and broadened mandate as compared to, the former Scientific Committees. The new system of Committees has been operating since November 1997 and is still in force at the time of writing. It is important to note, however, that the establishment of the European Food Authority, proposed for 2001, will alter the structure of these committees again. The Scientific Committees operating at present are the following:

- Scientific Steering Committee.
- Scientific Committee on Food: scientific and technical questions concerning consumer health and food safety associated with the consumption of food products and, in particular, questions relating to toxicology and hygiene in the entire food production chain, nutrition, and applications of agrifood technologies, as well as those relating to materials coming into contact with foodstuffs, such as packaging.
- Scientific Committee on Animal Nutrition: scientific and technical questions concerning animal nutrition, its effect on animal health, on the quality and health of products of animal origin, and concerning the technologies applied to animal nutrition.

---

12 COM (97) 183 Final of 30 April 1997.
13 OJ L169, 27.6.97.
14 OJ L237, 28.8.97.

- Scientific Committee on Animal Health and Animal Welfare: Sub-committee Animal Health: scientific and technical questions concerning all aspects of animal health, hygiene, animal diseases and therapies, including zoonoses of non-food origin and zootechnics. Sub-committee Animal Welfare: scientific and technical questions concerning the protection of animals, notably in regard to animal husbandry, herd management, transport, slaughter and experimentation.
- Scientific Committee on Veterinary Measures relating to Public Health: scientific and technical questions concerning consumer health and food safety, and relating to zoonotic, toxicological, veterinary and notably hygiene measures applicable to the production, processing and supply of food of animal origin.
- Scientific Committee on Plants: scientific and technical questions relating to plants intended for human or animal consumption, production or processing of non-food products as regards characteristics liable to affect human or animal health or the environment, including the use of pesticides.
- Scientific Committee for Cosmetic Products, and Non-food Products intended for Consumers: scientific and technical questions concerning consumer health relating to cosmetic products and non-food products intended for the consumer, especially substances used in the preparation of these products, their composition and use as well as their types of packaging.
- Scientific Committee of Medicinal Products and Medical Devices: scientific and technical questions relating to Community legislation concerning medicaments for human and veterinary use, without prejudice to the specific competences given to the Committee for Proprietary Medicinal Products and the Committee on Veterinary Medicinal Products[15] in the context of the evaluation of medicaments. Scientific and technical questions relating to Community legislation concerning medical materials and equipment.
- Scientific Committee for Toxicity, Ecotoxicity and the Environment: scientific and technical questions relating to examination of the toxicity and ecotoxicity of chemical, biochemical and biological compounds whose use may have harmful consequences for human health and the environment.

In May 1997, halfway through the three year mandate of the new Scientific Committees, the European Commission undertook a mid-term review of their achievements. Following the BSE crisis, the Commission's scientific advisory system had been completely restructured in November 1997. Since then,

---

15 Committees established in the European Agency for the Evaluation of Medical Products.

around 150 scientific opinions on questions relating to food safety, animal nutrition, animal health and welfare, plants, cosmetics, chemicals, pharmaceuticals or medical devices have been adopted and made publicly available on the internet. The eight new Scientific Committees and the Scientific Steering Committee have proved that transparent, excellent and independent scientific advice can contribute to regaining consumer confidence into the system which the BSE crisis had substantially damaged.

The majority of the opinions dealt with BSE-related questions, followed by opinions relating to the safety of genetically modified plants and the assessment of pesticides, food additives, food contact material and cosmetic ingredients. Antibiotics and other additives in animal feeding stuffs were another important issue. Although the Scientific Committees have an advisory role, many of these opinions have served as a basis for the Commission to propose legislation. The Scientific Committees are consulted whenever a legal act requires it. They are also increasingly consulted on a voluntary basis. In addition, they can act as a 'whistleblower' by drawing the Commission's attention to new risks for consumer health.

BSE

The multidisciplinary Scientific Steering Committee is the main advisory body of the Commission as regards BSE. Opinions were adopted on a number of complex questions, such as the listing of specified risk material, the UK's date-based export scheme, the risk of infection of sheep and goats with BSE, the safety of organic fertilisers, production standards for gelatine, tallow and meat and bone meal, to mention only a few. The Commission followed up most of these opinions with corresponding legislative proposals. On other issues, such as the safety of organic fertilisers derived from mammalians, legislation still has to be adapted to the last up to date scientific advice. Following a wide consultation process, work on the assessment of the geographical risk of countries and regions on the basis of a preliminary handbook is ongoing. An opinion on this risk has yet to be delivered.

Genetically modified organisms

The Commission submitted all applications for authorisation for placing on the market of genetically modified organisms (Directive 90/220/EEC) to the Scientific Committees for a safety check. Opinions were adopted on genetically modified organisms, ranging from pesticide resistant maize to tomatoes, Swede rape, cotton plants and potatoes. In the case of a genetically modified high-starch potato, the scientists concluded that the data for an adequate risk assessment were not complete. The experts also prepared, on their own initiative, a guidance document for applicants based on the experience of evaluating the first 13 dossiers.

Antibiotic resistance

This was another hot issue during the first 18 months of operation of the new committee system. The experts looked at the efficacy and risks of three antibiotics used as feed additives in view of widespread concern about increasing incidence of antimicrobial resistance. The Commission suspended the use of these substances as feed additives as a precautionary measure. An expert group with members of all the Scientific Committees is examining the problem of antibiotic resistance on a broad basis, taking into account all aspects of the use of antibiotics in humans, animals and plants. Opinions on the safety of carbadox and olaquindox, used for growth promotion in pigs, led to a ban of the use of these substances in the European Union (EU).

Pesticides

About 800 active substances are currently authorised for use in pesticides throughout the EU and new substances are constantly being developed. For the existing substances, which were authorised by the Member States before harmonised EU legislation entered into force, a review programme has been established. Before taking a decision on keeping an existing active substance on the market or before authorising a new active substance, the Commission consults experts. A number of opinions relating to pesticides – old ones, new ones and maximum residue levels for some pesticides on a rage of crops – have been adopted. The Commission based its proposals for maximum residue limits of pesticides in infant formulae and baby foods on two opinions, in order to ensure that young children's health is adequately protected. Advice is likewise given on the methodologies for carrying out chronic and acute risk assessments for pesticide residues in food.

BST and hormones

BST is a substance obtained by genetic engineering. It is similar to a cow's natural growth hormone and is injected into dairy cows to increase milk production. Prior to decisions on how to proceed with the moratorium of the EU prohibiting the marketing and use of BST which expired on 31 December 1999, the Scientific Committees were asked for their opinion on this question. The scientists recommended not using BST in dairy cows, as it causes significantly poorer welfare in the cows, particularly because of increased foot disorders and mastitis. The scientists likewise noted a potential risk of the use of BST to public health, which required further research.

Concerning the use of six growth hormones for growth promotion in cattle, the scientists identified a risk to the consumers, but with different levels of conclusive evidence. The natural hormone 17-b-oestrodiol was considered as a complete carcinogen, having both tumour initiating and tumour promoting effects. Following this opinion, which represents an up to date and comprehensive risk assessment respecting WTO requirements, the Commission agreed that there was no longer any question of lifting the existing ban on hormone-treated beef.

Food

A wide range of opinions was adopted, such as on food additives, packing materials, ingredients of energy drinks, ochratoxin A and on irradiation of foodstuffs. In the latter case, the scientists had no concerns about eight foodstuffs (frogs' legs, shrimps, gum arabic, casein, egg white, cereal flakes, rice flour, blood products) to the EU list of foods which may be irradiated. However, they emphasised that irradiation must not be used to cover negligence in handling foodstuffs or to mask their unsuitability for use as food. Regarding certain substances in 'energy drinks', the experts considered that the scientific data available were insufficient to conclude that the substances were safe in the concentrations reported. The scientists pointed to increasing concerns about ochratoxin A, a mycotoxin produced by fungi and occurring naturally in a variety of plants such as cereals, coffee beans, beans, pulses or dry fruit. They recommended reducing exposure to this substance as much as possible.

Chemical substances (phthalates, etc)

A big part of the work in this area was devoted to the evaluation of risks from phthalate migration from soft PVC toys and child care articles. Phthalates are used to soften PVC, but they are considered to be liable to provoke negative health effects when they are washed out by saliva while children suck or chew the toys. The experts considered that the margins of safety for child exposure to phthalates from these products in some cases raised some concern (DINP), and in others raised clear concern (DEHP). The Commission recommended to watch closely soft PVC child care articles intended to be put into the mouth and act if necessary while it considers possible risk management options (for example, immediate ban or limitations on the marketing and use of phthalates in the articles in question). Another opinion on endocrine disrupting chemicals will serve as a basis for possible Commission actions, including a Communication and further research. These substances are suspected to disrupt normal functions in both humans and animals, therefore possibly leading to – among other health effects – an increased risk of cancer and malformation of sexual organs. The main conclusions of the opinion do not, at this stage, substantiate the concerns as regards human health effects. They do so, however, as regards effects on wildlife.

Pharmaceuticals, medical devices

The committee did not see a 'recognisable risk' that Creutzfeldt–Jacob disease (CJD) can be transmitted by blood and blood products. However, as a precautionary measure, they recommended to continue excluding individuals having been or being at risk of CJD from blood donation. The experts also endorsed the present policy of recalling plasma derivatives which have been prepared with a donation from donors who subsequently developed new variant CJD as a precautionary measure.

CHAPTER 3

FOOD REGULATION IN THE UNITED KINGDOM

The main piece of legislation governing food in the UK is the Food Safety Act 1990. The Act's name is slightly misleading, in that the Act itself deals with the whole range of issues relating to food, including regulation and enforcement, and does not just deal with 'safety'. In addition to this Act, there are other Acts of Parliament and a huge number of pieces of secondary legislation, usually called regulations, which are published as statutory instruments.

FOOD SAFETY ACT 1990

Part 1 of the Act deals with preliminary issues. Section 1 defines what is meant by 'food' and other basic expressions used in the Act, such as 'food business', 'food premises' and 'food sources'. Section 2 provides a wide definition of the term 'sale' to include food supplied in the course of a business. Section 3 sets out presumptions applying to food and food ingredients, for example, that food commonly used for human consumption found on certain food premises is presumed to be intended for sale for human consumption. Section 4 lays down which ministers have functions under the Act. Section 5 identifies food authorities and authorised officers for the purposes of the Act and s 6 deals with the enforcement of the Act.

Part II of the Act contains the main provisions. Sections 7–13 deal with food safety, ss 14 and 15 with consumer protection.

Sections 16–19 cover the making of regulations under the Act. Section 16(1) gives the minister the power to make regulations on a wide range of issues relating to food safety and quality. Regulations may be made in respect of the composition of food (s 16(1)(a)), the means of ensuring that food is fit for human consumption (s 16(1)(b)), processes or treatments used in the preparation of food (s 16(1)(c)), hygiene (s 16(1)(d)), labelling, marking, presenting or advertising food and descriptions which may be applied to food (s 16(1)(e)).

The power to make regulations is not only conferred in respect of the food itself, but also applies to food sources and contact materials.

Sections 20–22 deal with defences and ss 23–26 contain miscellaneous and supplemental provisions.

The major offences provided for in the Food Safety Act are found in ss 7, 8, 14 and 15. The commission of any of these offences attracts criminal liability.

Food safety

Section 7 deals with the issue of 'rendering food injurious to health':

(1) Any person who renders food injurious to health by any of the following operations, namely –

    (a) adding any article or substance to the food;

    (b) using any article or substance as an ingredient in the preparation of the food;

    (c) abstracting any constituent from any food; and

    (d) subjecting the food to any other process or treatment with intent that it shall be sold for human consumption, shall be guilty of an offence.

(2) In determining for the purposes of this section and s 8(2) below whether any food is injurious to health, regard shall be had –

    (a) not only to the probable effect of that food on the health of a person consuming it; but

    (b) also to the probable cumulative effect of food of substantially the same composition on the health of a person consuming it in ordinary quantities.

(3) In this Part 'injury', in relation to health, includes any impairment. whether permanent or temporary, and 'injurious to health' shall be construed accordingly.

The offence contained in s 7 requires intention to sell the food for human consumption. To determine whether the food is injurious to health, it is necessary to look not only at the probable effect on the health of the consumer, but also at the probable cumulative effect (s 7(2)). Food will not be 'injurious' just because 'some exceptional individual is liable to have some particular injury done to his health', but only if a substantial portion of the population is likely to be affected by it.[1] This concept could, therefore, include food allergies or intolerance where the allergic reaction or intolerance is suffered by a significant number of people. Food will not be injurious to health if it causes an adverse reaction when consumed in abnormal or excessive quantities.

'Injury to health' is defined as any impairment, whether permanent or temporary (s 7(3)), and the section clearly covers potential injury as well as actual injury suffered.

This section would appear to provide consumers with complete protection, but it is so widely drafted that, in practice, prosecutions are never brought under this section. In most cases where this section would apply, there are specific regulations dealing with the issues which provide a more specific basis for legal action.

---

1   *Cullen v McNair* (1908) 6 LGR 753, p 758, *per* Lord Alverstone CJ.

Where a consumer has suffered injury as a result of consuming food which is 'injurious to health', they might also have an action for damages under the Consumer Protection Act 1987.

Section 8 deals with the offence of 'selling food not complying with the safety requirements' (s 8(1)). Section 8(2) goes on to define what those food safety requirements are:

(1) Any person who –

    (a) sells for human consumption, or offers, exposes or advertises for sale for such consumption, or has in his possession for the purpose of such sale or of preparation for such sale; or ...

    (c) deposits with, or consigns to, any other person for the purpose of such sale or of preparation for such sale, any food which fails to comply with food safety requirements shall be guilty of an offence.

(2) For the purposes of this Part food fails to comply with food safety requirements if –

    (a) it has been rendered injurious to health by means of any of the operations mentioned in s 7(1) above;

    (b) it is unfit for human consumption; or

    (c) it is so contaminated (whether by extraneous matter or otherwise) that it would not be reasonable to expect it to be used for human consumption in that state;

and references to such requirements or to food complying with such requirements shall be construed accordingly.

Section 8 makes it an offence to sell, offer, expose or advertise for sale or to have in one's possession for such purpose, food which fails to comply with the food safety requirements or to deposit with, or consign to, any other person, food for the purpose of such sale or for preparation for such sale (s 8(1)). The offence can, therefore, be committed at any stage of production, processing, importation or distribution.

Food will fail to comply with the food safety requirements if it has been (a) rendered injurious to health by any of the means outlined in s 7(1); or (b) if it is unfit for human consumption; or (c) if it is so contaminated that it would not be reasonable to expect it to be used for human consumption in that condition (s 8(2)).

In the case of food contaminated by micro-organisms or their toxins, a prosecution should be brought under this section of the Act.[2]

Whether food is unfit for human consumption is a question of fact. There is no requirement that the food must be harmful to the consumer. Food containing a harmless foreign body would not necessarily be unfit, but food

---

2   Code of Practice No 1, *Responsibility for Enforcement of Food Safety Act 1990*, 1991, London: HMSO.

which was decomposed almost certainly would be unfit, even if it posed no threat to health.

In *R v F and M Dobson*,[3] a chocolate containing the blade of a Stanley knife which caused injury to the consumer clearly failed to comply with the food safety requirements.

A loaf of bread which contained a dirty bandage[4] and a pork pie which had (harmless) black mould under its crust[5] were found to be unfit for human consumption. On the other hand, in two cases heard on the same day, a loaf containing a piece of string[6] and a cream cake containing a piece of metal[7] were held not to be unfit for human consumption. It is irrelevant that the seller did not know or was unaware of the state of the food.[8] These cases would now be brought under s 8(2)(c), which covers 'contaminated' food.

The Act does not define what is meant by contamination, but it is generally accepted that it is widely interpreted and is likely to include foreign bodies, mould, pesticide residues, the presence of heavy metal, mites or other infestation, radioactive contamination and the presence of unauthorised additives.[9]

If something which is not food is mistakenly sold as food, the offence will still be committed. In *Meah v Roberts*,[10] caustic soda was mistakenly sold as lemonade. This was held to be a sale of food. There is authority to suggest that the owner of a business will be deemed to have committed the offence where the sale was in fact made by an employee. This is consistent with the general law on vicarious liability, where employers are held liable for the acts of their employees when the latter are acting in the course of their business.

Under s 8(3), if the food is part of a lot, batch or consignment of the same class or description, it is presumed that all the food fails to comply with the food safety requirements unless the contrary is proved. It is for the person selling, offering, advertising or exposing for sale, to prove that the food is fit for human consumption and safe. This will be determined on the balance of probabilities.

---

3   (1995) The Times, 8 March.

4   *Chibnall's Bakeries v Cope Brown* [1956] Crim LR 263.

5   *David Greig v Goldfinch* (1961) 105 Sol J 307.

6   *Turner and Son Ltd v Owen* [1956] 1 QB 48; [1955] 3 All ER 565.

7   *J Miller Ltd v Battersea BC* [1956] 1 QB 43; [1955] 3 All ER 279; [1955] 3 WLR 559.

8   *Hobbs v Winchester Corporation* [1910] 2 KB 471.

9   Painter (ed), *Butterworths' Law of Food and Drugs*, Vol 2, para B63.

10   [1978] 1 All ER 97.

Consumer protection under the Food Safety Act 1990

Section 14(1) of the Food Safety Act provides that it is an offence for a person to sell to a purchaser's prejudice any food which is not of the nature, substance or quality demanded by the purchaser. The food must have been intended for human consumption. The term sale in the Act has a wide definition.

There is considerable overlap between s 8 and s 14 of the Act and food which is not of the nature, substance or quality demanded will often also not meet the safety requirements of s 8.

Section 2(1) of the Sale of Goods Act 1979 also applies in these circumstances.

Section 14 is worded in such a way as to create three separate offences. Enforcement authorities must make it clear, when bringing a prosecution, within which of the three categories the case falls. There is obviously considerable overlap between the three offences and, in many situations, more than one of the offences will have been committed.

Nature

Where food is not of the nature demanded, this usually implies that the purchaser has been sold a different variety of product from the one which was demanded. This will usually also be a breach of s 13 of the Sale of Goods Act (SGA) 1979, which implies into every contract for the sale of goods a term that the goods will correspond to the description in the contract. A breach of s 13 of the SGA allows a consumer to bring an action for damages. In *Meah v Roberts* (above, p 60), caustic soda was mistakenly sold as lemonade. It was held that the food supplied was not of the nature demanded by the purchaser. Caustic soda is not usually sold for human consumption, but in this case it purported to be the sale of lemonade and, therefore, the offence had been committed.

The food supplied need not be harmful to health for there to be an offence under s 14. In *Shearer v Rowe*[11] it was held that, where something purported to be 'minced beef', but in fact it contained 10% lamb and 10% pork, it was not of the 'nature' demanded by the purchaser. What needs to be determined is how the food was described and what the ordinary purchaser would understand by such a description.

Substance

This tends to cover cases where food has been adulterated, where there are foreign bodies in the food or where the food does not contain the proper

---

11   (1996) 84 LGR 196.

ingredients. In all the following cases it was held that the foreign body in the food rendered the food not of the substance demanded. In *Smedleys Ltd v Breed*,[12] a caterpillar was found in a tin of peas; in *Greater Manchester Council v Lockwood Foods Ltd*,[13] a beetle was found in can of strawberries; in *Watford Corporation v Maypole Ltd*,[14] penicillin mould was found in a fruit pie.

The object does not have to be harmful to health. In *Barber v Co-operative Wholesale Society Limited*,[15] a sterile drinking straw was found in a carton of milk. There was no danger to health, but it was still held that the milk was not of the substance, nor of the quality, demanded. Robert Goff LJ said that the test was whether the purchaser could reasonably object to the presence of the straw in the carton. This test would suggest that if food is supplied which contains a piece of extraneous material about which no reasonable person could complain, then no offence is committed (see, for example, *Edwards v Llaethdy Meirion Ltd*.[16] If food is supplied which contains something which cold cause injury, the courts will accept that it is not of the substance demanded (*Sothworth v Whitewell Dairies Ltd*, where a sliver of glass was found in a bottle of milk).

If there are statutory or other accepted trade standards relating to the composition of a particular food product, the food which fails to comply with those standards could be regarded as not being of the substance demanded. In *Tonkin v Victor Value*,[17] the defendants supplied 'mock salmon cutlets' which contained only 33% salmon. There were no statutory standards for such cutlets, but there was a standard for salmon fishcakes, which was that they should contain 35% salmon. It was held that, as a reasonable person would expect a 'cutlet' to be a superior product to a 'fishcake', they would not expect it to contain less salmon than the inferior product and therefore the cutlets were not of the substance demanded. The courts can also look at general trade practices.[18]

Quality

This means the quality demanded by a reasonable consumer. The issue of quality arises where a product contains more or less of an ingredient or the absence or presence of a particular ingredient. It could also include situations

---

12 [1974] AC 839.
13 [1979] Crim LR 593.
14 [1970] 1 QB 573.
15 (1983) 81 LGR 762.
16 (1957) 107 LJ 138.
17 [1962] 1 All ER 821.
18 *Per* Lord Parker CJ, p 823.

where a foreign body is found in the food. In *McDonalds v Windle*,[19] where a customer was supplied with ordinary Coke when they had asked for Diet Coke, it was held, in the circumstances, that the drink was not of the quality demanded because the defendant had displayed a notice giving the energy values of both ordinary and Diet Coke. This situation could also give rise to an offence because the product was not of the nature demanded. As indicated above, there is a considerable overlap between the offences. In *Newton v West Vale*, it was held that a fly found in a bottle of milk rendered the milk not of the quality demanded.

Whether a product is of the quality demanded might also depend on the price paid for it. Essentially, it is a question of fact in all the circumstances of the case. In *Goldup v John Masson Limited*,[20] cheap minced beef was sold. It contained 35% fat. Better quality beef was more expensive. No offence was committed where the cheaper beef contained a higher fat content because of the lower price. In *TW Lawrence and Sons v Burleigh*,[21] however, a butcher who sold minced beef containing 30.8% fat was held to have committed an offence under s 14 because the customer, having placed the order over the telephone, had no opportunity to inspect the meat and, therefore, a higher standard of quality was required.

For an offence to be committed under s 14, the food must be sold to the purchaser's 'prejudice'. This means that the food must be inferior or less in some way than what was demanded. It does not have to be harmful. Prejudice occurs because the purchaser does not get what he or she demanded. This means that the purchaser must actually have demanded food of a particular nature, substance or quality.[22]

Nowadays, of course, most people do most of their shopping in supermarkets where a lot of food is prepackaged and purchasers are often not in a position to make detailed or specific demands as to the 'nature, substance or quality' of the food they are buying. In these circumstances, courts will need to have regard to what an ordinary, reasonable purchaser might expect in order to determine whether a relevant demand has been made for the purposes of the s 14 offences. Account will be taken of statutory standards, trade practice, etc.

False and misleading descriptions

Under s 15 of the Food Safety Act, it is an offence falsely to describe, advertise or present food.

---

19 [1986] Tr LR 81.
20 [1981] 3 All ER 257.
21 (1981) 80 LGR 631.
22 *Collins Arden Products Ltd v Barking Corporation* [1943] 1 KB 419.

Labels

Under s 15(1), it is an offence for a person to sell, offer, expose or possess for the purposes of sale any food which is labelled in such a way that the label either falsely describes the food (s 15(1)(a)) or is likely to be misleading as to the nature or substance or quality of the food (s 15(1)(b)).

'Sale' here means sale for human consumption (s 15 (5)).

Section 15(1) only applies to descriptions on labelling and does not include oral descriptions.

The difference between 'false' and 'misleading' appears to be that 'a label is false if there is a clear factual misstatement', and that 'it is misleading if the label is false only by inference or omission'.[23]

The word 'false' implies a clear factual statement which is wrong. The word 'misleading' implies that one must ask what the ordinary consumer would understand by the description. The description must be 'likely' to mislead.

A label can be false or misleading not only when something has been stated on a label, but also when something has been omitted. A case which is often used to illustrate this is the case where two products which were substitutes for fresh cream were sold as 'Elmlea Single' and 'Elmlea Whipping'. It was held that the use of cartons such as the type in which fresh cream was sold, the use of the words single and whipping, the colouring of the words and the rural scene depicted on the carton might mislead consumers into believing that they were buying real cream. The fact that the product was clearly labelled as 'the real alternative to cream' made no difference as it was held that a consumer without special knowledge of such products could be misled by the label.[24] The label has to be 'likely' to mislead and this is a question of fact for the court to determine, having regard to the whole label or advertisement and not just to one single statement that might in itself be misleading.

Advertisements

Under s 15(2), it is an offence for someone to publish, or be party to the publication of, an advertisement which falsely describes any food or is likely to mislead as to the nature or substance or quality of such food. 'Advertisement' is defined in the Act as including any notice, circular, label, wrapper, invoice or other document, and any public announcement made orally or by any means of producing or transmitting light or sound (s 53(1)).

---

23 *Op cit*, Painter, fn 9, Vol 1, para B132.
24 *Van den Berghs and Jurgens Ltd v Burleigh* (1987) unreported.

The provision does not apply to a label given or supplied by the defendant which is covered by s 15(1).

It is important to note that, in respect of the offences relating to labels and to advertisements, s 15(4) makes it clear that it is not a defence to show that there was an accurate statement as to the composition of the food on the label or in the advertisement.

Presentation

Section 15(3) makes it an offence to sell, offer or expose for sale, or have in one's possession for the purposes of sale any food, the *presentation* of which is likely to mislead as to the nature, substance or quality of the food. The presentation of food includes its shape, appearance, and packaging as well as the way it is arranged when exposed for sale and the setting in which the food is displayed with a view to sale. Any form of labelling or advertising is, however, excluded from the definition of presentation (s 53(1)).

The s 15(3) offence is similar to the offences under the Food Labelling Regulations. The due diligence defence applies to s 15(3) offences.

It is also worth noting that there can be an overlap between s 15 of the Food Safety Act and s 1 of the Trade Descriptions Act 1968, which makes it an offence to apply a false trade description to any goods or to supply or offer to supply any such goods. The false description can be a description given verbally.[25]

Enforcement powers

Section 9 provides for the inspection and seizure of food. Sections 10–13 deal with improvement notices, prohibition orders, emergency prohibition notices and orders and emergency control orders respectively.

Inspection, seizure and destruction of suspected food (s 9)[26]

Section 9(1) provides that 'any authorised officer of a food authority may at all reasonable times inspect any food intended for human consumption' and if, as a result of that inspection, it appears that the food fails to comply with the food safety requirements, further action is permitted. This further action is outlined in s 9(3) and can involve the issuing of notices or the seizure of the food. Section 9(6) provides for the inspectors to apply to a court for an order for the food to be condemned and disposed of if it appears to the court that

---

25 Trade Descriptions Act 1968, s 4(2).
26 See Code of Practice No 4, *Inspection, Detention and Seizure of Suspected Food*, 1990, London: HMSO.

the food does not satisfy the food safety requirements. Where an enforcement officer applies to the court for further orders, he must issue a food condemnation warning notice which must state the reasons for issuing the notice and must give the person upon whom the notice is served the right to explain why the food should not be condemned.[27] If the court decides that the food does fail to meet the safety requirements, the food must be condemned and an order for its destruction or disposal will be issued. In reaching its decision, the court must take account of all the available evidence, including any evidence presented by the owner of the food concerned as well as evidence from the Public Health Laboratory Service.

If a notice issued under s 9(3) is withdrawn, or if the court does not condemn the food, then the food authority is required to pay compensation for the depreciation in the value of the food resulting from the action that was taken (s 9(7)).

There is no provision for an appeal against a decision to condemn food: the only remedy available to the owner of the food is to challenge the decision by way of judicial review. This, however, takes place after the event and is a review of the way in which the decision to condemn the food was reached. It will not prevent the food being destroyed in the first place.

Improvement notices (s 10)

Section 10 provides for improvement notices to be issued where food hygiene or food processing regulations have been contravened.[28] Where an improvement notice is served, the enforcement officer must state the grounds on which he believes the food business is failing, must state as precisely as possible the steps that must be taken in order to comply with the matters set out in the notice, and must also specify the time period within which these steps must be taken (s 10(1)).

If a person fails to comply with an improvement notice, then an offence is committed (s 10(2)).

Section 10 does not provide for the payment of compensation by the enforcement authority where an improvement notice has been wrongly or unreasonably served upon a food business.

Enforcement authorities are encouraged to comply with the guidance on good practice set out in Code of Practice No 5.[29]

---

27 Detention of Food (Prescribed Forms) Regulations 1990 (SI 1990/2614).

28 Food Safety Act 1990, s 10(1) and (3). The required format for the notice is set out in the Food Safety (Improvement and Prohibition – Prescribed Forms) Regulations 1991 (SI 1991/100).

29 *The Use of Improvement Notices*, 1991 (revised 1994), London: HMSO.

Prohibition orders (s 11)

Section 11 provides for prohibition notices to be issued by the courts where the proprietor of a food business has been convicted of an offence under food hygiene or food processing regulations to which the improvement notice regime applies (s 11(1)(a)). The court must be satisfied that the food business presents a risk to health (s 11 (1)(b)).

A food business presents a risk to health if there is a risk of injury to health resulting from the use of any process or treatment, the construction of premises, the use of any equipment or the state or condition of any premises or equipment (s 11(2)).

The nature of the prohibition order will vary depending on the nature of the risk posed. Where the enforcement authority is satisfied that a health risk no longer exists, it must issue a certificate, within three days, lifting the order (s 11(6) and (7)). The person upon whom the prohibition order was served is entitled to apply for a certificate, in which case the enforcement authority must make a decision as to whether there is still a health risk within 14 days (s 11(7)).

Guidance on the use of prohibition notices is contained in Code of Practice No 6.[30]

Emergency orders and food scares (s 12)

Section 12 provides emergency prohibition powers for use by authorised officers where there is an imminent risk of injury to health. There is provision for the immediate issue of an emergency prohibition notice in terms identical to those applying to prohibition notices. The enforcement authority can also apply to a magistrates' court for an emergency prohibition order (s 12(2)). Such an order will only be granted if one day's notice has been given to the proprietor of the food business (s 12(3)). Section 12(7) provides that, where a prohibition order has been issued, it will lapse unless an application is made to a magistrates' court for an order to the same effect under s 12(3). Where the court refuses to grant the prohibition order or where the enforcement authority decides not to make an application to the court, compensation will be payable to the proprietor of the food business (s 12(10)).

Section 13 gives ministers powers to make emergency control orders prohibiting commercial operations in relation to food, food sources or contact materials when there is an imminent risk of such items causing injury to health.

This procedure is particularly useful in the event of a 'food scare'.

---

30 *Prohibition Procedures*, 1991, London: HMSO, applies to s 11 and to the special provisions in s 12 concerning emergency orders.

In addition to the specific procedures outlined above, there is a system in the UK for alerting local enforcement authorities promptly of any potential dangers. The system aims to detect food hazards, evaluate them and to control them. If a food is identified as contaminated and a decision is taken to withdraw it, this decision must be communicated immediately to 60 local authorities, who then have the responsibility to pass on the information to other authorities within their general area. The European Commission must also be kept informed of the situation so that action can be taken at European level if necessary.

The necessary action to deal with a food hazard is contained in Code of Practice No 16.[31] The Code requires local enforcement authorities to determine the probable scale of the problem, to consider the possibility that the hazard was caused by a malicious act and to evaluate the extent of the risk to health.

Defences

Section 20 allows the enforcement authority to 'bypass' the immediate offender and to prosecute the real offender. Section 21 provides for a defence where defendants can prove to the court that they took all reasonable precautions and exercised all due diligence to avoid committing the offence. The defendant is deemed to have satisfied this due diligence defence in certain circumstances. These deemed due diligence defences are not available to a defendant who manufactured or imported the food. Section 22 contains a special defence for businesses who publish an advertisement in good faith.

The due diligence defence

This defence is important as a safeguard for the defendant who has done everything possible to prevent any offence being committed. The Act is a powerful tool in the hands of the enforcement authorities. If food is produced which is unfit for human consumption, an offence is committed and a prosecution can be brought. The offence is absolute and there is no need for the prosecution to establish any criminal intention on the part of the defendant. Hence the need for the defence. The onus is on the defendant to prove that he took all reasonable precautions and exercised all due diligence. He must prove both parts of the defence – they must not assume that the reasonable precautions are necessarily sufficient.

Section 21 provides that:

---

31 *Enforcement of the Food Safety Act 1990 in Relation to the Food Hazard Warning System*, 1993, London: HMSO.

(1) In any proceedings for an offence under any of the preceding provisions of this Part ... it shall, subject to section (5) below, be a defence for the person charged to prove that he took all reasonable precautions and exercised all due diligence to avoid the commission of the offence by himself or a person under his control.

The defence means that, if a person or a company has been trying to fulfil all legal requirements but, because of some unforeseen occurrence, fails to comply with the legal requirements, they will not be found guilty if they can show that they acted with due diligence and took all reasonable precautions. It is for the defendant to establish the defence ('... for the person charged to prove ...'). The prosecution simply has to demonstrate that the offence has been committed. A food business must take 'all reasonable precautions' to avoid breaking food law. What is 'reasonable' will depend on the nature and size of the food business. What might be considered reasonable for a large national company selling mass-produced products through major supermarket chains would not be reasonable for a small producer selling small quantities of possibly speciality products through a single outlet. A food business must also exercise 'all due diligence' and must not assume that the reasonable precautions are effective. The food business must demonstrate that they checked equipment, kept quality control systems under review, etc.

There are also a number of presumptions which determine the way in which the due diligence defence works. If a person who sells food under his own name or brand name has relied on information supplied to him by another person, it is presumed for the purposes of the defence that the seller has taken reasonable precautions and that he or some other person has carried out reasonable checks on the food and has no reason to suspect that an offence has been committed (s 21(3)).

Where a person does not sell under his own name or brand mark, then it is presumed that reasonable precautions have been taken where the seller has relied on information supplied by another and has no reason to suspect that an offence has been committed (s 21(4)).

It is for the courts to decide whether a defence has been established. Previous cases can sometimes help decide what is needed to satisfy the defence, but there is no detailed guidance. Every case will turn on its own facts.

Regulations under the Food Safety Act 1990

In addition to establishing the main offences outlined above, the Act contains many sections which confer on ministers the power to make regulations. In this respect it is essentially an 'enabling' Act delegating power to ministers to make secondary legislation containing the detailed provisions. Ministers are required to consult before issuing regulations unless the mater is one of such urgency that consultation is not possible. Draft regulations are usually issued and comments invited some time before the measures are published. Ministries have mailing lists of people and organisations they regularly contact for the purposes of consultation, but the process is also usually open to the general public, through public announcements, newsletters and the internet. Full details of secondary legislation can be found in Butterworths' *Law of Food and Drugs* and Sweet & Maxwell's *Practical Food Law Manual*.

Enforcement Codes of Practice

Under the Food Safety Act 1990, there is a provision (Section 40) which allows the Minister to issue enforcement Codes of Practice. This provision was included so as to provide a means of ensuring that the enforcement officers employed by local authorities operated to certain minimum national criteria. The Codes do not prescribe precisely what an officer must do but the Act ensures that, should a case come to court, the court can take into account the manner in which the enforcement officer has operated. In other words, if an officer has no good reason for ignoring the content of the Code, the defendant might be able to have the case thrown out 'on a technicality'.

Several Codes were issued quite rapidly after the passing of the Food Safety Act in 1990. Since then, they have been published from time to time, usually when new complex regulations have been adopted. It is often easier to Codes of Practice for complex and technical details than to put them in a Regulation.

The following is a list of the Codes and their date of publication:

1   *Responsibility for Enforcement of the Food Safety Act 1990*, 1991

2   *Legal Matters*, 1991

3   *Inspection Procedures – General*, 1991

4   *Inspection, Detention and Seizure of Suspect Food*, 1991

5   *The Use of Improvement Notices*, 1991 (revised 1994)

6   *Prohibition Procedures*, 1991

7   *Sampling for Analysis or Examination*, 1991 (revised October 2000)

8   *Food Standards Inspections*, 1991 (revised 1996)

9   *Food Hygiene Inspections*, 1991 (revised 1995 and again in October 2000)

10 *Enforcement of the Temperature Control Requirements of Food Hygiene Regulations*, 1991 (revised 1994)

11 *Enforcement of the Food Premises (Registration) Regulations*, 1991

12 *Quick Frozen Foodstuffs – Division of Enforcement Responsibilities*, 1991 (revised 1994)

13 *Enforcement of the Food Safety Act 1990 in Relation to Crown Premises*, 1992

14 *Enforcement of the Food Safety (Live Bivalve Molluscs and other Shellfish) Regulations 1992*, 1994

15 *Enforcement of the Food Safety (Fishery Products) Regulations 1992*, 1994

16 *Enforcement of the Food Safety Act 1990 in Relation to the Food Hazard Warning System*, 1993

17 *Enforcement of the Meat Products (Hygiene) Regulations 1994*, 1994

18 *Enforcement of the Dairy Products (Hygiene) Regulations 1995*, 1995

19 *Qualifications and Experience of Authorised Officers and Experts*, 1996 (revised October 2000)

20 *Exchange of Information between Member States of the EU on Routine Food Control Matters*, 1996

Codes 5, 6 and 8 are currently in the process of being revised. The texts of the Codes and the proposed amendments can be found on the Food Standards Agency website.

CONSUMER PROTECTION ACT 1987

The Consumer Protection Act (CPA) 1987 was enacted to give effect to Directive 85/374[32] and introduced strict liability for defective products, including food. The 'producer' of a product is strictly liable for any damage 'caused wholly or partly by a defect in a product' (s 2(1)).

The 'producer' of a product may be the person who actually manufactured the product, but the definition also includes those who have put their own brand name or mark on the product, thereby holding themselves out to be the producer of the product, and importers of a product into the EC from outside in the course of any business in order to supply the product to another. If the retailer of 'own brand' products wants to avoid liability, the product must indicate that it has been supplied to the retailer by including the words 'supplied to …' or 'made for …' on the label, immediately before the retailer's name and address.

---

32 Council Directive 85/374/EEC.

The supplier of the product can be held liable for any damage if he fails to supply to the person who has suffered the damage, within a reasonable time, the name of the producer, importer or the person who held himself out to be the producer of the product. The request for the information must be made within a reasonable time of the damage occurring and at a time when it is not reasonably practicable for the injured party to identify those persons (s 2(3)).

It is not only the 'producer' of the finished product who may be liable. Liability can lie with the supplier of a component or ingredient if the necessary proof that the injury was caused by that component or ingredient can be established.

The consumer must prove causation: that is, they must prove that their injury has been caused by the defective product. It is not sufficient to show that there is a foreign body in the food or that the food has decomposed.

'Defect' means that 'the safety of the product is not such as persons generally are entitled to expect' (s 3(1)). Factors to be taken into account include 'the manner in which and the purposes for which the product had been manufactured, its get up, the use of any mark in relation to the product and instructions for use, or warnings with regard to doing or refraining from doing anything in relation to the product' (s 3(2)).

Defences under the CPA 1987

There are a number of defences available under s 4.

Section 4(1)(a) provides that it is a defence where the defect 'is attributable to compliance with any requirement imposed by or under any enactment or with any Community obligation'. This means that any product which has been made to comply with compositional or other requirements provided under the Food Safety Act or any of the regulations made under it cannot give rise to liability under the CPA.

Section 4(1)(b) provides that it is a defence where 'the person proceeded against did not at any time supply the product to another'. This means that, where the manufacturer of a food product can identify the supplier of the ingredients, he will not be liable.

Section 4(1)(c) provides that it will be a defence where 'the only supply of the product to another by the person proceeded against was otherwise than in the course of a business of that person' or where the ingredients were supplied without a view to making a profit.

Section 4(1)(d) makes it a defence where the defect did not exist in the product at the relevant time.

Section 4(1)(e) provides what is known as the 'state of the art' defence. This provides that where 'the state of scientific and technological knowledge at the relevant time was not such that a producer of products of the same description as the product in question might be expected to have discovered the defect if it had existed in his products while they were under his control'. This means that there is a defence if the producer can demonstrate that the available scientific and technological knowledge at the time would not have enabled him to identify the defect. This defence could probably be used, at the moment, in the case of 'novel' foods.

Liability under the Act cannot be excluded by contract terms or by any other means (s 7).

No action in respect of personal injuries or loss of or damage to any property can be brought after the expiry of three years after the date on which the cause of action occurred, or the date of knowledge of the injury, loss or damage, whichever is the later.[33] No action may be brought after the expiry of 10 years from the relevant times.

Game and primary agricultural products

Under Art 2 of the EC Directive, Member States had the choice as to whether or not to include game and primary agricultural products (that is, vegetables, unprocessed meat or fish). The UK chose to exempt them from the CPA 1987. Agricultural products were defined as any product of the soil, of stock farming or of fisheries. There could be no liability in respect of such products unless they had undergone an 'industrial' process (s 2(4)). Jane Stapleton has argued that the 'exemption for game and unprocessed agricultural produce cannot be supported by any moral, economic or legitimate practical argument'.[34] At the time, the Government justified the exemption on the grounds that the Directive was intended to protect against 'risks inherent in modern technical production' and was therefore aimed at industrial goods. The English and Scottish Law Commissions have both rejected the exemption, arguing that farming today is a highly technological industry, involving, for example, chemicals, fertilisers and pesticides.[35]

In October 1997, following the experience of the BSE crisis, the European Commission adopted a proposal[36] to amend the Product Liability Directive to include primary agricultural produce. In preparing its proposal, the Commission took account of the public expectation of improved protection for consumer health, the existence in certain Member States of national laws on liability for primary agricultural products and the lack of evidence that the

---

33 Consumer Protection Act 1987, Sched 1 inserted a new s 11A into the Limitation Act 1980 and a new s 22A was inserted into the Prescription and Limitation (Scotland) Act 1973.

34 Stapleton, *Product Liability*, 1994, London: Butterworths, p 305.

35 Law Commission and Scottish Law Commission, *Liability for Defective Products*, Cmnd 9831, London: HMSO, paras 85–86.

36 OJ 1997 C337/54.

proposed inclusion of these products would have an adverse effect on agriculture. The proposal was adopted in March 1999.[37] In addition to the inclusion of game and primary agricultural produce, the Directive has also extended the limitation period to 20 years after the date on which the product was put on the market. This is a result of the experience with BSE, which clearly demonstrated that there can be an incubation period for diseases which may exceed the current limit of 10 years within which to bring an action. Member States had until 4 December 2000 to implement this amendment.

FOOD IMITATIONS

The Food Imitations (Safety) Regulations 1981[38] implement Directive 87/35[39] on products which, appearing to be other than they are, endanger the health or safety of consumers. It is an offence to supply, offer to supply, agree to supply, expose for supply or possess for the purpose of supplying manufactured goods which are ordinarily intended for private use and which are not food for human consumption, but which have a form, colour, odour or appearance, packaging, labelling, volume or size that is likely to cause people, especially children, to mistake them for food and put them into their mouths or suck them or swallow them, with the result that they might suffer death or personal injury. The Regulations do not apply to marbles, products for dolls houses or other model scene or setting or anything consisting entirely of articles or substances used as ingredients in the preparation of food. They also exclude items listed in s 11(7) of the CPA 1987.[40] A breach of these Regulations is an offence under the CPA.

SALE OF GOODS ACT 1979

Under s 14(2) of the Sale of Goods Act (SGA) 1979, 'where the seller sells goods in the course of a business, there is an implied term that the goods supplied are of satisfactory quality'. Section 14(2)(A) states that 'For the purposes of this Act goods are of satisfactory quality if they meet the standard that a reasonable person would regard as satisfactory, taking account of any description of the goods, the price (if relevant) and all the other relevant

---

37 European Parliament and Council Directive 99/34/EC (OJ 1999 141/20).
38 SI 1989/1291.
39 Directive 87/35 on products which appearing to be other than they are endanger the health or safety of consumers.
40 Growing crops, water, food, feeding stuff and fertiliser, gas, controlled drugs and licensed medicinal products.

circumstances'. Both of theses provisions apply to the sale of food. The effect of s 14(2) is to imply into every contract for the sale of goods, including food, a term that the goods will be of satisfactory quality. If the goods are not of satisfactory quality then, as well as any other remedy which might be available to the purchaser, they are entitled to a full refund. They do not have to accept an exchange.

GENERAL PRODUCT SAFETY

A general safety requirement exists in law in respect of all products, including food. This was introduced by Directive 92/59[41] and implemented in the UK by the General Product Safety Regulations 1994.[42] Like the Food Safety Act, the Regulations impose criminal liability on those who provide food which is unsafe. Regulation 7 states that 'no producer shall place a product on the market unless the product is a safe product'.

A safe product is defined as:

... any product which, under normal or reasonably foreseeable conditions of use, including duration, does not present any risk or only the minimum risks compatible with the product's use, considered as acceptable and consistent with a high level of protection for the safety and health of persons, taking into account in particular –

(a) the characteristics of the product, including its composition, packaging, instructions for assembly and maintenance;

(b) the effect on other products, where it is reasonably foreseeable that it will be used with other products;

(c) the presentation of the product, the labelling, any instructions for its use and disposal and any other indication or information provided by the producer; and

(d) the categories of consumers at serious risk when using the product, in particular children, and the fact that a higher level of safety may be obtained or other products presenting a lesser degree of risk may be available shall not of itself cause the product to be considered other than a safe product.

The usual defences that are available under the Food Safety Act are available under the Regulations.

Regulation 11 provides that food authorities are under a duty to enforce or secure enforcement of the Regulations. The Regulations provide that the sections of the Food Safety Act which allow officers to inspect and purchase food and submit food to be analysed apply 'as if these Regulations were food

41 Council Directive 92/59/EEC on general product safety.
42 SI 1994/2328.

safety requirements made under the Act'. Section 10 of the Food Safety Act, which allows officers to serve improvement notices, also applies 'as if these Regulations were made under Part II of the Act'.

FOOD STANDARDS AGENCY

Prior to the establishment of the Food Standards Agency the two government departments which had responsibility for food issues were the Ministry of Agriculture, Fisheries and Food (MAFF) and the Department of Health (DoH). The DoH was responsible for issues relating to the microbiological safety of food. MAFF was responsible for every other aspect. The main problem with this arrangement was that MAFF was perceived as being too closely involved with the producers of food, namely the food industry and the farming sector, to be able to be credible as a body concerned with consumer protection.

In the wake of the BSE crisis, there was a widespread view that there should be some kind of agency to regulate food.

Professor Philip James was asked by the Labour Party, then in opposition, to prepare a report setting out what was required in order to establish a food standards agency in the event of Labour winning the next general election. The report was prepared for Tony Blair personally, but was also intended for publication 'as part of the process of establishing an open system of communication and consultation'.[43]

The report was dated 30 April 1997. The election was held on 1 May 1997. The Report – *The Food Standards Agency: An Interim Proposal* – was presented to the new Labour Government shortly after it came into power and was immediately published for public consultation.

In January 1998, following the consultation period, the Government published a White Paper – *The Food Standards Agency: A Force for Change* – based on the James Report and the responses to the consultation. The White Paper itself was put out to consultation from January to March 1998 and, in January 1999, a draft Bill was presented for consultation in the Command Paper *The Food Standards Agency: Consultation on Draft Legislation*. The House of Commons Select Committee – the Food Standards Committee – published its report on the draft Bill in March 1999 and, in June 1999, the Bill in its definitive form was introduced into the House of Commons. In November 1999, the Bill received the royal assent and became the Food Standards Act 1999. On 3 April 2000, the Food Standards Agency became operational in accordance with the Act. Section 1(2) of the Act provides:

---

43 The Food Standards Agency Report – An Interim Proposal, Sir Philip James, 1997, Part I, para 1.

The main objective of the Agency in carrying out its functions is to protect public health from risks which may arise in connection with the consumption of food (including risks caused by the way in which it is produced or supplied) and otherwise to protect the interests of consumers in relation to food.

Section 6 outlines the functions of the Agency:

(1) The Agency has the function of –

   (a) developing policies (or assisting in the development by any public authority of policies) relating to matters connected with food safety or other interests of consumers in relation to food; and

   (b) providing advice, information or assistance in respect of such matters to any public authority.

Section 7 covers the provision of advice, information and assistance to other persons:

(1) The Agency has the function of –

   (a) providing advice and information to the general public (or any section of the public) in respect of matters connected with food safety or other interests of consumers in relation to food;

   (b) providing advice, information or assistance in respect of such matters to any person who is not a public authority.

Section 8 provides for the acquisition and review of information:

(1) The Agency has the function of obtaining, compiling and keeping under review information about matters connected with food safety and other interests of consumers in relation to food.

(2) That function includes (among other things) –

   (a) monitoring developments in science, technology and other fields of knowledge relating to the matters mentioned in sub-section (1);

   (b) carrying out, commissioning or co-ordinating research on those matters.

All aspects of food safety and standards are now the responsibility of the Food Standards Agency. The regulation of on-farm practices remains the responsibility of MAFF, however.

Aims and values

The Agency has been created to protect public health from risks which may arise in connection with the consumption of food, and otherwise to protect the interests of consumers in relation to food. The Agency will protect the interests of consumers by following three core values. It will:

(a) put the consumer first;

(b) be open and accessible;

(c) be an independent voice.

The Agency's functions are to:

- provide advice and information to the public and to the Government on food safety from farm to fork, nutrition and diet;
- protect consumers through effective enforcement and monitoring;
- support consumer choice through promoting accurate and meaningful labelling.

It will:

- base its decisions and advice on the best evidence available;
- consult widely before it takes action and makes recommendations unless urgent action is essential;
- obtain independent expert advice from its advisory committees;
- commission research to support its functions;
- be prompt in making public its advice to the Government.

The Agency has a policy of openness and transparency and provides full information on its aims, values, structures and committees on its website.

The Agency's structure

The Food Standards Agency is led by a Board which has been appointed to act in the public interest, not to represent particular sectors. Its members bring a wide range of relevant skills and experience.

The Agency is accountable to Parliament through Health Ministers, and as a UK body to the devolved administrations for its activities within their areas. To safeguard its independence, it has the unique legal power to publish the advice it gives to the Government.

Its UK headquarters are based in London, and there are offices in Scotland, Wales and Northern Ireland. The Meat Hygiene Service is now accountable to the Food Standards Agency.

The UK headquarters comprise three main groups incorporating a range of specialist divisions established to fulfil the tasks of the Agency.

I Food Safety Policy Group

This group deals with all aspects of food safety and nutrition. Most of these functions were previously split between MAFF and the Department of Health. The group also includes the new Food Chain Strategy Division, which will undertake focused studies on food safety and standards across the food chain from the farm onwards.

Additives and Novel Foods Division

This division is responsible for developing policy and setting standards for food additives, food contact materials, novel foods (including genetically modified foods) and novel processes.

Animal Feed Division

This division negotiates and administers international standards for the composition and labelling of animal feeds, for example, on additives in feed, maximum permitted levels of contaminants, labelling, and rules on official inspections and approval of establishments.

Chemical Safety and Toxicology Division

This division determines safety limits for chemicals in food through the development of risk assessments, develops policy and advises on food allergy and the safety of natural toxicants, and ensures consumer interests are taken into account in the safety assessments of pesticides and veterinary medicines.

Contaminants Division

This division is responsible for policy development on heavy metals, mycotoxins, organic chemicals, nitrates, radionuclides and other chemical contaminants in food. It manages an extensive programme of surveys and investigations to monitor the levels of those contaminants in food which pose significant health threats. It also provides advice on the analysis and sampling of food and includes the Radiological Safety Unit (RSU), which sets standards for radioactive waste disposals to ensure these do not affect food safety, takes action in cases of unacceptable contamination of food, and provides advice on the scientific aspects of food irradiation.

Food Chain Strategy Division

This division undertakes one of the new functions of the Food Standards Agency, namely, to develop a strategic view of food safety and standards throughout the food chain from farm to fork. It will also have responsibility for leading focused investigations into food safety and standards in specific areas from the farm onwards, drawing on expertise both within and outside the Food Standards Agency.

Microbiological Safety Division

This division is charged with promoting the microbiological safety of food throughout the food chain. It will take on the new task of developing a strategy for reducing food-borne illness. It also promotes a hazard analysis-based approach to food safety management and provides guidance for producers, retailers, caterers and the general public. It works with the EU to improve food hygiene regulations, works closely with the Public Health Laboratory Service and supports local public health officials in dealing with microbiological food hazards and outbreaks of food-borne disease.

This division also takes the lead in the handling of major outbreaks and hazards with wider national or international implications.

Nutrition Division

This division provides authoritative factual information about the nutrient content of individual foods and of the diet as a whole. It secures expert scientific advice on the relationship between diet, nutritional status and health and provides information on a healthy balanced diet, so as to promote and protect public health.

Research Co-ordination Unit

This unit will develop a strategy and framework for managing the Agency's research budget, and liaises with other food research organisations.

II Enforcement and Food Standards Group

This group includes two new divisions established to help local authorities improve the effectiveness of local enforcement of food standards legislation. In addition, it will bring together, and develop, the work on enforcing food law which was previously divided between the Department of Health and MAFF. This encompasses food hygiene, composition, authenticity and other trading standards.

Food labelling, standards and Consumer Protection Division

The work of this division is to ensure that food meets appropriate quality standards and to promote informed consumer choice. It will focus on the development of international standards and UK and EU food law to ensure adequate protection of consumers. It will work with EU partners to seek to establish a food labelling regime which delivers the information consumers need in a clear and accurate way. It is responsible for co-ordinating the UK contribution to the setting of international standards in Codex. It will manage a programme of surveys and investigations to check the level of food adulteration, misdescription and fraud; will ensure that the Agency's policies recognise the needs of groups with particular characteristics, such as food allergy sufferers and low income groups; will develop and improve links with consumer groups and ensure that their views are taken into account in all the Agency's activities.

Local Authority Enforcement (Policy) Division

This is a new division which will set standards for local authorities' enforcement of food law and monitor and audit their performance against established standards.

Local Authority Enforcement (Support) Division

This is a new division which will work with local authority enforcement services to improve standards by providing advice, guidance and training on technical, professional and legislation issues. It takes over responsibility for the existing food hazard warning system, and policy on statutory enforcement powers and import controls on fish and food of non-animal origin.

Meat Hygiene Division

This division is responsible for standards of meat hygiene in licensed plants. It develops policy on red meat; poultry meat; farmed and wild game; hygiene standards; and meat inspection charges. The division works closely with the Meat Hygiene Service, which is responsible for enforcing these standards, and with the Veterinary Public Health Unit (see below). It develops and implements strategy for the food safety aspects of BSE controls, advises on meat inspection charges, and publishes monthly enforcement reports.

Veterinary Public Health Unit (VPHU) HQ team

This unit is responsible for the licensing of meat plants and designation of Official Veterinary Surgeons and for the meat hygiene legislation and policy relating to these areas. The unit provides veterinary public health advice to the Meat Hygiene Division.

The Field team supports the HQ team in its licensing function by carrying out inspection visits to various meat premises such as slaughterhouses, cutting premises and cold stores. It organises, manages and carries out the audit of the Meat Hygiene Service.

Food Emergencies Unit

This unit develops standards and protocols for the Food Standards Agency's handling of emergencies, and develops generic risk management approaches for use in internal incident plans.

III Corporate Resources and Strategy Group

This group supports the Agency as a whole through the work of its three divisions:

- Corporate Strategy Division

  This division provides the secretariat to the Food Standards Agency Board and support to the Board on strategic and cross-Agency issues. It co-ordinates liaison with international organisations and with other government departments, provides economics, statistics, and operational research support to the whole organisation and leads on risk management and communication issues (working with the Communications Division). It will be responsible for developing and implementing strategies on openness and consultation.

- Finance, Procurement and IT Division

  This division is responsible for financial management and strategy, financial systems procurement, IT support and system development, and the webmaster.

- Personnel and Establishments Division

  This division is responsible for strategic and operational personnel issues, training and development, internal communications, and organisational development, accommodation and related support services.

Communications Division

This division helps all parts of the Food Standards Agency to communicate effectively with the public and the media, and supports the work of the Corporate Strategy Division on risk communications. It has a press office and deals with media relations, and provides editorial and publishing support for Food Standards Agency publications.

Legal Services

There is provision for legal advice and legislative drafting for the Food Standards Agency and the Meat Hygiene Service. They undertake quality assurance and supervision of litigation and other legal services provided by other departments or the private sector.

An investigation branch investigates suspected breaches of meat hygiene legislation.

The Board

The Board of the Agency comprises a Chairman, Deputy Chair, Chief Executive and 12 Board members. The Agency Board is responsible for overall strategic direction, ensuring the Agency fulfils its legal obligations so that its decisions or actions take proper account of scientific advice, the interests of consumers and other relevant factors. The Board members have been appointed to act collectively in the public interest, not represent specific sectors.

The Chairman and Deputy Chair were jointly appointed by the Secretary of State for Health, Scottish Ministers, the National Assembly for Wales and Northern Ireland Office Ministers. The Chief Executive was appointed by the Secretary of State for Health with the approval of the Head of the Civil Service under the normal Civil Service Commission.Two Board members were appointed by Scottish Ministers, one by the National Assembly for Wales and one by Northern Ireland Office Ministers; these members are to have special responsibility for Scottish, Welsh and Northern Irish issues. Special Advisory Committees have been established for Scotland, Wales, and Northern Ireland to advise on food safety and standards issues which are specific to each devolved administration. All these committees will be chaired by a relevant Board member. The other eight Board members were appointed by the Secretary of State for Health. The members all demonstrate substantial achievement at a senior level and while many have expertise in food matters, they represent a wide range of other backgrounds. Integrity and freedom from conflicts of interest were key considerations in their selection.

Scottish, Welsh and Northern Irish Executives

These three executives of the Food Standards Agency have been established to develop and implement policies on food issues that are specific to each country, within the framework set by the Agency as a whole. They provide support to their Parliament/Assembly and ministers on the Agency's local activities, and prepare legislation as needed to implement the Agency's policies (modified as necessary to reflect local needs). The Food Standards Agency is accountable to the relevant devolved legislatures for its activities within and for their geographical areas.

The Executives work closely with local partners such as the Public Health Laboratory Service in Wales, the Food Safety and Promotion Board in Northern Ireland and the Food Safety Authority for Ireland, and the Scottish Centre for Infections and Environmental Health.

Welsh Executive

The Welsh Executive of the Food Standards Agency was launched on 6 April 2000 as part of the new, UK-wide independent body, accountable both to Parliament and the National Assembly. The Welsh Executive, which comprises the Director and 12 staff plus the Chairman of the Advisory Committee for Wales (who is also a member of the UK Board), is based in Cardiff and will carry out those food safety functions formerly discharged by public health and agriculture staff of the National Assembly for Wales.

Under the terms of the legislation, an Advisory Committee for Wales will be established to provide advice or information to the Agency on matters relating to its functions in Wales. The Agency is required to take the advice of the Advisory Committee into account when carrying out its functions or advising the National Assembly or ministers.

The main role of the Advisory Committee will be to provide advice or information to the Agency and the Assembly on a range of issues, including the development of strategies, the aims and objectives and their application to Wales; the Agency's plan of work, budgets and targets; major food safety issues; the development of the Agency's working relationships with others and the Agency's own working in terms of openness, transparency and consultation.

Food Standards Agency Scotland

The Food Standards Agency Scotland was launched on 3 April 2000. It handles issues in Scotland involving:

(a) food standards, nutrition and diet;

(b) general food hygiene, fish, shellfish and milk hygiene;

(c) hygiene controls on meat and meat products;

(d) regulation of animal feeding stuffs;

(e) novel foods, radiological safety and emergencies.

Food safety and standards are devolved matters and legislation governing Scotland is determined by the Scottish Parliament. In Scotland, the Food Standards Agency will provide advice on proposed legislation to the Minister for Health and Community Care in the Scottish Executive.

Food Standards Agency Scotland operates within the UK Food Standards Agency. This ensures consistency of approach while allowing for specific

Scottish circumstances to be fully taken into account in the implementation of food safety and standards policy in Scotland. There are two Scottish members of the main Food Standards Agency Board – the independent body which governs the operation of the UK Agency.

The Agency is accountable for its actions to both the Scottish and Westminster Parliaments. There is also a statutory Scottish Food Advisory Committee which provides Food Standards Agency Scotland with independent information and advice on all food safety and standards issues in Scotland, taking into account, where necessary, the advice of the independent scientific advisory committees working in the food safety and standards area. The Committee will focus, in particular, on Scottish circumstances and consider Agency Board proposals for activities which affect Scotland, offering advice to Food Standards Agency Scotland which in turn advises the Scottish Executive and ministers on particular food safety and standards priorities. Its 11 members provide a wide base of knowledge of food and food-related issues and include the two Scottish Board members. The officials who will carry out the Agency's work in Scotland comprise the Director Scotland, two Deputy

Directors and some 50 members of staff with a range of policy and professional expertise. They have taken on the food safety work and functions previously carried out by the Food Standards and Safety Division of the Scottish Executive.

Northern Ireland Executive

The Northern Ireland Executive of the Food Standards Agency was launched on 3 April 2000 as part of the new, UK-wide independent body, accountable both to Parliament and the Northern Ireland Assembly.

The Northern Ireland Executive, which will initially comprise the Director and 13 staff, plus the Chairman of the Advisory Committee for Northern Ireland (who is also a member of the UK Board), will be based in Belfast and will carry out those food safety functions formerly discharged by public health and agriculture staff of the Northern Ireland Central Government Departments.

Under the terms of the legislation, an Advisory Committee for Northern Ireland will be established to provide advice and information to the Agency on matters relating to its functions in Northern Ireland. The Agency is required to take the advice of the Advisory Committee into account when carrying out its functions or advising the Northern Ireland Assembly.

The main role of the Advisory Committee will be to provide advice and information to the Agency and information to the Assembly on a range of issues, including:

(a) the development of strategies, the aims and objectives and their application to Northern Ireland;

(b) the Agency's plan of work, budgets and targets;

(c) major food safety issues;

(d) the development of the Agency's working relationships with others; and

(e) the Agency's own working in terms of openness, transparency and consultation.

In a press release issued on 3 April 2000, the day on which the Agency started work, the Agency announced its intention to introduce a scheme for setting and auditing standards for the enforcement of food law by local authorities.[44] Service planning guidance were issued to local authorities in September 2000. The new arrangements were due to be implemented in April 2001 and the Agency intends to work collaboratively with local authorities to improve enforcement standards and to ensure that the Agency's decisions and recommendations take account of the practical implications of enforcing them. Representatives from Scotland, Wales and Northern Ireland were involved in

---

44 Food Standards Agency, *Local Authority Food Law Enforcement Monitoring and Audit Accountability Framework.*

the discussions and the Agency's Executive will consider the implications of similar schemes adapted to meet local circumstances.

The White Paper *The Food Standards Agency – A Force for Change* identified the need for stronger links between central and local government on food law enforcement. It also identified the Food Standards Agency as having a key role overseeing local authority enforcement activities. It envisaged the Agency setting and monitoring standards and auditing local authorities' food law enforcement activities to ensure such work was effective and undertaken on a more consistent basis. Powers to enable the Agency to monitor and audit local authorities are contained in the Food Standards Act 1999.

Following consultation on the White Paper, the Joint Food Safety and Standards Group (JFSSG) held a series of meetings, in the first part of 1998, with a number of industry, enforcement and consumer organisations to discuss food law enforcement in the context of the Food Standards Agency. This led to further, more detailed work, to examine the current links with local authorities on food law enforcement and how these links could be strengthened. In particular, work has focused on two key aspects of the Agency's relationship with local authority enforcement, namely, the setting and monitoring of enforcement standards and the development of a national scheme to audit local authority food law enforcement work. The necessary components to form this accountability framework have been identified as:

(a) a service (business) planning processes operating in a structured and consistent way in all local authorities;

(b) enforcement standards setting out key aspects of enforcement responsibility arising from legislation, Food Safety Act Codes of Practice and other centrally issued guidance;

(c) an enhanced enforcement monitoring scheme providing quantitative information on activity, including where appropriate outcomes of that activity; and

(d) an audit scheme providing in depth qualitative information on enforcement activity.

The 'farm to fork' approach in the Food Standards Agency

A project was undertaken by ADAS Consulting Ltd on behalf of the Joint Food Safety and Standards Group (JFSSG). The purpose of this study was to assess the need for an 'on farm' function within the Food Standards Agency, assess the expectations of key stakeholders and Government departments, identify the functions to be carried out, and recommend the level of resources required and mode of operation.

The main conclusion was that 'there is a need for the Agency to develop a specialist function to examine food safety and standards issues in depth' throughout the whole food chain from 'farm to fork', not just 'on farm'.

In its Summary of Conclusions, ADAS concluded that:

A new specialist function within the Agency is required to examine food safety and standards throughout the whole food chain from farm to fork, not just 'on farm'. This should, however, have particular emphasis on primary production, at least initially. All policy divisions within the Agency should adopt a farm to fork approach within their respective responsibilities, rather than the Agency creating a new Division specifically devoted to food safety policy 'on farm'. Such a function would be free from day-to-day policy development and implementation responsibilities.

The new function will need to consult the key stakeholders when developing its work programme. The studies undertaken by the new function should take account of regulatory, commercial and practical factors affecting food production. Food production practices are evolving rapidly in response to new technologies. The function should be particularly mindful of the implications of these developments.

The function should comprise a small core of expertise, supplemented by studies and information commissioned from outside experts.

The function will need to maintain effective communications and relationships with internal and external stakeholders.

The function could be called 'The Food Chain Strategy Division'.

On the day the Agency began work, the Chairman, Sir John Krebs, stated:

The Food Standards Agency is a new Government department. It will deal with all aspects of food safety and standards throughout the food chain. It is a unique organisation. The UK is in the lead internationally in setting up a Government department to deal with food safety and standards in such a comprehensive way.

At the heart of all the Agency's activities will be the clear commitment to serve the best interests of consumers, and operate in an open and independent way.

One of the features of the Agency that has been emphasised by its Chairman is its commitment to openness. The Board decided to meet in public from its first formal meeting in May 2000. This will help to ensure that all policy debate and discussion will be accessible to everyone.

The Agency also held a public 'open forum' in the West Midlands on 31 May 2000, to discuss how the Agency will do business. Agendas and notes of Board meetings will be published on the website, as well as regular reports on the Agency's scientific work and surveillance, and food safety information.

Consumer choice

The Agency will undertake annual consumer surveys which will help to establish what people expect, and track what people think, of the Agency and its work and help the Agency to respond to their real concerns.

Nutrition

The Agency will contribute to the Government's targets to reduce coronary heart disease and stroke. One activity will be to identify new ways to help disadvantaged consumers improve their diets. The Agency will appoint a dedicated staff member to ensure that their interests are fully taken into account in all that the Agency does.

It is still far too early to say whether or not the ambitious objectives of the Agency will be met. There is concern that although the Agency is not a Government department, it might nevertheless find it difficult to remain truly independent in the face of political and diplomatic pressures. There were a number of early criticisms of the Agency, including criticism of its attitude towards organic farming. There was also unease over its refusal to recommend the banning of French beef in the UK in November 2000 when it became apparent that the incidences of BSE in the French herd were far more numerous than had originally been thought and that there was a risk that banned beef products were entering the UK market.

It is too early yet to say whether the Agency is going to be a truly effective champion of food safety, but there are many who sincerely hope that it will.

Advisory committees

In the UK, there is a well established system of advisory committees which inform government ministers on aspects of food.

Food Advisory Committee (FAC)

This committee was established in its present form in 1983; it is a non-statutory body. Its terms of reference are to assess the risk to humans of chemicals which are used in or on food and to advise on the exercise of powers in the Food Safety Act 1990 relating to the labelling, composition and chemical safety of food. The Committee will also advise on general matters relating to food safety. In exercising its functions, the Food Advisory Committee will take the advice and work of the Committee on Toxicity of Chemicals in Food, Consumer Products and the Environment (CoT), the Advisory Committee on Novel Food and Processes (ACNFP), the Advisory Committee on the Microbiological Safety of Food (ACMSF) and other relevant advisory committees into account. Recent topics covered by the FAC include caffeine in soft drinks, labelling of products containing ingredients designed to help lower cholesterol, nutrition claims – and an open forum on food labelling.

Advisory Committee on Novel Foods and Processes (ACNFP)

This committee was established in1988; it is a non-statutory body. Its terms of reference are to advise on any matters relating to the irradiation of food or to the manufacture of novel foods and foods produced by novel processes having regard, where appropriate, to the views of relevant expert bodies. Recent topics dealt with by ACNFP include post market health surveillance of novel foods and new approaches to the assessments of genetically modified foods.

Advisory Committee on Animal Feedingstuffs (ACAF)

This committee was established in 1999; it is a non-statutory body. Its terms of reference are to advise on the safety and use of animal feeds and feeding practices, with particular emphasis on protecting human health and with reference to new technical developments. In carrying out its functions, the Advisory Committee on Animal Feedingstuffs will liaise with other relevant advisory committees as appropriate. Recent topics dealt with by this committee include genetically modified organisms and animal feed, labelling of animal feed, the use of sewage sludge in French animal feed, and dioxin contamination in Belgian animal feed.

Advisory Committee on the Microbiological Safety of Food (ACMSF)

This committee was established in its present form in 1990; it is a non-statutory body. Its terms of reference are to assess the risk to humans of micro-organisms which are used, or occur in or on food, and to advise on the exercise of powers in the Food Safety Act relating to the microbiological safety of food. Recent topics covered by this committee include microbial antibiotic resistance, food-borne viral infections, poultry meat, salmonella in eggs (work ongoing).

Committee on Toxicity of Chemicals in Food, Consumer Products and the Environment (COT)

This committee was established in its present form 1978; it is a non-statutory body. Its terms of reference are:
(a) to assess and advise on the toxic risk to man of substances which are:

- used or proposed to be used as food additives, or used in such a way that they might contaminate food through their use or natural occurrence in agriculture, including horticulture and veterinary practice or in the distribution, storage, preparation, processing or packaging of food;
- used or proposed to be used of manufactured or produced in industry, agriculture, food storage or any other workplace;
- used or proposed to be used as household goods or toilet goods and preparations;
- used or proposed to be used as drugs, when advice is requested by the Medicines Control Agency;
- used or proposed to be used or disposed of in such a way as to result in pollution of the environment.

(b) to advise on important general principles or new scientific discoveries in the connection with toxic risks, to co-ordinate with other bodies concerned with the assessment of toxic risks and to present recommendations for toxicity testing.

Recent topics include a review of enzyme preparations, an examination of the safety assessment of flour treatment agents and an assessment of the safety of phytoestrogens in infant food.

Committee on Mutagenicity of Chemicals in Food, Consumer Products and the Environment (CoM)

This committee was established in its present form in 1978; it is a non-statutory body. Its terms of reference are:

(a) to assess and advise on the mutagenic risk to man of substances which are:

- used or proposed to be used as food additives, or used in such a way that they might contaminate food through their use or natural occurrence in agriculture, including horticulture and veterinary practice or in the distribution, storage, preparation, processing or packaging of food;
- used or proposed to be used or manufactured or produced in industry, agriculture, food storage or any other workplace;
- used or proposed to be used as household goods or toilet goods and preparations;
- used or proposed to be used as drugs, when advice is requested by the Medicines Control Agency;
- used or proposed to be used or disposed of in such a way as to result in pollution of the environment.

(b) to advise on important general principles or new scientific discoveries in connection with mutagenic risks, to co-ordinate with other bodies concerned with the assessment of mutagenic risks and to present recommendations for mutagenic testing.

Committee on Carcinogenicity of Chemicals in Food, Consumer Products and the Environment (CoC)

This committee was established in its present form in 1978; it is a non-statutory body. Its terms of reference are:

(a) to assess and advise on the carcinogenic risk to man of substances which are:

- used or proposed to be used as food additives, or used in such a way that they might contaminate food through their use or natural occurrence in agriculture, including horticulture and veterinary practice or in the distribution, storage, preparation, processing or packaging of food;
- used or proposed to be used or manufactured or produced in industry, agriculture, food storage, or any other workplace;
- used or proposed to be used as household goods or toilet goods and preparations;
- used or proposed to be used as drugs, when advice is requested by the Medicines Control Agency;
- used or proposed to be used or disposed of in such a way as to result in pollution of the environment.

(b) to advise on important general principles or new scientific discoveries in connection with carcinogenic risks, to co-ordinate with other bodies concerned with the assessment of carcinogenic risks and to present recommendations for carcinogenicity testing.

Scientific Advisory Committee on Nutrition

This committee, which is currently being established, replaces the Committee on Medical Aspects of Food and Nutrition Policy, which has been wound up. The new committee's terms of reference are to advise on scientific aspects of nutrition and health with specific reference to:

- nutrient content of individual foods and advice on diet as a whole including the definition of a balanced diet, and the nutritional status of people;
- monitoring and surveillance of the above;
- nutritional issues which affect wider public health policy issues including conditions where nutritional status is one of a number of risk factors (for example, cardiovascular disease, cancer, osteoporosis and / or obesity);

- vulnerable groups (for example, infants and the elderly) and inequality issues;
- research requirements for the above.

Spongiform Encephalopathy Advisory Committee (SEAC)

This committee was established in 1990 and reviewed in 1996. It is a non-statutory body. Its terms of reference are to provide scientifically based advice on matters relating to spongiform encephalopathies, taking account of the remits of other bodies with related responsibilities. Its recent food safety topics include a review of the over 30 month rule for cattle; an epidemiological update on BSE case predictions and the numbers of potentially infective animals likely to enter the human food chain; and an investigation into the inclusion of porcine meat and bone meal in poultry feed and an investigation into sheep transmissible spongiform encephalopathies.

Expert Group on Vitamins and Minerals (EVM)

This group was established 1998. Its terms of reference are:
- to establish principles on which controls for ensuring the safety of vitamin and mineral supplements sold under food law can be based;
- to review the levels of individual vitamins and minerals associated with adverse effects;
- to recommend maximum levels of intakes of vitamins and minerals from supplements, if appropriate;
- to report to the Food Advisory Committee. The Group will also be able to advise on the levels of vitamins and minerals in fortified foods, if it considers that this is appropriate.

It has recently undertaken a study into the safety of vitamins and minerals.

Food working parties

Working Party on Chemical Contaminants in Food

This working party was established in its present form in 1997. Its terms of reference are:
- to advise on the scope of future surveys and related research on chemical contaminants for funding;
- to consider the results of surveys and relevant research on chemical contaminants and advise on the implications for JFSSG, consumers, industry and other interested parties;

- to consider and review the causes of human exposure to chemical contaminants in food in the UK;
- to advise on the appropriate fora for release of survey results;
- to produce a contribution to the annual surveillance report;
- to report to the Food Advisory Committee.

Working Party on Chemical Contaminants from Food Contact Materials and Articles

This working party was established in 1984. Its terms of reference are:

- to keep under review the possibility of contamination of any part of the UK food and drink supply by chemicals arising from all types of materials and articles in contact with food or drink (for example, packaging, cookware, bottles, cutlery, food preparation surfaces and parts of industrial machinery);
- to advise on the cost-effective research and surveillance necessary to ensure that both industry and consumers in the UK are adequately protected from the consequences of migration of chemicals from materials and articles into food or drink, and to consider the results of such research and surveillance;
- to report, via the Working Party's Chairman and Secretariat, to the Food Advisory Committee on the achievements in the surveillance programme that was carried out in the previous financial year.

Working Party on Dietary Surveys

This working party was established in 1991. Its constitution, terms of reference and future priorities are currently under review, but its current terms of reference are:

- to propose, or when requested, advise on the planning, analysis and interpretation of dietary surveys for the Food Advisory Committee in order to determine normal and extreme intakes of dietary constituents in groups of the population; and to oversee the Total Diet Study;
- to advise other committees and departments when requested to do so;
- to report at intervals to the Food Advisory Committee and, where appropriate, to request publication of the results.

Working Party on Food Additives

This working party was established in 1986. Its terms of reference are:

- to keep under review intakes of food additives in the UK, both by the population as a whole and by consumers in appropriate sub-groups of the population;
- to advise on cost-effective research and surveillance necessary to ensure the maintenance of consumer protection with regard to the use of food additives;
- to report annually, via the Working Party's Chairman and Secretariat, to the Food Advisory Committee on progress in the above areas.

Working Party on Food Authenticity

This working party was established in 1992. Its terms of reference are:
- to identify and advise on priorities in areas of food authenticity to be studied;
- to consider what methods of analysis can be applied to detect adulteration and misdescription, and advise on the significance of results;
- to advise where work is needed to identify suitable methods to detect adulteration and misdescription;
- to monitor the Agency's programme on adulteration and authenticity;
- to encourage industry and enforcement authorities to apply existing and new techniques, as appropriate;
- to ensure product authenticity.

Working Party on Nutrients In Food

Established in 1991, its constitution, terms of reference and future priorities are currently under review. At the present time, its terms of reference are:
- to identify areas in which information on the content and availability of nutrients in foods is required to ensure that the nation's food supplies and diets can be adequately monitored;
- to review nutrient surveillance programmes in order to maintain *McCance and Widdows on the Composition of Foods* and the Ministry's nutrient databank;
- to assess priorities; and to propose means of obtaining information;
- to oversee the preparation of data from the Ministry's nutrient surveillance programme and elsewhere for publication in the *McCance and Widdows on the Composition of Foods* series;
- to advise other committees and departments when requested to do so;
- to report at intervals to the Food Advisory Committee and, where appropriate, to request publication of the results.

Working Party on Radionuclides In Food

Established in 1988, the terms of reference of this working party are:

- to develop and maintain comprehensive, continuous environmental surveillance programmes to ensure that radioactive discharges from licensed nuclear sites and other industries do not result in unacceptable levels of radionuclides in foods;
- to quantify more accurately the actual or potential doses to humans from radionuclides in foods and to ensure that these are within acceptable limits;
- to carry out *ad hoc* surveys to investigate the impact of changes to the operation of nuclear plants or commencement of new processes and to ensure that surveillance programmes adapt where necessary to maintain comprehensive coverage;
- to investigate the geographical and temporal variation of naturally occurring radionuclides in food and agriculture, and their pathways to the consumer;
- to develop and maintain environmental surveillance programmes around non-nuclear industrial sites where enhanced levels of natural anthropogenic radioactivity may be found;
- to develop appropriate survey design, analytical methodology and quality assurance in support of surveillance programmes for radioactivity in foodstuffs;
- to provide the necessary scientific and technical information to official bodies and the public sector to demonstrate that food and agriculture are being adequately safeguarded in the context of radioactive substances;
- to establish baseline data on radionuclide levels in food and agricultural produce around nuclear sites and nationwide against which any subsequent contamination by accidental release of radioactivity can be compared.

Meat Hygiene Service

The Meat Hygiene Service (MHS) became an executive agency of the Food Standards Agency on 1 April 2000. The values and new working methods adopted by the Food Standards Agency will also apply to the MHS. The MHS will play an important role in contributing to the aim of the Food Standards Agency, which is 'to protect public health from risks which may arise in connection with the consumption of food, and otherwise to protect the interests of consumers of food'.

The MHS was first established as an Executive Agency of MAFF on 1 April 1995 when it took over meat inspection duties from 300 local authorities.

The MHS operates in England, Scotland and Wales, providing consumers and the meat industry with a single independent enforcement agency with consistent standards, and providing consistent inspection and enforcement services. The MHS is accountable to the Food Standards Agency and to Parliament via Health Ministers.

It provides a unified inspection service under veterinary supervision acceptable to European Union and third country trading partners.

The MHS mission statement is:

... to be a service which has the full confidence of all its customers, including the meat industry, consumers and Ministers, through the achievement of improving standards and increasing efficiency.

The aim of the MHS is:

... to safeguard public health and animal welfare through fair, consistent and effective enforcement of hygiene, inspection and welfare regulations.

A sub-committee of the Food Standards Agency provides a strategic overview of the MHS, and put forward recommendations on major issues to the Agency Board. This sub-committee is called the 'MHS Supervisory Board' and it is chaired by the Deputy Chairman of the Food Standards Agency and includes some other Agency Board members.

Policy and legislative control for animal welfare issues, however, remain with MAFF, and following devolution, with The National Assembly for Wales and the Scottish Executive Rural Affairs Department. The MHS continues to have an important role in this area by enforcing animal welfare at slaughter legislation on behalf of these departments.

MHS objectives and functions

The principal objectives of the MHS are:

- to provide supervision, inspection and health marking in all licensed meat plants;
- to ensure hygienic production of meat and meat products;
- to promote best practice in standards of hygienic operation and animal welfare at slaughter;
- to apply the principles of Service First and in particular to maintain or improve the quality of services to its stakeholders;
- to deliver value for money in the provision of efficient and high quality services; and

- to achieve the financial and performance targets which will be set by the Food Standards Agency.

The principal functions of the MHS undertaken on behalf of the Food Standards Agency are:

- the enforcement of hygiene legislation in licensed meat plants, meat inspection and health marking in licensed meat plants;
- the enforcement of hygiene controls in meat products, meat preparations and minced meat plants which are integrated or co-located (on the same site) with licensed meat plants;
- the enforcement of controls over specified risk material and other animal by-products in licensed meat plants.

The MHS also undertakes the following work on behalf of the Ministry of Agriculture, Fisheries and Food, The National Assembly for Wales and the Scottish Executive Rural Affairs Department under a Service Level Agreement:

- the enforcement of animal welfare at slaughter;
- legislation in licensed red meat slaughterhouses, poultry meat slaughterhouses and farmed game handling facilities;
- the enforcement of controls on veterinary medicines residues in licensed slaughterhouses;
- collection and dispatch of samples on behalf of the Veterinary Medicines Directorate (VMD) and the State Veterinary Service (SVS);
- cattle identification checks at licensed slaughterhouses;
- provision of export certification when required either by the importing country or by EU legislation.

The MHS also discharges the responsibilities of the Intervention Board Executive Agency (IBEA) under a Service Level Agreement for the supervision, inspection and monitoring of the Over Thirty Months Slaughter (OTMS) Scheme and Selective Cull Scheme in premises licensed or approved in England, Scotland and Wales.

The MHS may also deliver services through Service Level Agreements or contracts, to other public or private sector customers, subject to the approval of the Food Standards Agency, in accordance with its general aims and objectives as set out above, and HM Treasury guidelines on selling to the wider market.

The principle objective of the MHS is to ensure the hygienic production of meat and meat products whilst maintaining animal welfare at slaughter. This is undertaken by meat inspection and official veterinary surgeon staff at some 1600 licensed premises throughout the UK, day or night for 365 days a year (including Christmas Day). This is a statutory requirement placed upon the Meat Hygiene Service.

MHS hygiene and inspection teams

MHS duties and responsibilities at plant level are carried out by teams of Official Veterinary Surgeons (OVSs) and Meat Hygiene Inspectors (MHIs). These teams are supported by Meat Technicians (MTs) at licensed fresh (red) meat plants and Poultry Inspection Assistants (PIAs) at licensed poultry meat plants.

Official Veterinary Surgeons are the team leaders of the MHS hygiene and inspection teams in their respective plants. They are fully responsible for ensuring compliance with the structural, hygiene, inspection, health marking and animal welfare requirements at licensed premises.

Meat Hygiene Inspectors carry out the post mortem inspection of carcasses, health marking and where necessary they assist the OVS in ante mortem inspections. Under the direction of the OVS or Senior MHIs, the Meat Hygiene Inspectors ensure that the necessary standards of hygiene are observed throughout the production process. MHIs assist the OVS in the monitoring of animal welfare standards. They also collect samples for the residues sampling and disease control programmes. MHIs are responsible for supervising compliance with Specified Risk Material controls, particularly checking the dentition status of cattle and sheep, and maintaining accurate records of the eligibility of animals for slaughter for human consumption by checking cattle passports. MHS hygiene and inspection teams are present on a permanent basis at licensed plants whilst slaughtering and dressing is occurring. Their role comprises four main stages: ante mortem inspection of animals; the maintenance of hygienic process control throughout all stages of slaughter and processing, post mortem inspection of carcasses and health marking. Each stage plays an important role in minimising the risk to public health from zoonotic disease and bacterial pathogens.

Ante mortem inspection

MHS staff inspect every animal before it is slaughtered and reject any that are sick or show signs of diseases transmissible to man. In addition, it is recognised that slaughtering dirty animals is a known route for E-coli and other harmful bacteria to enter the food chain. MHS staff therefore reject for slaughter any animal that does not meet required standards of cleanliness to prevent contamination of meat later in the production process and thus reduce the risks to public health.

Hygiene control

Compliance with hygiene legislation is the responsibility of plant operators. However, MHS plant staff, in addition to their inspection duties, work with plant operators to ensure that hygienic controls are maintained throughout the slaughter process to minimise further the risk of cross contamination. Specifically, MHS staff enforce legislative requirements aimed at ensuring that premises operate to recognised hygiene standards. Failure to meet these requirements will lead to enforcement action against premises and ultimately to prosecution.

Post mortem inspection

Through post mortem inspection, individual carcasses are inspected. Only those carcasses presented with no signs of visible contamination or pathological lesions will be passed by MHS staff as safe, wholesome and fit for sale for human consumption.

Health marking

Fresh meat for sale for human consumption produced in licensed slaughterhouses must be stamped, marked or labelled with the MHS official health mark. It is an internationally recognised symbol indicating that the meat bearing the stamp has been: produced under veterinary supervision; complies fully with all relevant legislation, and has been inspected and passed as fit for sale for human consumption.

The health mark stamp is the MHS's guarantee to consumers and to Great Britain's international trading partners that the meat is fit and wholesome and fulfils all regulatory standards. MHS Inspectors are in no doubt that they must not stamp any carcass which shows any evidence of contamination. MHS Operational Managers ensure that this requirement is kept at the forefront of the mind of the front-line inspectors.

MHS staff also undertake other responsibilities:

Specified risk material (SRM) controls

Specified risk materials are those parts of the animal, notably the brain, spinal cord, thymus, tonsils, spleen, and head, considered to be most likely to harbour the infective agent of BSE. Plant operators must comply strictly with the SRM controls introduced to protect public and animal health from any risk from Bovine Spongiform Encephalopathy (BSE) infected material. By providing constant supervision in slaughterhouses, MHS hygiene and inspection teams ensure the full and complete removal of SRM from cattle and sheep carcasses; its separation from meat for human consumption; its staining with blue dye, and its dispatch to an approved premises for disposal.

Cattle traceability

New rules on when to register the birth, death or movement of all cattle came into effect from September 1998. Cattle passports have now been issued for all cattle born, or imported into Great Britain (GB), since July 1996. MHS inspection teams in red meat slaughterhouses are responsible for reconciling each animal with its passport and checking that the documentation is correct before allowing the animal to be accepted for slaughter.

Over Thirty Months Slaughter (OTMS) scheme

MHS staff has responsibility for supervising the slaughter and processing of animals under the OTMS scheme. MHS inspection staff check the eligibility of cattle presented for slaughter and undertake ante and post mortem inspections. They also supervise the staining and disposal of OTMS material ensuring that it does not enter the human food chain.

Hygiene Assessment System (HAS)

The HAS is a risk-based, objective method of assessing hygiene standards at licensed plants. The resulting HAS score is an important guide to the hygiene performance of licensed abattoirs and cutting premises in GB measured over a period of time. These scores are used to monitor hygiene standards and best practice in plants over the long term.

During 1998/99, the MHS, together with MAFF and industry representatives, completed a review of the guidance provided to Official Veterinary Surgeons (OVSs) for hygiene assessment. This resulted in new guidance procedures which came into effect from 1 July 1999 (HAS 99).

ENFORCEMENT OF FOOD LAW IN THE UK

Since the implementation of the EU Official Control of Foodstuffs Directive, there has been a requirement for Member States to send information to the European Commission indicating the extent of enforcement activity. All local authorities must complete a standard form which is then submitted to MAFF, which then prepares the comprehensive UK return.

Local government

Since the beginning of food law in the UK, it has been the job of local authorities to protect the consumer in a particular area. Local authorities have to employ the officers who monitor compliance and who then have the responsibility to take appropriate enforcement action. Responsibility for food law enforcement has been split between two different professions – the Environmental Health Officers (EHOs) and Trading Standards Officers (TSOs).

Environmental health officers (EHOs)

Environmental health officers have been in existence since the 1970s. Their role developed from the earlier role of the public health officer. Their title reflects their responsibilities which include housing, pollution, pest control and, of course, aspects of food law enforcement. Environmental health officers are responsible for monitoring the hygienic operation of food businesses and for the investigation and control of food poisoning outbreaks.

Trading standards officers (TSOs)

Trading standards officers used to be known as Inspectors of Weights and Measures, a title they still use when they are enforcing the legislation on weights and measures. They have responsibility for a number of trading issues including advertising, labelling and safety testing.

Food businesses are therefore subject to inspections by both EHOs and TSOs.

LACOTS[45]

LACOTS stands for the Local Authorities Co-ordinating Body on Food and Trading Standards. The role of LACOTS is to encourage sensible and consistent enforcement of food and trading standards laws and promote best practice by local regulatory authorities. LACOTS was set up in 1978 and has a nationwide responsibility to all local authorities in England, Wales, Scotland and Northern Ireland. Enforcement coordination is the cornerstone of the activities.

Home authority principle

With the locally based enforcement structure, problems arise when a company operates across the country. A company with many retail outlets may be subject to different advice on hygiene and on food labelling. A manufacturer who makes a mistake on a label could be faced with prosecutions from all the local authorities for the same problem. The food industry has often complained about the problems it faces brought about by this locally based structure.

---

45   Further information can be obtained from the LACOTS website at www.lacots.com

To overcome the problem LACOTS has developed the 'home authority principle'. Under the principle, one authority – the 'home authority' – takes the lead in providing advice to a food business. Other authorities can then refer issues relating to that business to the 'home authority'. In this way, the 'home authority' can develop a clear picture of the overall management of the business and take appropriate action. The principle does not prevent any local authority from taking action on an incident in its own area. Where a food business has followed the advice of officers from the home authority this will help to establish a defence of due diligence in any legal proceedings.

The LACOTS website contains the following information on the Home Authority principle:

1   The Home Authority Principle is supported by local authority food and trading standards services throughout the United Kingdom.

2   A local authority acting as a home or originating authority will place special emphasis on the legality of goods and services originating within its area. It aims to prevent infringements by offering advice and guidance at source in order to maintain high standards of public protection at minimum cost.

3   The Principle underpins the principles of free trade 'in fit products and services' and acknowledges that local priorities need to be considered in the context of national and European obligations.

In summary: Businesses recognise that the Home Authority Principle enables them to reduce compliance costs and implement the law in a spirit of consultation rather than confrontation. Good enforcement practices are also effective in minimising duplication and reducing public expenditure.

It is made clear that the Guidelines cannot remove the onus of compliance from business itself or remove the primary responsibility for enforcement from the authority in whose area a specific incident has taken place.

Chemical analysis

Public analysts are scientists who provide chemical analysis and other related testing and who form the scientific base for the UK's public protection enforcement service.

A public analyst can provide a definitive statement as to the content of a particular foodstuff which could be used in a prosecution relating to food contamination.

The Food Safety Act gives the public analyst a special status in that their certificate can be taken as a factual statement as to the content of the food. The certificate can be challenged but this is unusual. To become a public analyst requires the person to pass recognised examinations.

Public analysts can be either employed by a local authority or can work as independent consultants. The Food Safety Act (s 27) requires a food authority to have a public analyst – some therefore have employed their own whilst other local authorities have a contract with a consulting public analyst laboratory. The provision of public analyst laboratories in the UK has been subject to a review, which reported in October 1998.

To be fully recognised, a laboratory has to meet certain minimum standards. One of these is to take part in a proficiency scheme. In the UK, the Central Science Laboratory (CSL) operates a proficiency scheme known as FAPAS (Food Analysis Performance Assessment Scheme).

If a court believes that the result of an analysis by a public analyst may be suspect or where there has been challenge that raises some doubt as to the validity of the analysis a further sample can be sent to the 'Government Chemist' for a definitive statement.

The professional body for public analysts is the Association of Public Analysts (APA).[46]

Microbiological examination and surveillance

There is a distinction in the Food Safety Act between 'analysis' which is physical or chemical based and 'examination' which is microbiological. The person who is qualified to undertake microbiological work on food is therefore the 'food examiner'. Whilst the function of the public analyst has been established for over a hundred years, the food examiner was only introduced in the Food Safety Act 1990. There are Regulations prescribing certain requirements for a person to be recognised as a food examiner – they are, however, less prescriptive than the equivalent requirements for public analysts.

When there is a suspected food poisoning incident there has to be close collaboration between the various professionals involved. Food poisoning is a notifiable disease and once a doctor suspects that a patient is suffering from food poisoning she must report the suspicion to the local public health laboratory, part of the Public Health Laboratory Service (PHLS) and the relevant local authority would be notified. Environmental Health Officers would then start investigating the source of the outbreak and trying to prevent further incidents occurring. To provide a national picture, the local public health laboratories report to the Central Public Health Laboratory (CPHL), who will then gather and analyse data to establish any links between individual cases.

---

46 Further information can be obtained from the APA website at www.the-apa.co.uk.

Institute of Food Science and Technology

The Institute of Food Science and Technology (IFST) is the independent incorporated professional qualifying body for food scientists and technologists. Its purposes are:

- to serve the public interest by furthering the application of science and technology to all aspects of the supply of safe, wholesome, nutritious and attractive food, nationally and internationally;
- to advance the standing of food science and technology, both as a subject and as a profession;
- to assist members in their career and personal development within the profession;
- to uphold professional standards of competence and integrity.

In recent years, the Institute had published many detailed reports and has developed a very extensive set of web pages.[47]

BSE INQUIRY

The establishment of the BSE Inquiry, chaired by Lord Phillips, was announced by the Minister of Agriculture, Fisheries and Food and the Secretary of State for Health on 22 December 1997. The first hearing was held on 9 March 1998.

Bovine spongiform encephalopathy is a slowly progressive and ultimately fatal neurological disorder of adult cattle. Creutzfeldt-Jakob disease is a human spongiform encephalopathy. The Government was advised by an expert committee of scientists in 1996 that a new variant of CJD had been identified and that it seemed likely to be linked with BSE found in cattle. The Department of Health releases monthly figures on BSE and CJD.

Figures covering the period from 1985 to 31 October 1999 show that there have been 58 definite and probable cases of variant CJD in the UK.

The Inquiry heard oral evidence from various groups including scientists, farmers, private industry, senior civil servants, local authorities, former ministers and families of victims of new variant CJD. It received written evidence from many more people.

It was a non-statutory inquiry; statutory inquiries would have legal powers to require individuals to supply evidence or to attend. The Committee observed however that it had received considerable assistance from those involved without the need for legal powers to compel this.

---

47   Further information can be obtained from the IFST website at www.easynet.co.uk/ifst.

The Report of the Inquiry[48] is very detailed, reflecting the depth and thoroughness of the Inquiry. Below is an extract from Volume I. The extract explains what happened and why.

Volume 1: Findings and Conclusions

Introduction

The story in a nutshell

What happened?

This is a summary of the more significant events in the BSE story. In responding to the emergence of BSE, the Ministry of Agriculture, Fisheries and Food (MAFF) and the Department of Health (DH) took the lead. For the most part, Wales, Scotland and Northern Ireland followed that lead. This summary will focus on the action taken by MAFF and DH.

A TSE known as scrapie has been endemic in the sheep population of the UK for nearly 200 years. In the later stages of the disease the fabric of the brain is attacked. The pathologist can diagnose the disease by the spongiform appearance of the diseased brain. At the end of 1986 pathologists at the Central Veterinary Laboratory (CVL) identified similar degenerative changes in the brain samples of diseased cattle from two different herds. These were early cases of BSE.

By May 1987 this novel disease had been confirmed in four herds. No publicity, even within the State Veterinary Service (SVS), had been given to these early cases and it is likely that others had gone unrecognised and unreported. From May, however, the fact of the existence of a novel disease was gradually disseminated and Mr John Wilesmith, head of the CVL's Epidemiology Department, was asked to investigate its cause.

Over the next six months, as he carried out his task, reported incidents of the disease proliferated. By 15 December 1987 there were 95 confirmed cases on 80 farms. Mr Wilesmith had formed the provisional view that the cause of the outbreak was contaminated meat and bone meal (MBM) that had been incorporated in cattle feed. His confidence in this theory grew stronger early in 1988, and he concluded that the likely contaminant was offal of scrapie-infected sheep, rendered down to make MBM. Enquiries of feed compounders tended to confirm this view.

On 18 May 1988 Mr John MacGregor, the Minister of Agriculture, on the advice of Mr William Rees, the Chief Veterinary Officer (CVO), decided on what proved to be the principal step taken to eradicate BSE. A prohibition on feeding ruminant protein to ruminants ('the ruminant feed ban') was introduced on 14 June 1988 to take effect on 18 July. This was, at the time, regarded as a measure to protect animal health. The risk that BSE posed to human health had not, however, been ignored.

---

48 Full report available at www.bse.org.uk.

Officials at MAFF had been concerned from the outset at the possibility that BSE might pose a risk to human health. Diseased cattle were going into the human food chain. Scrapie was not transmissible to humans, but there was no certainty that the same would be true of BSE. By 19 February 1988, 264 cases of BSE from 223 farms had been confirmed. On 24 February Mr Derek Andrews, the Permanent Secretary, forwarded a submission to Mr MacGregor. This recommended that BSE should be made a notifiable disease and that a policy of compulsory slaughter with compensation should be introduced. Mr MacGregor had reservations about such a policy and accepted the suggestion that the advice of Sir Donald Acheson, the Chief Medical Officer (CMO), should be sought on the implications that BSE had for human health.

Sir Donald, in turn, recommended that an expert working party should be set up to advise on the implications of BSE. This was done. The Working Party was chaired by Sir Richard Southwood.

Before the first meeting of the Southwood Working Party, and at the same time that the ruminant feed ban was introduced, Mr MacGregor, on the advice of his officials, introduced a requirement for compulsory notification of all cases of BSE.

On 21 June 1988 the Southwood Working Party made interim recommendations that included the compulsory slaughter of animals showing symptoms of BSE and the setting up of a committee to advise on research. The Government accepted these recommendations and, on 8 August 1988, an Order came into force making slaughter of BSE suspects compulsory. Compensation of 50 per cent of the sound value of the animal was paid if, on post mortem, it was shown to have had BSE and 100 per cent if it did not. Although made under the Animal Health Act 1981, the primary object of this measure was to take sick animals out of the human food chain.

By 13 January 1989, 2,296 cases of BSE had been confirmed on 1,742 farms.

The Southwood Report was submitted to Ministers on 9 February 1989. This endorsed Mr Wilesmith's conclusion that the source of infection was probably scrapie-infected meat and bone meal. It concluded that it was 'most unlikely that BSE would have any implications for human health'. It recommended that the Health and Safety Executive (HSE) and the authorities responsible for human and veterinary medicines, which had already been alerted by the Working Party, should take appropriate measures to address possible risks posed by BSE, and advised manufacturers of baby foods not to include in their products ruminant offal including thymus, which, from what was known about scrapie, would be most likely to be infective. Sir Richard Southwood clarified later in February that this offal did not include liver or kidney.

The Working Party concluded that the risk posed by BSE-infected animals which had not yet developed clinical signs did not justify any further measures to protect human food. The Government accepted this, and on publication of the Southwood Report announced that secondary legislation would make it illegal to sell baby food containing the types of offal identified by the Report. MAFF Ministers, however, had concerns which, after discussion with officials and with DH and after wide consultation, led, on 13 November 1989, to the introduction of a ban on the use for human consumption of Specified Bovine Offals (SBO), namely those tissues in cattle considered most likely to be infective. This became known as 'the human SBO ban'. Tissues from cattle aged under six months were exempt from the ban on the basis that scrapie infectivity had not been found in lambs of this age.

Meanwhile, on 27 February 1989, the establishment of a committee chaired by Dr David Tyrrell was announced. The Tyrrell Committee was to advise on research in relation to BSE, thus implementing one of the first recommendations of the Southwood Working Party. This Committee met three times and delivered to the Minister of Agriculture and the Secretary of State for Health what they described as an 'Interim Report' on 13 June 1989. This identified the key research questions that needed to be answered and set in an order of priority the research studies needed to answer those questions.

The Report was not published until 9 January 1990. By this time funding had been put in place which enabled the Food Minister, Mr David Maclean, to announce that all projects identified by the Tyrrell Committee as 'urgent' or of 'high priority' had either been put in train or would start as soon as possible. Experiments to check the belief that BSE was transmissible had been put in hand at an early stage. In September 1988 transmission to mice by intracerebral inoculation of brain tissue had been confirmed. By February 1990 transmission to cattle had been established by the same route and transmission to mice by oral ingestion had been achieved.

Meanwhile, on 28 July 1989, the EU banned the export of UK cattle born before 18 July 1988 and of offspring of affected or suspect females. This was the first of a number of restrictions placed by the EU on the export from the UK of live cattle and (from June 1990) of beef.

By the end of 1989, 10,091 cases of BSE had been confirmed in the UK.

Anxiety had been expressed in many quarters that 50 per cent compensation might be inadequate to procure full compliance with the requirement to notify BSE suspects and, on 14 February 1990, Mr John Gummer, who had succeeded Mr MacGregor as Minister of Agriculture, introduced entitlement to 100 per cent compensation.

On 1 March 1990 the EU restricted exports of live cattle to those aged less than six months. Importing Member States were required to ensure that these were slaughtered before they reached that age. Offspring of whatever age of affected or suspected females continued to be banned from export.

On 3 April it was announced that Dr Tyrrell was to chair a new expert committee – the Spongiform Encephalopathy Advisory Committee (SEAC). The Committee had a wider membership than the Tyrrell Committee and wider terms of reference:

To advise the Ministry of Agriculture, Fisheries and Food and the Department of Health on matters relating to spongiform encephalopathies.

It was government policy in relation to BSE to act on 'the best scientific advice'. Thereafter the Government was to look to SEAC to provide that advice.

One of the recommendations of the Southwood Working Party had been the need for surveillance of CJD cases in order to detect whether there were any changes in their incidence that might be attributable to BSE. In May 1990 the CJD Surveillance Unit was set up under Dr Robert Will, a consultant neurologist at the Western General Hospital in Edinburgh.

On 10 May 1990 it was announced that a Siamese cat had died of a spongiform encephalopathy – the first known case of feline spongiform encephalopathy (FSE). This resulted in a rash of media comment, speculating that the cat had caught BSE and that humans might be next. Humberside Education Authority had already banned beef from school meals and a number of other Authorities threatened to follow this example. Public statements by the CMO and by Mr Gummer that beef was safe to eat failed wholly to reassure. The House of Commons Agriculture Committee announced an Inquiry into BSE. After receiving evidence from most of the key players in the BSE story, the Committee reported on 12 July 1990 that, while there were too many unknowns to say anything with absolute certainty, 'we heard no evidence of any sort to constrain those taking a more balanced view of the risks from eating beef'. The measures taken by the Government 'should reassure people that eating beef is safe'.

On 8 June 1990 the EU Council of Ministers agreed that bone-in beef exported from the UK must come from holdings where BSE had not been confirmed in the previous two years, while boneless beef was required to have obvious nervous and lymphatic tissue removed.

Meanwhile, there had been controversy as to whether the SBO that had been banned from human food should be permitted to be fed to animals. Pet food manufacturers had voluntarily ceased to incorporate it in their products. UKASTA, the feed producers' trade association, had pressed strongly for a ban on including SBO in the material rendered to make MBM for inclusion in pig and poultry feed, and advised their members to exclude it. MAFF officials and Ministers opposed a ban on the ground that it was without any scientific justification. SEAC was about to advise on this question when, early in September, a pig, which had been inoculated with BSE-infected brain tissue, succumbed to the disease. In an emergency meeting SEAC advised that, as a precautionary measure, SBO should not be fed to any animals. MAFF, which had anticipated this possibility, immediately banned the incorporation of SBO or its products in animal feed ('the animal SBO ban'). Export of feed containing SBO to the EU was also banned. This was followed in July 1991 by a ban on the export of material derived from SBO to third countries.

Among the many matters on which SEAC was asked to advise were slaughterhouse practices. There was concern that the removal of brain and spinal cord (both SBO) in slaughterhouses might contaminate meat going for human consumption. There was also concern about the practice of the mechanical recovery of remnants of meat and other tissues adhering to the vertebral column, in that these might include scraps of spinal cord not cleanly removed by slaughterhouse operators. SEAC advised that head meat should be removed before brain, but that no further measures were necessary provided that the rules were properly followed and supervised. This advice was implemented first by guidance and then, in March 1992, by statutory regulation.

By the end of 1990, 24,396 cases of BSE had been confirmed in the United Kingdom.

One of a number of recommendations of the House of Commons Agriculture Committee was that the Government should 'establish an expert committee to examine the whole range of animal feeds and advise on how industries which produce them should be regulated'. Some debate ensued as to how to implement this recommendation, but on 6 February 1991 MAFF announced the establishment of an Expert Group on Animal Feedingstuffs chaired by Professor Eric Lamming. It met on 14 occasions over the next year and reported on 15 June 1992. The Group considered the steps taken to prevent the BSE agent being transmitted to animals in feed and concluded that they were satisfactory and adequate. In particular the Group considered whether the practice of feeding animal protein to animals should be discontinued. It decided that there was no scientific justification for such a step. It did, however, recommend that:

> ... an independent Animal Feedingstuffs Advisory Committee be established to take an overview of all feedingstuffs issues.

Although the Government initially accepted this recommendation, it subsequently decided not to proceed with it.

With compulsory slaughter of sick animals and the human SBO ban to deal with potentially infective tissues in apparently healthy animals incubating BSE, the Government considered that there were in place appropriate measures to deal with the risk that BSE might be transmissible to humans in food. Action was taken to see that medicinal products both for humans and for animals were not sourced from potentially infective bovine tissues. Ruminants were protected by the ruminant feed ban and other animals by the animal SBO ban. No further major measures were considered necessary to protect human or animal health in the period with which we are concerned. In March 1992 SEAC concluded 'that the measures at present in place provide adequate safeguards for human and animal health'. Several relatively uneventful years were to pass before it became apparent that the measures in place were not achieving all that had been expected of them.

Because of BSE's lengthy incubation period, it was appreciated when introducing the ruminant feed ban that years would pass before it would have a visible effect. What was not known was the rate at which cattle had been infected in the period up to 18 July 1988, when the ruminant feed ban came into force. At the time of the Southwood Report suspected cases of BSE were being reported at the rate of about 400 a month. It was considered that these had been infected with scrapie and that this source would have continued to infect cattle until the ban at about the same rate. Whether, or to what extent, recycling of BSE might have increased the rate of infection was not known.

It soon became apparent from the numbers of BSE cases reported[49] that the rate of infection had not reached a plateau, but had been increasing rapidly in the years leading up to the ruminant feed ban, and that the reason for this was the effect of recycling the BSE agent in MBM.

Thus the Government found it had to deal with many more cases infected before the ban than it had expected. But of even more concern were cases in cattle that had been born after the ban (BABs). The first of these was announced on 27 March 1991.

When exploring the possible sources of infection of the BABs, the CVL epidemiologists were able to rule out maternal transmission in most cases. The likely source of infection of the earlier BABs was thought to be ruminant feed in which ruminant protein had been incorporated before the ban and which was in the distribution pipeline, or still unused on farms when the ban came into force. This remained the view of MAFF officials at the beginning of 1994, by which time Mrs Gillian Shephard had succeeded Mr Gummer as Minister of Agriculture. Cross-contamination of ruminant feed by non-ruminant feed in the feedmills was considered, but discounted after September 1990, when the animal SBO ban should have prevented SBO from being incorporated in any animal feed.

In the course of 1994 opinions changed as to the source of infection of BABs. By August the CVL had reached the conclusion that the more recent BABs had been infected by feed which had been contaminated in the feedmill by feed containing ruminant protein. Two factors had led to this conclusion. First, there had been an increasing volume of evidence, some of it cogent, of widespread infringement of the animal SBO ban, so that SBO was contaminating non-ruminant feed. Second, interim results of an experiment, which started in 1992, indicated that a single quantity of as little as 1 gram of infective material – the size of two peppercorns – had sufficed to infect cattle to which this had been fed.

MAFF officials approached the problem of the cross-contamination of cattle feed on two fronts. Their primary emphasis was on tightening up the implementation of the animal SBO ban. This was facilitated by the transfer of enforcement functions in slaughterhouses to central government. What had

---

49   For statistics, see Vol 16: Reference Material.

been the responsibility of some hundreds of individual local authorities became the task of a new national Meat Hygiene Service (MHS) from 1 April 1995. A revised statutory scheme was introduced that required SBO to be identified by a distinctive blue dye and kept separate at all times from other material. At the same time plants rendering SBO were required to do so in separate facilities. The consultation process was thorough and lengthy, with the result that the introduction of the new Regulations was not completed until August 1995. Their introduction was combined with a campaign of more rigorous enforcement and monitoring of the Regulations by the MHS and the Veterinary Field Service (VFS).

At the same time as tightening up on the implementation of the animal SBO ban, MAFF officials took steps to address cross-contamination in feedmills. So far as these were concerned, effective monitoring of compliance with the ruminant feed ban had been initially impossible for want of any method of testing for the presence of ruminant protein in animal feed. It had been hoped that an 'ELISA test' would be perfected within about 12 months, capable of detecting this. In the event, it was not until 1994 that the test was ready for use, and even then its results were not sufficiently reliable to provide evidence that would support a prosecution for breach of the Regulations. The test was, however, employed on a voluntary basis, with cooperation from UKASTA, and resulted in at least some feedmills taking steps to reduce the possibility of cross-contamination.

Hindsight confirms that, between 1989 and 1994, the ruminant feed ban had resulted in a steady but substantial year-on-year reduction in the numbers of infections, and that the measures taken in 1994 and 1995 radically accelerated this decline (see Volume 16, Figures 3.2 and 3.34).

The years 1994 and 1995 also saw developments in relation to the risks posed by BSE to human health. An interim result of a pathogenesis experiment conducted by the CVL demonstrated infectivity in the distal ileum (small intestine) of a calf within six months of oral infection with BSE. This led MAFF, with the agreement of DH, to extend the human SBO ban to include the intestines and thymus of calves which had died aged over two months.

On 27 July 1994 the European Commission decided that existing restrictions on the export of UK beef should be replaced with two measures. One was a ban on export of bone-in beef except from cattle which had not been on holdings where BSE had been confirmed in the previous six years. The other measure affected beef from cattle which had been on such a holding within that time. This could not be exported unless it was deboned with adherent tissues removed. In December 1994 the Commission amended this decision to exempt from these measures beef from cattle born after 1 January 1992. Subsequently in July 1995 this exemption was replaced with one that exempted beef from cattle less than 30 months of age at slaughter.

In July 1994 Mrs Shephard was succeeded by Mr William Waldegrave, who oversaw the introduction of the MHS. He in turn was succeeded by Mr Douglas Hogg in July 1995. At the direction of Mr Hogg, the MHS set about raising standards of meat inspection, a task that was to prove to require the employment of several hundred additional staff.

More rigorous monitoring of slaughterhouses in 1995 disclosed a number of occasions on which Meat Inspectors had applied the health stamp to a carcass to which fragments of spinal cord remained attached. This led SEAC to recommend a ban on the practice of extracting mechanically recovered meat (MRM) from the spinal column of cattle. MAFF accepted that advice and introduced the ban in December 1995.

In the course of 1995 a number of events served to increase public anxiety that it might be possible to contract CJD as a consequence of eating beef. Cases of CJD were reported in farmers whose herds had had BSE and in several young people – the latter being particularly significant because up until then the disease had almost invariably struck down its victims late in life. A distinguished scientist questioned the safety of beef offal. These events received wide media coverage. The CMO and the Secretary of State for Health each responded with public assurances that it was safe to eat beef.

The first two months of 1996 saw the CJD Surveillance Unit and SEAC concerned at an increasing number of young victims of CJD. On 16 March SEAC advised the Government that a new variant of CJD had been identified in young people and that the most likely explanation was that these were linked to exposure to BSE before the introduction of the SBO ban in 1989. A series of urgent meetings of Ministers and then of the Cabinet ensued, and SEAC's advice was sought as to further precautionary measures.

On 20 March 1996 the Government announced the likelihood that the recent cases of CJD in young people had resulted from exposure to BSE before 1989 and stated its intention to adopt further precautionary measures in accordance with SEAC's advice. These were that carcasses from cattle aged over 30 months must be deboned and that the use of MBM in feed for all farm animals would be banned. These measures proved inadequate to reassure the public and, within two weeks, were replaced with a total ban on cattle over the age of 30 months being used for human food or animal feed.

By 20 March 1996 approximately 160,000 cattle affected by BSE had been slaughtered. In addition about 30,000 cattle suspected of BSE, but not confirmed to have the disease, were slaughtered. These figures can be compared with over 3.3 million cattle slaughtered and destroyed under the Over Thirty Month Scheme in the period from March 1996 to the end of 1999.

This brief narrative has concentrated on events that have been most in the public eye. As we explained above, we shall also cover in later chapters of this volume precautionary measures taken in areas which, while important, did not come to the attention of the general public. These include medicines, cosmetics and occupational health.

Why did it happen?

The Report of an Inquiry such as this inevitably focuses on the areas where things went wrong. It is those areas that government and the public are most anxious to have thoroughly explored. For this reason we think it desirable to give at the outset an overview of why things happened in the way that they did.

Why initially a cow or cows developed BSE will probably never be known. Why the early case or cases began a chain of transmission that ended with hundreds of thousands of cattle becoming infected is now clear. It was because of the practice of rendering cattle offal, including brain and spinal cord, to produce animal protein in the form of meat and bone meal (MBM), and including MBM in compound cattle feed. This resulted in the recycling and wide distribution of the BSE agent.

Many have expressed the view that it was not surprising that a practice as unnatural as feeding ruminant protein to ruminants should result in a plague such as BSE. Had BSE emerged soon after this practice was introduced, there might have been force in this reaction. However, the practice of feeding MBM to animals in the UK dates back at least to 1926, when it was given statutory recognition in the Fertilisers and Feedingstuffs Act of that year. It is a practice which has also been followed in many other countries. It was recognised that it was important that the rendering process should inactivate conventional pathogens. Experience had not suggested that the practice involved any other risks. In these circumstances we can understand why no one foresaw that the practice of feeding ruminant protein to ruminants might give rise to a disaster such as the BSE epidemic. Accusations have been made both against the Government and against renderers of causing BSE by relaxing rendering standards. As we shall explain, changes in rendering practices and regulatory requirements are unlikely to have made any substantial difference.

There were a number of factors that made it inevitable that, whatever measures were taken in response to its emergence, BSE would be a tragic disaster:

- it had an incubation period of five years on average;
- it tended to strike a single cow in a herd;
- it had clinical signs which were similar to those of a number of other diseases in cattle;
- it was impossible to diagnose before clinical signs appeared; and
- it was transmissible to human beings, but with a much longer incubation period than that in cattle.

These factors had the following consequences:

- the emergence of the disease may well have gone undetected for ten years or more from the time of the first cases. A farmer would not be likely to send a single casualty for a post mortem. It was only when, by chance, several cases were experienced on the same farm that the pathology was carried out that disclosed the new disease;

- by the time that BSE was identified as a new disease, as many as 50,000 cattle are likely to have been infected;[50]
- it is also likely that by this time some of the human victims had been infected;
- it was not until nearly ten years after BSE was identified as a new disease in cattle that the first human victims succumbed to the disease, thus showing that, contrary to expectation, it was transmissible to humans.

Given the practice of pooling and recycling cattle remains in animal feed, this sequence of events flowed inevitably from the first cases of BSE. It was inevitable that, whatever measures were taken, many thousands of cows would succumb to the disease in the years to come. It was inevitable that if humans were susceptible to the disease, some would be infected with it before its existence was even suspected.

The measures that were taken in response to the emergence of BSE greatly reduced the scale of the disaster. The MBM component of feed was diagnosed as the vector responsible for the disease with commendable speed, and the ruminant feed ban was a swift and appropriate response. That ban reduced the rate of infection by 80 per cent overnight and established a diminishing trend which would, ultimately, have resulted in the eradication of the disease. Unhappily, as the cases born after the ban were to demonstrate, there were shortcomings in formulating and carrying out both the ruminant feed ban and the animal SBO ban, which should have provided a second line of defence against infection of cattle feed. These shortcomings had serious consequences. Over 41,000 cattle that developed clinical signs of BSE in the years that followed were infected after the ruminant feed ban came into effect. Many more must have been infected but slaughtered before the signs developed. When the link between BSE and the new variant of CJD became apparent in March 1996, the Government was unable to demonstrate that the source of infection had been completely cut off. Had they been able to do so, some of the drastic measures that followed might have been avoided. The reasons for these shortcomings receive detailed consideration in our Report.

There is a popular misconception that the Government did nothing to protect the public against the risk BSE might pose to human health until the likelihood of transmissibility was demonstrated in 1996. It is important to emphasise that the most significant measures to protect human health were taken at a time when the likelihood of transmissibility to humans was considered to be remote. Those were the compulsory slaughter and destruction of sick animals introduced in August 1988 and later, in November 1989, the human SBO ban, which was intended to remove from the human food chain those parts of apparently healthy cattle most likely to be infective if the animals were incubating BSE. At the same time steps were taken to ensure that bovine ingredients of medicines came from BSE-free sources.

---

50 S9 Anderson para 1.

These were vitally important measures. For a period of nearly ten years continuous consideration was given to addressing the possibility that BSE might be transmissible to humans, although few believed that there was any likelihood of it. This is a matter for commendation.

Yet again, however, there were shortcomings: shortcomings which led to delay in introduction of the precautionary measures, and shortcomings in formulating and carrying out the ban. Despite the SBO ban, some potentially infective bovine tissues continued to enter the human food chain. The reasons for these shortcomings also receive detailed consideration in our Report.

The other casualty of the BSE story has been the destruction of the credibility of government pronouncements. Those responsible for public pronouncements – or at least some of them – were aware of the possibility that humans might have become infected before the slaughter policy and the SBO ban were introduced. They saw no reason to draw attention to this. They believed that the measures taken had effectively removed the 'theoretical risk' of infection. They were concerned that the public should not be misled by scaremongers or the media into believing that it was dangerous to eat beef when this was not the case. Ministers and, on occasion, the Chief Medical Officers, made statements about the safety of beef which were intended to reassure the public. Insofar as these statements were believed, many clearly treated them as assurances that BSE posed no danger to human beings. In the case of some, there was a growing scepticism as the media reported cases of possible human victims of BSE which were then challenged by the Government. When on 20 March 1996 it was announced that cases of new variant CJD were probably attributable to contact with BSE before precautionary Regulations were introduced, the reaction of the public was that they had been misled, and deliberately misled, by the Government.

We have examined with care the public pronouncements that were made about the risks posed by BSE, and have concluded that allegations of a government 'cover-up' of the risks posed by BSE cannot be substantiated. There were, however, mistakes in the way risk was communicated to the public, and there are lessons to be learned from these.

The key conclusions, contained in the Executive Summary of the Report of the Inquiry are as follows:

Key conclusions

BSE has caused a harrowing fatal disease for humans. As we sign this Report the number of people dead and thought to be dying stands at over 80, most of them young. They and their families have suffered terribly. Families all over the UK have been left wondering whether the same fate awaits them.

A vital industry has been dealt a body blow, inflicting misery on tens of thousands for whom livestock farming is their way of life. They have seen over 170,000 of their animals dying or having to be destroyed, and the precautionary slaughter and destruction within the United Kingdom of very many more.

BSE developed into an epidemic as a consequence of an intensive farming practice – the recycling of animal protein in ruminant feed. This practice, unchallenged over decades, proved a recipe for disaster.

In the years up to March 1996 most of those responsible for responding to the challenge posed by BSE emerge with credit. However, there were a number of shortcomings in the way things were done.

At the heart of the BSE story lie questions of how to handle hazard – a known hazard to cattle and an unknown hazard to humans. The Government took measures to address both hazards. They were sensible measures, but they were not always timely nor adequately implemented and enforced. The rigour with which policy measures were implemented for the protection of human health was affected by the belief of many prior to early 1996 that BSE was not a potential threat to human life. The Government was anxious to act in the best interests of human and animal health. To this end it sought and followed the advice of independent scientific experts – sometimes when decisions could have been reached more swiftly and satisfactorily within government. In dealing with BSE, it was not MAFF's policy to lean in favour of the agricultural producers to the detriment of the consumer.

At times officials showed a lack of rigour in considering how policy should be turned into practice, to the detriment of the efficacy of the measures taken.

At times bureaucratic processes resulted in unacceptable delay in giving effect to policy.

The Government introduced measures to guard against the risk that BSE might be a matter of life and death not merely for cattle but also for humans, but the possibility of a risk to humans was not communicated to the public or to those whose job it was to implement and enforce the precautionary measures.

The Government did not lie to the public about BSE. It believed that the risks posed by BSE to humans were remote. The Government was preoccupied with preventing an alarmist over-reaction to BSE because it believed that the risk was remote. It is now clear that this campaign of reassurance was a mistake. When on 20 March 1996 the Government announced that BSE had probably been transmitted to humans, the public felt that they had been betrayed. Confidence in government pronouncements about risk was a further casualty of BSE.

Cases of a new variant of CJD (vCJD) were identified by the CJD Surveillance Unit and the conclusion that they were probably linked to BSE was reached as early as was reasonably possible. The link between BSE and vCJD is now clearly established, though the manner of infection is not clear.

CHAPTER 4

FOOD QUALITY

In the UK, issues relating to food quality are dealt with under ss 14 and 15 of the Food Safety Act 1990 and under the Food Labelling Regulations 1996. Section 14 covers offences relating to the nature or substance or quality of food. Section 15 makes it an offence falsely to describe, advertise or present food.

'Quality' is a rather abstract term and can be rather difficult to define, particularly in relation to what one regards as 'good quality' food. It can be a very subjective matter. In food law, the issues of quality usually arise in relation to the composition of food. Prior to 1985, EC legislation attempted to lay down compositional requirements for certain types of food, but since 1985, there has been a move away from so called 'vertical' harmonisation, where rules were set down for individual products, to 'horizontal' approximation of laws, where general rules are set down which apply to all, or many types of food (such as labelling requirements).

In its 1985 Communication on the completion of the internal market in the foodstuffs sector, the Commission indicated that, in future, it would not bring forward proposals for vertical legislation imposing qualitative specifications for particular categories of foodstuffs. The Commission indicated that it would, instead, be relying on the use of labelling and the application of voluntary instruments as the basis for mutual recognition of national rules in accordance with the principles of free movement of goods. Part III, para 7 of the Green Paper on Food Law makes it clear that there will be no further measures on the compositional or quality standards of specific groups of foods. Member States are permitted to keep existing national compositional standards as long as they do not conflict with the principles of free movement of goods and with the operation of the internal market. By 1985, prior to this new approach, there were compositional standards for certain sugars, honey, fruit juices and certain similar products, certain partly or wholly dehydrated and preserved milk products, fruit jams, jellies, marmalades and chestnut puree, coffee and chicory extracts, cocoa products and chocolate products.

PRODUCT-SPECIFIC DIRECTIVES

Milk, sugar, fruit juices

In January 2000, the Council of Ministers reached a political agreement on three vertical directives on foodstuffs relating to certain partly or wholly dehydrated preserved milk for human consumption, certain sugars intended for human consumption and fruit juices and certain similar products intended for human consumption. These Directives are part of a process of simplification and will replace the current rules contained in Directives 76/118/EEC (preserved milk), 73/43/EEC (certain sugars) and 73/437/EEC (fruit juices).

The aim of the new Directive on milk is to set down common definitions and treatment rules for partly or wholly dehydrated preserved milk so that they are consistent with general EC law on foodstuffs, particularly the legislation on labelling, additives, hygiene and health.

The aim of the Directive on sugars is to establish definitions and common rules on the manufacturing characteristics, packaging and labelling of the products concerned, which include semi-white sugar, sugar, extra-white sugar, invert sugar solution and syrup, glucose syrup, dextrose and fructose, in order to achieve consistency with general EC legislation on labelling, colouring and other additives, extraction solvents and methods of analysis.

The aim of the Directive on fruit juices is to establish common rules on the manufacturing and marketing conditions for fruit juices and certain similar products, relating to labelling, colouring, sweeteners and other additives. There will be a distinction, in terms of the product name, between fruit juices made from fresh or chilled fruit and fruit juices made from concentrate. Mixtures of fruit juice or nectar with concentrate of fruit juice or nectar will also be clearly labelled.

Fruit jams, jellies and marmalades

In March 2000, the Council reached political agreement, subject to the reconsultation of the European Parliament, on a proposed Directive relating to fruit jams, jellies, marmalades and certain puree intended for human consumption.

The proposal is part of a group of five vertical Directives on food (the others being the three Directives discussed above, and honey) based on Art 37 (ex Art 43) of the EC Treaty and submitted by the Commission to the Council in May 1996. Their purpose is to simplify and replace the existing rules on certain foods. This new proposal will replace Council Directive 79/693/EEC relating to fruit jams, jellies, marmalades and chestnut puree.

The new Directive sets down and updates common rules relating to composition, including authorised colouring agents, sweeteners and other additives, manufacturing specifications and labelling of the products concerned. The Directive defines in great detail the products that come within its scope (jam, extra jam, jelly, extra jelly, marmalade, jelly marmalade and sweetened chestnut puree), and specifies the ingredients and raw materials which may be used in their manufacture. The text specifies labelling conditions subject to which the general rules on labelling contained in the framework labelling Directive (79/112) apply.

Member States will be required to comply with the Directive within 18 months following its entry into force (20 days after publication in the Official Journal). Products which do not comply with the terms of the new Directive will be prohibited after 30 months after the Directive's entry into force.

Honey

In May 2000, the Council reached political agreement on the text of a new Directive on honey. This was the last vertical Directive based on Art 37 of the Treaty and first presented by the Commission in June 1996 in the framework of a simplification exercise.

The aim of the Directive is to lay down rules regarding the composition and definition of honey, specifying the different types of product which can be placed on the market under appropriate names. It also specifies rules as to the labelling, presentation and indication of origin for these products. This Directive will repeal Directive 74/409/EEC. Member States will be required to comply with this Directive within 18 months of its publication in the Official Journal.

Chocolate

Directive 73/241 was originally introduced because differences between national laws on cocoa and chocolate products in different Member States were creating barriers to free trade. Article 1 of the Directive provides that in future only the definitions listed in Annex 1 will be permitted as trade descriptions. The Directive defined cocoa powder, drinking chocolate, cocoa butter, chocolate, plain chocolate, chocolate flakes and milk chocolate. All the definitions contain the compositional/quality requirements of the product so that it can be correctly labelled. The Directive also stipulates the different weights in grammes by which the products may be sold, which are 100, 125, 150, 200, 250, 300, 400 and 500 grammes. There are also further labelling requirements relating to the minimum percentage of cocoa solids for certain products and the type of chocolate used and the net weight of filled chocolate. The product must indicate the name or trade name and the address or registered office of the manufacturer or packer or of a seller within the European Union.

The Directive has been amended nine times since it was adopted. In its definition of cocoa and chocolate products, the Directive did not make any provision for the inclusion of vegetable fats to replace cocoa butter in the production of chocolate. Following the accession of the UK, Ireland and Denmark to the European Communities, an exemption was introduced to allow the use of vegetable fats up to a limit of 5% in those three countries, to reflect the rules applicable in them. The exemption was agreed to for an indefinite period until such time as the issue was resolved by an amendment to the original Directive. Portugal, Austria, Finland and Sweden are also permitted to add up to 5% of vegetable fat other than cocoa butter to chocolate. The Directive also allows the UK and Ireland to sell in their countries a product labelled as 'milk chocolate' with a higher milk and lower cocoa content than 'milk chocolate' made and sold in the rest of the EU.

In 1984, and again in 1992, the Commission put forward a proposal for a harmonising measure to authorise the 5% limit. On both occasions, the proposal was rejected by the European Parliament and was not enacted.

In 1996, the Commission issued a further proposal aimed at simplifying the various vertical Directives in the foodstuffs sector, including the Directive on chocolate. The proposed new amendments to the 1973 Directive would allow Member States the option of using vegetable fats other than cocoa butter in chocolate production up to a limit of 5% by weight of the end product. The progress of these amendments has proved extremely slow and contentious. In October 1997, the European Parliament voted to allow the use of up to 5% vegetable fats, but agreed very stringent conditions as to the labelling of such chocolate. The wording must read 'contains vegetable fats other than cocoa butter' and must be placed on the front of the label. As far as the term 'milk chocolate' was concerned, the European Parliament voted in favour of an amendment that would mean that milk chocolate made in the UK or Ireland would be labelled as 'milk chocolate with a high milk content' and in France it would be labelled as 'household chocolate'. The Commission proposed that the term 'milk chocolate' should apply to chocolate with 25% cocoa solids and 14% milk solids. The EP also voted in favour of an amendment that would prevent the Directive from coming into force until such time as there was a reliable scientific method of testing the substitute fat content of chocolate and until the Commission had carried out a study on the impact of the Directive on developing countries dependent on cocoa exports. The Commission opposed both these amendments, because research was already being undertaken into finding reliable scientific testing methods for assessing substitute fats and because it regarded the issue of the impact of the Directive on developing nations as a separate matter. By November 1997, there was complete deadlock. The issue rumbled on and finally, after more than two years of negotiations, the Council agreed a common position.[1] In February 2000, the Committee on the Environment, Public Health and Consumer

---

1   Common Position (EC) No 1/2000 adopted by the Council on 28 October 1999 with a view to adopting Directive 2000/36/EC of the European Parliament and of the Council relating to cocoa and chocolate products intended for human consumption.

Protection decided to recommend that the EP should adopt the Council's common position, almost unchanged. The rapporteur, Paul Lannoye (Greens/EFA) opposed some of the key points in the common position, in particular excluding the possibility of using vegetable fats other than cocoa butter and the Council's proposals on labelling. He also emphasised the serious consequences for the cocoa producers of the developing world, but his views were not supported. The Committee called for a ban on the use of genetic or enzymatic engineering in cocoa or chocolate products in the light of consumer concerns about these processes. The Committee also asked the Commission to consider how the interests of the cocoa producing countries could be protected, for example, by promoting fair trade. Under the proposal, up to 5% of the finished product may consist of fats other than cocoa butter, but only six types of vegetable fat may be used, all of which are of tropical origin. Coconut oil will be allowed only in ice cream and other similar frozen products. Chocolate products which contain these fats will have labels which clearly state 'also contains fats in addition to cocoa butter'. This must be placed in the same field of vision as the list of ingredients, clearly separated from that list, in letters at least as large and in bold. An amendment demanding that this information appear on the front of the product was defeated.

In March 2000, the European Parliament agreed the proposal and in May 2000, the Council accepted the EP's amendments to its common position and adopted the Directive. The Directive will repeal the existing Directive 73/241 and will finally create a single market for chocolate within the EU while still recognising the different chocolate making traditions of the various Member States. The new Directive will still allow the UK and Ireland to produce 'milk chocolate' to a different standard from that produced in the rest of the EU, but if it is to be exported, then it must be labelled as 'family milk chocolate'.

There are also other pieces of specific legislation on compositional standards and quality for natural mineral waters, spirit drinks, the marketing of milk and milk products and spreadable fats, including butter and margarine and minced meat.

Directive 80/777 on natural mineral waters[2] (as amended by Directive 96/70/EC)[3]

As there were different definitions in the Member States as to what constituted 'natural mineral water', the Commission deemed it necessary to specify rules for such waters in order to prevent the possibility of hindering free movement of these products. In order to ensure free movement of these products, it was

---

2   Commission Directive 80/777/EEC (OJ 1980 L229/1).
3   Commission Directive 96/70/EC (OJ 1996 L299/26).

determined that Member States must allow into their territory any 'natural mineral waters' which were recognised as such by any of the other Member States. The labelling of natural mineral water is subject to the provisions contained in the framework labelling Directive (79/112). In Annex 1(1) of the Directive, natural mineral water is described as 'microbiologically wholesome water originating in an underground water table or deposit and emerging from a spring tapped at one or more natural or bore exits'.

The natural mineral water must be recognised as such by a competent national authority with responsibility for ensuring that the producer of the water is following all the provisions of Directive 80/777. Member States are required to notify the Commission of the mineral waters they have recognised under the Directive, and this information will be published in the Official Journal.

Art 4 of the Directive provides that natural mineral water may not be subject to any treatment or addition except:

(a) the separation of its unstable elements such as iron or sulphur compounds;

(b) the total or partial elimination of free carbon dioxide;

(c) the introduction or re-introduction of carbon dioxide according to the requirements in Annex 1(3) which provide that it should be labelled 'naturally carbonated natural mineral water', 'natural mineral water fortified with gas from the spring' or 'carbonated natural mineral water'.

The Directive prohibits any kind of disinfectant treatment, the addition of any bacteriostatic elements or any other kind of treatment which might alter the viable colony count of the water. The Directive provides that the containers used for packaging the water must be fitted with closures that will ensure that there is no possibility of adulteration or contamination of the water.

On the label, the product should be described as 'natural mineral water' or by one of the descriptions listed above if carbon dioxide has been added. The original Directive stated that the label should also include either the words 'composition in accordance with the results of the officially recognised analysis of [date of analysis]' or a statement of the analytical composition, listing its characteristic constituents, the place where the spring is exploited and the name of the spring. Following the amendments introduced by Directive 96/70, both pieces of information are required. Member States are allowed to demand that the country of origin is specified on the label except in the case of water from within the EU. Water from one source may not be marketed under more than one trade description. It is prohibited to attribute to any natural mineral water properties suggesting that it can prevent, treat or cure any human disease. Member States may adopt special provisions concerning the suitability of a natural mineral water for consumption by infants. Member States may not introduce any national measures which would threaten the free movement of natural mineral water unless those measures can be justified on the grounds of public health, prevention of fraud or protection of industrial or commercial property. The sampling methods required to check the microbiological and compositional characteristics of natural mineral water are set out in Annexes to the Directive.

Directive 96/70 introduced new definitions and compositional standards for 'spring water'. It also introduced a procedure providing for co-ordinated action by Member States in the event of an emergency which threatens public health. This followed the problem with contaminated Perrier water.

Milk and milk products

Regulation 1898/87[4] applies to milk and milk products intended for human consumption and which are marketed in the EU. At the time the Regulation was introduced, there was a surplus of milk within the Community and it was thought that this surplus could be reduced if milk was marketed as a quality product. To achieve this, it was decided to introduce rules on the compositional standards of milk and milk products together with rules on labelling.

The Regulation consists of specific definitions and compositional requirements for 'milk' and 'milk products'. The Regulation established a system under which Member States must inform the Commission, before 1 October every year, about developments in the market for milk and milk products and competing products. Under this system, Member States are able to vary the indicative list of those products every Member State regards as a product corresponding to the products designated as milk or milk products under the Regulation. Member States are also permitted to retain national measures which restrict the production and marketing, within their territory, of products that do not comply with the compositional requirements outlined in the Regulation.

Regulation 2991/94 on spreadable fats[5] (as amended)[6]

With the increase in the variety of margarine and other similar products, the Commission believed that it was necessary to introduce compositional and quality standards for these new products in order to provide protection for consumers and avoid confusion. Accordingly, the Regulation provides that the terms 'butter' and margarine' may only be used for certain categories of product with a clearly defined fat content. The general rules on labelling as

---

4   Council Regulation 1898/87 (OJ 1987 L182/36) on the protection of designations used in the marketing of milk and milk products.

5   Council Regulation 2991/94/EC (OJ 1994 L316/2).

6   Regulation 2991/94 has been amended by Commission Regulation 577/97/EC (OJ 1997 L87/3) and Commission Regulation 1278/97/EC (OJ 1007 L175/6).

contained in the framework labelling Directive (79/112) must be complied with, but additional information is also required, namely, the indication of the total fat content and the fat constituents composed of animal and plant fats that are contained in the product. Imports of these products from third countries are subject to equivalent measures.

The Regulation specifies compositional and quality standards for spreadable fat products 'with a fat content of at least 10% but less than 90% by weight, intended for human consumption' (Art 1) and for products which remain solid at a temperature of 20ºC and which can be used as spreads (Art 2). As well as the usual labelling requirements, the product must also indicate:

(a) the sales description as defined in the Annex, for example, 'butter', 'margarine', blended spread' etc. The Annex contains a description of the specific product, its sales description and its composition which must be mentioned on the label;

(b) the total percentage of fat content by weight;

(c) the vegetable, milk or other fat content in decreasing order of weight importance as a percentage by total weight;

(d) the percentage salt content must be indicated in the list of ingredients.

An exception to these rules is that the term 'reduced fat' may be used for products with a fat content of more than 41% but less than 62%. The terms 'low fat' or 'light' may be used for products with a fat content of 41% or less. These exceptions are due for review in 2001, after which date the Commission will review their application and decide whether they should continue for a further period of time (at the time of writing, this review has not yet occurred). Subject to the provisions contained in the Regulation, Member States are permitted to adopt or maintain national regulations which contain different quality standards as long as these national measures do not discriminate against products from other Member States.

In 1998, an amendment was introduced which provided that, from 1 September 1998, a composite product whose main ingredient is butter should only be allowed to use the proprietary name 'butter' if the final product contains at least 75% dairy products and has been manufactured solely from butter (as defined in the Annex to Regulation 2991/94) and the dairy ingredient(s) are listed on the food label. Products which contain less than 75% but more than 62% of dairy fats should be referred to as 'butter preparations' on the label, in a prominent and clearly visible place.

Minced meat and meat preparations

Directive 94/65[7] was introduced in order to ensure a uniform development of the market in these products and with a view to ensuring consumer safety.

7   Council Directive 94/65/EC (OJ 1004 L368/10).

The Directive introduced public health requirements for the products covered by it and also established a system of approval for establishments at which these products are produced. It sets out rules for the production, placing on the market and importation of minced meat and meat products. It does not cover such products which are produced in retail shops or in premises adjacent to sales points, with a view to sale to the consumer, as these establishments are already subject to national measures governing the retail trade. The Directive provides detailed requirements regarding conditions for the approval of establishments producing minced meat and meat products, conditions for the production of these products, inspection of establishments, marking, labelling, wrapping, packaging, storage and transport, compositional and microbiological requirements and the type of health certificate required in order to be able to trade in these products.

In 1996, a Commission Decision[8] adapted the Directive and introduced equally stringent conditions regarding public health and health certification for minced meat and meat products imported from third countries.

QUALITY LEGISLATION SPECIFIC TO THE AGRICULTURAL SECTOR

Two Regulations were introduced in 1992, following the Council's Resolution of 1989 which re-launched the EC's consumer protection policy, to provide quality symbols which would provide consumers with extra information and protection regarding the characteristics of certain agricultural products and foodstuffs and enable consumers to choose products accordingly.

Agricultural certificates of specific character

Regulation 2082/92[9] lays down the rules under which agricultural products listed in Annex II of the Treaty on European Union and foodstuffs listed in the Annex of the Regulation may be awarded a Community certificate of specific character. The agricultural products include all those for which there is EC legislation, such as meat, milk, cheese, fish, eggs, fruit and vegetables. The foodstuffs include beer, chocolate, cocoa, confectionery, bread, cakes, pastry, biscuits, pasta (cooked, uncooked or stuffed), precooked meals, condiment sauces, soups, beverages made from plant extracts, ice cream and sorbets.

Certificate of specific character (CSC) designation is open to products which can demonstrate their traditional character and have a name which is

8   Commission Decision of 17 December 1996 (OJ 1996 L12/33).
9   Council Regulation 2082/92 on agricultural certificates of specific character (OJ 1992 L208/9).

traditional or customary. They may be based on a traditional recipe which, for example, has been used for at least 25 years or, if abandoned, has been revived.

A 'specific character' is defined in the Regulation as 'the feature or set of features which distinguishes an agricultural product or foodstuff clearly from other similar products or foodstuffs belonging to the same category'. Specific character may not be restricted to the qualitative or quantitative composition of the product, nor to a specific production method stipulated in EC or national legislation or standards, unless these provisions have been adopted specifically to define the particular character of a product.

Only a 'group' (producer groups/trade associations, etc) may apply to register an agricultural product or a foodstuff for a certificate. The Commission is charged with maintaining a register of existing certificates. Article 4(1) of the Regulation states that 'in order to appear in the register, an agricultural product or foodstuff must either be produced using traditional raw materials or be characterised by a traditional composition or a mode of production and/or processing, reflecting a traditional type of production and/or processing'.

'Traditional' is not defined, and this has caused problems for applicants, since most natural ingredients can be described as traditional in the sense that they have been used for many years to make the product. An application for a certificate of specific character must include the following information:

(a) the name of the product in one or more languages;

(b) a description of the method of production, including the nature and characteristics of the raw material used and method of preparation;

(c) aspects allowing the appraisal of traditional character;

(d) a description of the characteristics (physical, chemical, microbiological, organoleptic) which related to the specific character;

(e) the minimum requirements and inspection procedures to which specific character is subject.

In 1994, Regulation 2515/94[10] introduced an EU-wide symbol which can be used in the labelling, presentation and advertising of products which have a certificate of specific character. Under the Regulation, a named food or drink is given protection against imitation throughout the Community.

In May 2000, traditional Farmfresh Turkey became the first British product to receive protected status under a CSC. In a press release issued by the Ministry of Agriculture, Fisheries and Food (MAFF), the Minister of State said: 'Registration is a guarantee to consumers that the product is authentic and unique. Research has shown that across Europe consumers are becoming increasingly interested in where the food and drink they buy is coming from.'

---

10   Council Regulation 2515/94/EC (OJ 1991 L275/1).

The UK currently has 31 products registered under the protection of designations of origin (PDO) and protection of geographical indicators (PGI) schemes (see below), but Farmfresh Turkey is the first under the CSC.

There are now eight products in the EU with CSC status, compared with over 500 products registered on the basis of a geographical link under the PDO and PGI schemes. Changes to the arrangements for processing CSC applications are under way and both the UK and the Commission want to encourage more CSC applications. Under the ongoing 'Safeguarding Britain's Food Heritage' campaign which MAFF is conducting, more CSC applications relating to beer and meat are envisaged.

Agricultural geographical indicators

As many Member States had already introduced 'registered designations of origin' quality systems, it was felt that EU rules would be appropriate for the benefit of consumers, particularly because of the diversity in national practices.

Regulation 2081/92[11] lays down rules on the PDO and PGI of agricultural products referred to in Annex II of the Treaty on European Union and foodstuffs or agricultural products listed in the Annexes to the Regulation itself. Theses products are beer, natural mineral waters and spring waters, beverages made from plant extracts, bread, cakes, pastry, confectionery, biscuits, natural gums and resins (foodstuffs) and hay and essential oils (agricultural products).

Only product groups or associations working with the same agricultural product or foodstuff are eligible to apply for these certificates. Names that become 'generic' may not be registered. According to the Regulation, a 'generic' name is one which 'although it relates to the place or region where this product or foodstuff was originally produced or marketed, has become the common name of an agricultural product or foodstuff'.

In relation to PDOs, the Regulation makes it clear that names of products that have become generic may not be registered under the procedure laid down in the Regulation. In 1995, the Greek authorities made an application to the Commission to register the name 'feta' as a PDO. The Commission conducted a consumer poll and, in 1996, concluded that the name had not become generic and therefore registered it as a PDO. Cases were brought by Denmark, Germany and France against the Commission in the European Court of Justice (ECJ).[12] The ECJ held that the Commission had unjustly prevented other Member States from marketing their own cheeses as 'feta'

11 Council Regulation 2081/92/EC (OJ 1992 L208/1).
12 Cases C-289, 293 and 299/96 *Denmark, Germany and France v Commission, supported by Greece.*

and that 'feta' was a long established generic name and could no longer be claimed only by its place of origin, Greece.

Protected designations of origin (PDO)

A PDO is defined as the name of a region, specific place or, in exceptional circumstances, a country, used to describe the agricultural product or foodstuff originating in that region, specific place or country and the quality or characteristics of which are essentially or exclusively due to a particular geographical environment with its inherent natural and human factors, and the production, processing and preparation of which take place in the defined geographical area.

Protected geographical indicators (PGI)

A PGI is defined as the name of a region, specific place or, in exceptional circumstances, a country, used to describe an agricultural product or foodstuff originating in that region, specific place or country and which possesses a specific quality, reputation or other characteristic attributable to that geographical region and the production and/or processing and/or preparation which take place in the defined geographical area.

The difference between the two is not great. The one appears to relate to a specific geographical environment and the other to a specific geographical origin. The test of geographical origin is the more popular of the two and is the easier to demonstrate.

In relation to agriculture there are, of course, certain pieces of legislation covering quality standards. These are in respect of organic products, certificates of a specific character and protected geographical indicators.

ORGANIC PRODUCTS

With organic food the crucial quality issue relates to the way in which the food is produced.

In its Briefing Paper on organic food and farming, the Soil Association has described organic agriculture as:

... a safe, sustainable farming system producing healthy crops and livestock without damage to the environment.

It avoids the use of artificial fertilisers and pesticides on the land, relying instead on developing a healthy, fertile soil and growing a mixture of crops. In this way the farm remains biologically balanced, with a wide variety of beneficial insects and other wildlife to act as natural predators for crop pests and a soil full of micro-organisms and earthworms to maintain its vitality.

130

Animals are reared without the routine use of the army of drugs, antibiotics and womers which form the foundation of most conventional livestock farming.

'Organic' is a term defined by law.

European Community Regulation 2092/91 on organic production[13] lays down rules relating to the organic production of agricultural products and the quality requirements for these products, including specific provision regarding vegetables.

In July 1999 an amendment was made to the Directive,[14] which extended its scope to include livestock and livestock products.

Regulation 2092/91 has been implemented in the UK by the Organic Products Regulations 1992[15] (as amended).[16] It is illegal to use the term 'organic' unless the food has been produced in accordance with the Regulations and by a registered producer. Those who are involved in the preparation of organic food or in importing it from countries outside the EU must also be registered.

All food sold as organic must come from growers, processors or importers who are registered and subject to regular inspection. In the UK it is the United Kingdom Register of Organic Food Standards (UKROFS) that has responsibility for ensuring that Regulation 2092/91 is properly applied by the various bodies in the UK which register and regulate organic food.

UKROFS defines organic production systems as being 'designed to produce optimum quantities of food of high nutritional quality by using management practices which aim to avoid the use of agro-chemical inputs and which minimise damage to the environment and wildlife'.

UKROFS comprises an inspection board appointed by the Ministers for Agriculture and a Secretariat provided by the Ministry for Agriculture, Fisheries and Food.

There are six bodies in the UK which register and inspect organic businesses: the Soil Association, the Biodynamic Agricultural Association, the Irish Organic Farmers and Growers Association, Organic Farmers and Growers, the Organic Food Federation and the Scottish Organic Producers Association. All registered operators are subject to inspection from their sector bodies and from UKROFS to ensure the application of organic standards.

Consumers who choose organic products do so for a variety of reasons, including concern over animal welfare, concern for the environment and

---

13   Council Regulation 2092/91 on organic production (OJ 1991 L198/1).

14   Regulation 1804/99.

15   The Organic Products Regulations 1992 (SI 1992/2111).

16   The Regulations have been amended by the Organic Products (Amendment) Regulations 1993 (SI 1993/495), the Organic Products (Amendment) Regulations 1994 (SI 1994/2286) and the Organic Products (Amendment) Regulations 1997 (SI 1997/163).

scarce resources and for health reasons believing that organic production involves less cruelty to animals, less damage to the environment and less chance of chemical contamination.

In its 'Position Paper' on organic food, the Food Standards Agency of the UK concludes that 'there is not enough information available at present to be able to say that organic foods are significantly different in terms of their safety and nutritional content to those produced by conventional farming'. With regard to the issue of nutrition, the Paper concludes that:

> From a nutritional point of view the composition of individual food is relatively unimportant. What matters is the nutrient content and overall balance of the diet as a whole. A varied and balanced diet, which includes plenty of fruit, vegetable sand starchy foods, should provide all of the nutrients that a healthy individual requires, regardless of whether the individual components are produced by organic or conventional methods.

While there may be no nutritional difference between a conventionally grown apple and an organically grown one, in that they will probably both have roughly the same amount of vitamins, fibre and so on, the difference lies in the way in which the apples are produced and that is what interests and concerns consumers who choose organic foodstuffs.

The Paper goes on to consider the issues of microbiological safety, pesticide and veterinary residues and mycotoxin contamination. Concern has been expressed, however, that organic product may be more prone to mycotoxin contamination and more likely to cause food poisoning than conventionally produced food, through pathogenic transfer into the food chain.

It its Paper, the Food Standards Agency concludes that 'There is no firm evidence at present to support the assertion that organic food is more or less microbiologically safe than conventionally farmed produce' and that 'There is no evidence to indicate that organic food is more prone to mycotoxin contamination than conventionally grown food'.

The Position Paper, while providing useful information, does not appear fully to acknowledge the moral and ethical reasons why an increasing number of people are choosing organically produced foods.

CHAPTER 5

FOOD LABELLING

As consumers become increasingly concerned about exactly what is in the food they buy and eat, the way in which food is labelled and the nature of the information contained on the label has become increasingly important for legislators and food producers alike.

In the absence of a comprehensive system of EC law on the composition of foodstuffs, it was acknowledged by the Commission that it would be necessary to institute a coherent system for the labelling, presentation and advertising of food products within the EC.[1]

The main framework directive was Directive 79/112,[2] as amended by a number of other Directives

Different rules on labelling in the different Member States were a hindrance to the free movement of goods and free trade generally and Directive 79/112 was intended to provide general rules which would apply horizontally to all foodstuffs and which would help to inform and protect the consumer.

Directive 79/112 and its amending Directives have now been consolidated in Directive 2000/13/EC.

The Directive defines 'labelling' as meaning 'any words, particulars, trade marks, brand name, pictorial matter or symbol relating to a foodstuff and placed on any packaging, document, notice, label, ring or collar accompanying or referring to such foodstuff' (Art 1(3)(a)).

Under the Directive, the labelling and presentation of foodstuffs must not be such as to mislead the purchaser, particularly as regards the characteristics of the foodstuffs (its properties, composition, durability, method of manufacture or production), by attributing to the foodstuff attributes or properties which it does not possess or by suggesting that the foodstuff possesses special characteristics which, in fact, all similar foodstuffs possess. It is not permitted to attribute to any foodstuff the possibility of preventing, treating or curing of a medical condition or to refer to such properties by a particular product.

Article 3 of the Directive lists the compulsory pieces of information which must be included on any food label. These are:

---

1 European Parliament and Council Directive 2000/13/EC (OJ 2000 L300/13).

2 Commission Communication, *Completion of the Internal Market: Community Legislation on Foodstuffs*.

1   the name under which the product is sold;

2   the list of ingredients;

3   the quantity of certain ingredients or categories of ingredients, as provided for in Art 7;

4   in the case of prepackaged foods, the net quantity;

5   the date of minimum durability; or, in the case of foodstuffs which, from the microbiological point of view, are highly perishable, the 'use by' date;

6   any special storage conditions or conditions of use;

7   the name or business name and address of the manufacturer or packager or of a seller established within the Community;

8   particulars of the place of origin or provenance in the cases where failure to give such particulars might mislead the consumer to a material degree as to the true origin or provenance of the foodstuff;

9   instructions for use when it would be impossible to make use of the foodstuff in the absence of such instructions;

10 for beverages containing more than 1.2% by volume of alcohol, the actual alcoholic strength by volume [this was added by Directive 86/197].[3]

Amendments to Directive 79/112

Directive 89/395

In the interests of the completion of the internal market and to provide greater protection for the consumer this Directive abolished the derogations which had been available to Member States in the original Directive (public health, fraud, protection of industrial and commercial property rights).

This Directive also makes it mandatory for Member States to apply the provisions of the 1979 Directive to 'mass caterers' such as hospitals, restaurants, etc. Originally, this had been optional.

The Directive also introduced the 'use by' date for highly perishable goods (see above).

Directive 91/72[4]

This Directive dealt specifically with the issue of how flavourings should be designated on a label. The Commission felt that it was necessary to harmonise the legislation in this area because the different national laws of the Member States regarding the way in which flavourings were indicated on a label could potentially threaten the free movement of foodstuffs.

3   Council Directive 86/197/EEC (OJ 1986 L144/38).

4   Commission Directive 91/72/EEC (OJ 1991 L42/27).

The Directive adds a new Annex 3 to the 1979 Directive on the 'designation of flavourings in the list of ingredients'. It provides that flavourings must be designated either by the word 'flavouring(s)' or by a more specific name or description of the flavouring. The word 'natural' can only be used in conjunction with a flavouring if it satisfies the definition for such a flavouring under Directive 88/388/EEC on flavourings. Vegetable or animal derived flavourings can only be called 'natural vegetable flavouring' if it has been derived almost exclusively from the vegetable source concerned. The same applies in the case of 'natural' animal origin flavourings.

Directive 93/102[5]

This Directive replaced Annexes 1 and 2 of the original Directive with new Annexes. Annex 1 lists the categories of ingredients which may be designated on the label by the name of the category (for example, 'starch', 'fish', 'poultry meat') rather than by their specific name.

Annex 2 lists the categories of ingredients which must be designated by the name of the category to which they belong followed by their specific name or EEC number (for example Color E211, Stabiliser E453, etc).

Directive 94/54[6]

Under this Directive, foodstuffs whose durability has been extended by the use of packaging gases must be labelled as 'packaged in a protective atmosphere'. This Directive was amended by Directive 96/21[7] to include specific labelling requirements for sweeteners.

Directive 97/4[8]

This Directive provides that the use of the customary sales name indicated in the Member State in which the food product is manufactured should also be allowed in the case of food products to be sold in another Member State, unless there would be a possibility of confusion amongst consumers, in which case the sales name must be supplemented by other descriptive information which should appear in proximity to the sales name.

As far as ingredients are concerned, this Directive amends Art 3, so that in addition to the list of ingredients being part of the food label, the quantity and categories of ingredients as contained in Annexes 1 and 2 must also now be

---

5   Commission Directive 93/102/EEC (OJ 1993 L291/14).

6   Commission Directive 94/54/EC (OJ 1994 L300/14).

7   Council Directive 96/21/EC concerning the compulsory indication on the labelling of certain foodstuffs of particulars other than those provided for in Council Directive 79/112/EEC (OJ 1996 L88).

8   Commission Directive 97/4/EC (OJ 1997 L43/21).

indicated on the food label. This requirement is known as the quantitative ingredient declaration (QUID).

Quantitative ingredient declarations

The QUID provisions are set down in Art 7. In principle, the QUID requirement applies to all food, including beverages, with more than one ingredient. There are certain exceptions.

The Directive also provided that QUID would apply to products hitherto exempt from ingredient listing. In these food products, the ingredient quantity must be indicated in or immediately next to the name under which the product is sold, unless a list of ingredients is voluntarily indicated on the labelling, in which case the quantity may appear in that list.

QUID does not apply to food products that are already regulated at Community level.

The QUID requirement does not apply to constituents that are naturally present and which have not been added as ingredients; for example, caffeine in coffee.

In an advisory document, the Commission has provided guidance as to how the QUID provisions should be applied, while acknowledging that the official interpretation of the legislation remains the 'the exclusive reserve of the judicial powers'.[9]

QUID declarations are compulsory in the following cases:

... where the ingredients or category of ingredients concerned appears in the name under which the foodstuff is sold or is usually associated with that name by the consumer.[10]

Where the *ingredient* is included in the name of the food, for example, 'cheese and *mushroom* pizza', '*raspberry* yoghurt', '*date* and *walnut* loaf', it is the italicised ingredient that must be quantified.

Where the *category* of ingredient is included in the name of the food, for example, 'vegetable pasty', 'nut loaf', the QUID declaration need only relate to the total vegetables, nuts, etc.

Category of ingredients is the generic term which Annex 1 of the Directive allows to be used as names for ingredients and any similar generic terms which, though not permitted as names for ingredients in ingredients lists, are legitimately or customarily used in the name of a food. Where Member States

---

9   General guidelines for implementing the principle of Quantitative Ingredient Declaration (QUID) – Directive 79/112/EEC, Art 7, as amended by Directive 97/4/EC (III/5260rev 5/98 - EN).

10 Directive 97/4/EC, Art 7(2)(a), now Directive 2000/13/EC.

have food products whose names refer to ingredients they do not actually contain, then the QUID requirements do not apply, for example, 'water biscuits'. When a compound ingredient appears in the name (for example, 'biscuits with a cream filling') it is the percentage of the compound which should be indicated. If a specific ingredient of the compound ingredient is mentioned, its percentage must also be given (for example, biscuits with a cream filling containing butter).

> ... where the ingredient or category of ingredients concerned is emphasised on the labelling in words, pictures or graphics.[11]

This requirement will apply where a particular ingredient is emphasised on the label other than in the name under which the food is sold, for example, by information such as 'with butter', 'with cream', or by use of a different size, colour and/or style of lettering to refer to particular ingredients elsewhere on the label other than in the product name.

The provision will also apply where a pictorial representation is used to emphasise selectively one or more ingredients or where an ingredient is emphasised by an image evoking its origin, for example, a picture of a cow to emphasise dairy products. The provision would not apply where there is a picture depicting a 'serving suggestion' for the product, or where a picture illustrates all the ingredients in the product without emphasising one in particular. The provision would not apply in the case of a food mix where there is a pictorial representation showing how to prepare the product.

> ... where the ingredient or category of ingredients concerned is essential to characterise a foodstuff and to distinguish it from products with which it might be confused because of its name or appearance.[12]

This provision is intended to protect consumers in some Member States where the composition of certain foodstuffs is regulated and/or where consumers associate certain names with specific composition. The only two examples identified in the guidance are marzipan and mayonnaise. In order for the QUID provisions to apply in these circumstances, the ingredient or category of ingredient must be essential both to characterise the food and to distinguish it from products with which it might be confused because of its name or appearance.

> In any other cases determined by the Standing Committee on Foodstuffs, in conjunction with the Commission.

QUID declarations are not required in the case of:

> ... an ingredient or category of ingredients the drained net weight of which is indicated in accordance with Art 8(4).[13]

---

11 Directive 97/4/EC, Art 7(2)(b), now Directive 2000/13/EC.
12 *Ibid,* Art 7(2)(c).
13 *Ibid,* Art 7(3)(a) (first indent).

This Article requires that where a solid food is presented in a liquid medium, the drained net weight as well as the actual net weight should be included on the label. 'Liquid medium' means water, brine, fruit or vegetable juice (in the case of preserved fruit or vegetables) and aqueous solutions of salts, food acids, sugars or other sweetening substances. These can also be in mixtures, frozen and quick-frozen. This means that any product which includes the drained net weight as well as the total net weight, in accordance with Art 8(4), is exempt from the need to give a separate QUID declaration.

> ... an ingredient or category of ingredients the quantities of which are already required to be given on the labelling under Community provision.[14]

This refers to the legislation contained in Annex A.

> ... an ingredient or category of ingredients which is used in small quantities for the purposes of flavouring.[15]

This exemption applies whether or not pictorial representations are included on the label. The label must, of course, comply with the requirements of Directive 88/388/EEC on flavourings; the exemption is not confined to flavourings as defined in that Directive, but applies to any ingredient or category of ingredients used in small quantities to flavour food, for example, garlic, herbs and spices. It is for Member States to determine what constitutes 'small quantities'.

> ... an ingredient or category of ingredients which, while appearing in the name under which the food is sold, is not such as to govern the choice of the consumer in the country of marketing because the variation of quantity is not essential to characterise the foodstuff or does not distinguish it from similar foods.[16]

This provision provides for exemption from the QUID requirements where the quantity of an ingredient mentioned in the name of a food does not affect the consumer's purchasing decision, for example 'malt whisky'.

> ... where specific Community provisions stipulate precisely the quantity of an ingredient or of a category of ingredients without providing for the indication thereof on the labelling.[17]

At present, there do not appear to be any Community provisions which come within the scope of this Article.

QUID declarations are also not required 'in the cases referred to in the fourth and fifth indents of Art 6(5)(a) of Directive 79/112/EEC',[18] namely

---

14 Directive 97/4/EC, Article 7(3)(a) (second indent), now Directive 2000/13/EC.
15 *Ibid*, Art 7(3)(a) (third indent).
16 *Ibid*, Art 7(3)(a) (fourth indent).
17 *Ibid*, Art 6(3)(b).
18 *Ibid*, Art 7(5)(c).

foods that are mixtures of fruit and vegetables or mixtures of spices or herbs where no ingredient in the mixture significantly predominates by weight.

The quantity indicated on the label must be expressed as a percentage and must correspond to the quantity of the ingredient(s) at the time of its (their) use. Member States may derogate from this stipulation provided that they have the approval of the Standing Committee on Foodstuffs in conjunction with the Commission. The indication of the quantity of ingredients must appear in or immediately next to the name under which the foodstuff is sold or in the list of ingredients in connection with the ingredients or categories of ingredients in question.

Directive 99/10[19] provides for certain specific derogations from the QUID declarations and also gives directions as to how QUID should be calculated for finished products that have lost moisture, products that contain volatile ingredients or products which contain concentrated or dehydrated ingredients that are reconstituted during the manufacturing process by the consumer adding water. Member States were required to allow products complying with this Directive to move freely within their territory by 1 September 1999 and to prohibit trade of products not complying with it by 1 February 2000. Products that were marked or labelled before 14 February 2000 (the deadline for the implementation of Directive 97/4) may still be traded.

In its White Paper on Food Safety, the Commission identified further areas which needed addressing which include the following:

The abolition of the 25% rule

As the law stands at present, where a compound ingredient (that is, an ingredient that is itself derived from several other ingredients) is less than 25% of the weight of the ingredients used, then a label can simply identify the compound ingredient, and it is not necessary to list the component ingredients although additives used in the compound ingredient must be declared. It is now the view that this does not provide enough information to the consumer, and the provision is to be removed, although it is possible that the 25% limit will only be reduced in line with a recent amendment to the Codex General Standard on Food Labelling, rather than abolished altogether.

The labelling of allergens

There appears to have been an increase in recent times in the number of people who suffer from allergic reactions to certain foods, for example, nuts, gluten derived from wheat, and shellfish. Some of these reactions can be very serious, even fatal, and therefore there is a need to identify foods which

---

19   Commission Directive 99/10/EC (OJ 1000 L69/22).

contain potentially dangerous ingredients. In the White Paper, the Commission states: 'For ingredients that are known allergens, but where only the name of the category needs to be indicated, an indication as to the presence of such allergens will be considered in order to enable susceptible consumers to avoid such allergens.'

Consideration is being given to a proposal which would make it a requirement that food and ingredients that cause known allergic reactions should always be specifically identified in the list of ingredients. The following foods, ingredients or products containing them would have to be identified: cereals containing gluten, eggs and egg products, crustaceans, fish and fish products, peanuts, soya beans, milk and milk products, including lactose, tree nuts and nut products, sesame seeds and sulphide at concentrations of 10 mg/kg or more. These products are the same as those identified by the Codex Alimentarius Commission at their meeting in 1999.

Claims

The Commission has indicated in the White Paper that it will 'consider whether specific provision should be introduced in EU law to govern "functional claims" (for example, claims related to beneficial effects of a nutrient on certain normal bodily functions) and "nutritional claims" (such as claims which describe the presence, absence or the level of a nutrient, as the case may be, contained in a foodstuff or its value compared to similar foodstuffs)'.

Consolidation

As indicated above, EC labelling requirements have now been consolidated into one new Directive. In March 2000, the Council adopted a Directive on the approximation of the laws of the Member States relating to the labelling, presentation and advertising of foodstuffs. This Directive consolidates Directive 79/112 (which will be repealed) and the amending directives. Consolidation is a technical, legal procedure and the new Directive does not introduce substantive changes to the existing provisions.

Nutrition labelling

Directive 90/496 on nutrition labelling for foodstuffs[20]

There is growing interest and awareness of the importance of diet for maintaining health. Consumers are increasingly concerned to know about the nutritional composition of the food they eat. The Commission took the view that knowledge of the basic principle of good nutrition and the appropriate nutrition labelling of foods would enable consumers to make better informed choices about the food they purchased. For these reasons, and in order to facilitate the operation of the internal market, it was decided that nutrition labelling should be presented in a standardised form throughout the EC. All forms of nutrition labelling which did not conform to the Directive would be prohibited. Food products which did not carry any nutrition label would be allowed to circulate freely within the EC. The rules contained in this Directive reflected the Codex Alimentarius guidelines on nutrition labelling. The Directive also took account of the rules contained in the framework Directive 79/112 and its subsequent amendments.

The Directive deals with the nutrition labelling of foodstuffs which are intended for sale to the ultimate consumer as well as foodstuffs intended to be supplied to restaurants, hospitals, canteens, and other similar 'mass caterers'. The Directive does not cover natural mineral water (which is covered by Directive 80/777) on food supplements.

For the purposes of the Directive, 'nutrition labelling' is defined as information contained on a label which relates to:

- energy; and
- the following nutrients: protein, carbohydrate, sugars, fat, saturates, fibre and sodium, vitamins and minerals listed in the Annex and their recommended daily allowances (RDAs).

The provisions of the Directive are voluntary for food manufacturers, but become mandatory if the food manufacturer makes what is called a 'nutritional claim' concerning the food product they produce. A 'nutritional claim' is defined as any representation and any advertising message which states, suggests or implies that a foodstuff has particular nutritional properties due to the amount of energy it provides or the level of nutrients it contains.

Where nutrition information is given it may be presented in one of two ways: either (a) energy value and the amounts of protein, carbohydrate and fat, or (b) energy value and the amounts of protein, carbohydrate, fat, sugars, starches, fibre and sodium.

---

20   Council Directive 90/496/EEC (OJ 1990 L276/40).

Additional information may be provided on the amounts of starch, polyols, monounsaturates, polyunsaturates, cholesterol and any of the vitamins and minerals listed in the Annex and present in amounts relative to their RDAs.

The information provided for in the Directive must be presented together in one place in tabular form, with the numbers aligned if space permits. If space does not permit, the information may be presented in linear form. Member States are asked to ensure that the information appears in a language which can be understood by consumers, although it may appear in more than one language. Member States are not permitted to introduce national rules on nutritional labelling more detailed than those contained in the Directive.

CODEX AND THE INTERNATIONAL CONTEXT

Codex Food Labelling Committee

This Committee has developed a number of standards: in particular, the Codex General Standard for the Labelling of Pre-packaged Foods, which was first issued in 1985 and was influenced by EC Directive 79/112. Section 4.2.1.3 of the General Standard originally contained the same provision relating to the 25% rule for compound ingredients as the EC legislation. In 1999 however at the Codex Commission meeting the level was changed to 5% and the new s 4.2.1.4 relating to hypersensitivity was included.

    4.2.1.3   Where an ingredient is itself the product of two or more ingredients, such a compound ingredient may be declared, as such, in the list of ingredients, provided that it is immediately accompanied by a list, in brackets, of its ingredients in descending order of proportion Where a compound ingredient (for which a name has been established in a Codex standard or in national legislation) constitutes less than 5% of the food, the ingredients, other than food additives which serve a technological function in the finished product, need not be declared.

    4.2.1.4   The following foods or ingredients are known to cause hypersensitivity and shall always be declared:

- cereals containing gluten: that is, wheat, rye, barley, oats, spelt or their hybridised strains and products of these;
- crustacea and products of these;
- eggs and egg products;
- fish and fish products;
- peanuts, soya beans and products of these;

- o   milk and milk products (lactose included);
- o   tree nuts and nut products; and
- o   sulphite in concentrations of 10 mg/kg or more.

Labelling issues are also becoming very important in international trade. At the FAO/WHO Conference on International Food Trade Beyond 2000, held in October 1999, a paper was presented entitled 'Harmonization, mutual recognition and equivalence: labelling and nutritional requirements – how much information is necessary?'.[21]

The paper considered the background to the debate on labelling and considered the current state of food labelling, including issues such as product information; nutritional values and presentation format; nutritional claims. The conclusions and recommendations were as follows:

45 Experience suggests that the rationale for food labelling is best served if decisions are science-based and principles are applied systematically. It is the relentless pursuit of science and an adherence to principles that will take us to the maximal level of harmonization. Moreover, science-based decisions are most likely to stand the test of time and thus serve harmonization best. Other legitimate factors have not clearly emerged.

46 Discussions about the current status of food labelling also suggest some pragmatic observations. One observation is that more consumer involvement in food labelling is likely, and this must be accompanied by consumer education. Another observation is that while the food label can serve diverse needs, it is nonetheless tiny and can carry only a limited informational burden. Perhaps most obvious but least understood is the fact that harmonization must be considered early in the process. Certainly, in the end, food labelling decisions must be respectful of provisions that are intended to give individual nations the right to protect public health at levels their authorities find to be appropriate. But this apparent inconsistency with the goal of harmonization can often be resolved by identifying as a principle the likelihood that increased understanding and scientific data are the key to harmonizing such national decisions. When all nations face the same, sound scientific conclusions, they may not take the same public health actions but the chances that they will do so are much greater with the availability of the scientific evidence than without it. Finally, as controversies arise, an important consideration is that the potential conflict between the consumers' need to know and their interest in knowing, as well as the interplay of manufacturing and trade interests, must not be short-circuited. Harmonization cannot be superimposed, it must evolve and will entail adjustment of laws, regulations, policies, standards, and practices between different jurisdictions so as to minimize dissonance and facilitate commercial activity.

47 The following are general recommendations for FAO/WHO/WTO and member governments that are intended to provide for an adequate and

---

21 Delivered by Dr Christina J Lewis from the Center for Food Safety and Applied Nutrition, Food and Drug Administration, US.

acceptable science base for the food label and to provide some guidance when the science itself is at issue or lacking:

- Support efforts to resolve technical issues such as chemical definitions for nutrients and acceptable analytical procedures.
- Support scientific research to explore the impact of nutrition on health and to better elucidate human nutritional requirements so that dietary standards can be candidates for harmonization; promote nutrition monitoring in all regions of the world.
- Collect information about consumer skills, perceptions, beliefs and motivations concerning food, nutrition and food safety, and actively work to educate consumers about these topics.
- Anticipate the need for science-based decisions by rapidly identifying emerging issues and working group discussions with relevant science; support targeted research to resolve controversies.
- Ensure transparency for the decision-making process.

UK LABELLING REGULATIONS

In the UK, the Food Labelling Regulations 1996 implement Council Directive 79/112 (as amended).[22]

They also implement Commission Directive 87/250[23] on the indication of alcoholic strength by volume in the labelling of alcoholic beverages for sale to the ultimate consumer, Council Directive 89/398[24] on the approximation of the laws of Member States relating to the labelling of foodstuffs for particular nutritional uses; Council Directive 90/496 on nutrition labelling for foodstuffs and Commission Directive 94/54 (as amended by Council Directive 96/21).

The Regulations have been amended by the Food Labelling (Amendment) Regulations 1999,[25] which implemented Directive 97/41/EC (see above), providing for the introduction of QUID information on labels. The Regulations apply in Great Britain and contain the requirements laid down in the relevant Directives.

There are certain foodstuffs which are exempted from the Regulations. These are: drinks bottled before 1 January 1982 having an alcoholic strength greater than 1.2% by volume and meeting the labelling requirements in force at the time of bottling; any food prepared on domestic premises for sale for the benefit for the person preparing it by a registered society; any food not prepared in the course of a business by the person preparing it.

---

22 As amended by Council Directives 85/7, 86/197, 89/395 and Commission Directives 91/72, 93/102.

23 Commission Directive 87/250/EEC (OJ 1987 L113).

24 Council Directive 89/198/EEC (OJ 1989 L186).

25 SI 1999/747.

Part II deals with foods which are to be delivered to the ultimate consumer or caterer. It must comply with the provisions laid down in Art 3 of Directive 79/112 as to the list of information which must be given. There are, however, certain exemptions. These are: specified sugar products; cocoa and chocolate products; honey; condensed and dried milk for delivery to a catering establishment (unless prepared and labelled for infant consumption); coffee and coffee products (including designated chicory products) for delivery to catering establishments.

There are also certain foods which are not subject to the controls of Part II in so far as their labelling is regulated by other Regulations. These are: hen eggs; spreadable fats; wines or grape musts; sparkling wines and aerated sparkling wines; liqueur wines; semi-sparkling wines and aerated semi-sparkling wines; spirit drinks; fresh fruit and vegetables; preserved sardines; preserved tuna; and bonito additives (s 4(2)).

In the case of the products listed above, they must, however, carry statements relating to packaging gases and sweeteners.

Apart from the exemptions, all foods must be marked with the information laid down in Art 3 of the Directive. Section 5 lists the general labelling requirements.

Name under which a product is sold (ss 6–11)

The name under which a particular foodstuff is sold shall be the name laid down by whatever laws, regulations or administrative provisions apply to the foodstuff in question. In the absence of any such name, the name customary in the Member States where the product is sold to the ultimate consumer should be used. If this is not possible, then a description of the product should be used together with, if possible, a description of its use which is sufficiently precise to inform the purchaser of its true nature and to distinguish it from food products with which it could be confused. No trade mark, brand name or 'fancy' name may be substituted for the name under which the product is sold.

The name of the product must be accompanied by details of its physical condition or of any specific treatment it has undergone (for example, powdered, freeze-dried, frozen, concentrated, smoked), where the omission of these details could confuse the consumer.

List of ingredients (ss 12–18)

Ingredients need not be listed in the case of fresh fruit or vegetables, cheese, butter, fermented milk and cream and products consisting of a single ingredient where confusion is likely to occur for the consumer if ingredients were listed in these cases.

The list of ingredients should be headed or preceded by 'ingredients' (or a heading which includes the word 'ingredients').

Order of ingredients

Ingredients to be listed in weight descending order, determined as at the time of their use in the preparation of the food, except for the following:

s 13(2) water and volatile products used as ingredients shall be listed in order of their weight in the finished product. The weight of water is calculated by subtracting from the weight of the finished product the total weight of the other ingredients used;

s 13(3) if an ingredient is reconstituted from concentrated or dehydrated form during preparation of the food, it may be positioned according to its weight before concentration or dehydration;

s 13(4) if a food is to be reconstituted during use by the addition of water, its ingredients may be listed in order after reconstitution provided there is a statement 'ingredients of the reconstituted product' or 'ingredients of the ready to use product' or similar indication;

s 13(5) if a product consists of mixed fruit, nuts, vegetables, spices or herbs and no particular one of these ingredients predominates significantly by weight, the ingredients may be listed in any order provided that for foods consisting entirely of such a mixture the heading includes 'in variable proportion' or other words indicating method of listing and for other such foods the relevant ingredients are accompanied by such a statement.

Names of ingredients

The name of an ingredient shall be:

(a) the name which would be used if the ingredient were sold as a food, including, if appropriate, either 'irradiated' or 'treated with ionising radiation' (other appropriate indications must be given if a consumer could be misled by its omission) (s 14(1) and (2)); or

(b) the generic name given in Schedule 3 (s 14(4)).

A flavouring shall be identified by the word 'flavouring' or 'flavourings' or a more specific name or description of the flavouring; it may be supplemented by the word 'natural' (or similar) only where the flavouring component(s) of the ingredient consist(s) exclusively of a flavouring substance obtained by physical (including distillation and solvent extraction), enzymatic or microbiological processes, from material of vegetable or animal origin which material is either raw or has only been subjected to a process normally used in preparing food (including drying, torrefaction and fermentation), and/or, a flavouring preparation(s); in addition, if the name refers to a vegetable or animal nature or origin, the word 'natural' (or similar), it must be derived solely or almost solely from that vegetable or animal source (s 14(5), (6), (7)).

Additives shall be listed by either the principal function they serve, as given below, followed by its name and/or serial number (subject to the notes) or where the function is not given, its name.

Compound ingredients

Where a compound ingredient is used in the preparation of a food, names of the ingredients of a compound ingredient may be given either instead of the compound ingredient or in addition (and immediately following the name of the compound ingredient); except only the name of the compound ingredient need be given if the compound ingredient:

- need not bear an ingredients' list if it were being sold;
- is identified by a generic name; or
- is less than 25% of the finished product, but in this case, any additives used and needing to be named must be listed immediately following the name of the compound ingredient.

Water

Section 16 provides that water which is added as an ingredient of a food must be declared unless:

(a) it is used solely for reconstitution of an ingredient which is in concentrated or dehydrated form;

(b) it is used as, or as part of, a medium which is not normally consumed;

(c) it does not exceed 5% of the finished product; or

(d) it is permitted under EEC frozen or quick-frozen poultry regulations (s 16(2)).

Ingredients not needing to be named (s 17)

(a) Constituents of an ingredient which have temporarily become separated and later reintroduced (in the original proportions);

(b) additives which were in an ingredient and which serve no significant technological function in the finished product;

(c) any additive used solely as a processing aid;

(d) any substance (other than water) used as a solvent or carrier of an additive (and used only at level which is strictly necessary).

Foods which need not bear a list of ingredients (s 18)

(a) Fresh fruit and vegetables which have not been peeled or cut into pieces;

(b) carbonated water (consisting of water and carbon dioxide only, and the name indicates that the water is carbonated);

(c) vinegar derived by fermentation (from a single basic product) with no added ingredients;

(d) cheese, butter, fermented milk and fermented cream to which only lactic products, enzymes and micro-organism cultures essential to manufacture have been added, or, in the case of cheese (except fresh curd cheese and processed cheese), any salt required for its manufacture;

(e) any food consisting of a single component (including flour containing only legally required nutritional additives);

(f) any drink with an alcoholic strength by volume over 1.2%.

For (c) and (d), if other ingredients are included, only those other added ingredients need be listed if the list is headed 'added ingredients' or similar.

Appropriate durability indication

Minimum durability (s 20)

The minimum durability of a food product can be indicated as follows:

• by the words 'best before' followed by the date up to and including which the food can reasonably be expected to retain its specific properties if properly stored, and details of the storage conditions necessary for the properties to be retained until that date. The date must be expressed in the form day/month/year. If the date is within three months, then only the day/month are required; or

• 'best before end' followed by the month/year if date is from three to 18 months, or 'best before end' and month/year or year if date is more than 18 months;

• either the date only or the date and storage conditions may be elsewhere on the packet if reference is made to the position after the 'best before' statement.

In the case of certain highly perishable foodstuffs, the Directive allows Member States to require the words 'use by' to be indicated. They must advise the Commission and other Member States if they intend to demand this additional requirement and they must indicate the products to which this requirement applies, in order to ensure the free movement of goods. In addition to these dates, the Directive allows for a non-compulsory description of the storage conditions which must be observed if the product is to remain fresh for the specified period.

The UK Regulations provide as follows: the 'use by' date is to be indicated by 'use by' followed by the date (expressed in day/month or day/month/year) up to and including which the food, if properly stored, is recommended for use. Details of any necessary storage conditions must also be given. Either the date only or the date and storage conditions may be elsewhere on the packet if reference is made to the position after the 'use by' statement.

Certain foods are exempted from stating an appropriate durability indication. These are:

(a) fresh fruit and vegetables (including potatoes, but not including sprouting seeds, legume sprouts and similar products) which have not been peeled or cut into pieces;

(b) wine, liqueur wine, sparkling wine, aromatised wine and any similar drink obtained from fruit other than grapes and certain other drinks made from grapes or grape musts (see Regulations);

(c) any drink made from grapes or grape must comply with certain specific EC provisions;

(d) any drink with an alcoholic strength by volume of 10% or more;

(e) any soft drink, fruit juice or fruit nectar or alcoholic drink sold in a container of more than 5 litres (intended for catering);

(f) flour, confectionery and bread normally consumed within 24 hours of preparation;

(g) vinegar;

(h) cooking and table salt;

(i) solid sugar and products consisting almost solely of flavoured or coloured sugars;

(j) chewing gums and similar products;

(k) edible ices in individual portions.

Omission of certain particulars

Extensive and detailed provisions are given in ss 23–34.

Manner of marking or labelling

General (s 35)

When sold to the ultimate consumer, the required markings shall be either:

(a) on the packaging; or

(b) on a label attached to the packaging; or

(c) on a label visible through the packaging.

If sold otherwise than to the ultimate consumer, as an alternative, the details may be on relevant trade documents (except that the name of the food, its appropriate durability indication and the name and address of manufacturer, packer or seller must appear on the outermost packaging).

Further details are outlined in s 36.

Milk (s 37)

In the case of milk that is contained in a bottle, particulars may be given on the bottle cap. However, in the case of raw milk, the statement relating to health (see above) shall be given elsewhere than on the bottle cap.

Intelligibility (s 38)

Any marking or notice should be easy to understand, clearly legible and indelible and, when sold to the ultimate consumer, easily visible (although, at a catering establishment where information is changed regularly, information can be given by temporary media, for example, chalk on a blackboard). They shall not be hidden, obscured or interrupted by written or pictorial matter.

Field of vision (s 39)

When required to be marked with one or more of the following, the required information shall appear in the same field of vision:

(a) name of food;

(b) appropriate durability indication;

(c) indication of alcoholic strength by volume;

(d) the cautionary words in respect of raw milk;

(e) the warning required on products consisting of skimmed milk with non-milk fat;

(f) statement of net quantity as required by the Weights and Measures Act 1985 or any order or regulation made thereunder.

The requirements of (b), (c) and (f) do not apply to foods falling within the section on small packages and certain bottles above (see above).

Claims and nutrition labelling

These issues are dealt within Part III of the Act.

Section 40 and Sched 6 provide that certain claims are prohibited. These are:

- a claim that a food has tonic properties (except that the use of the word tonic in the description 'Indian tonic water' or quinine tonic water' shall not of itself constitute this claim);

- a claim that a food has the property of preventing, treating or curing a human disease or any reference to such a property (except that the use of the claim described below under 'claims relating to foods for particular nutritional uses' shall not of itself constitute this claim).

Certain other claims in the labelling or advertising of a food are only permitted where the conditions specified in the Regulations are met. When considering whether a claim is being made, a reference to a substance in an ingredients list or in any nutrition labelling shall not constitute a claim.

Claims relating to foods for particular nutritional uses

That is, a claim that a food is suitable, or has been specially made, for a particular nutritional purpose which includes requirements either of people whose digestive process or metabolism is disturbed, or of people who, because of special physiological conditions, obtain special benefit from the controlled consumption of certain substances, or of infants (0–12 months) or young children (1–3 years) in good health:

1 the food must be capable of fulfilling the claim;

2 the food must be marked or labelled with an indication of the particular aspects of composition or process which give the food its particular nutritional characteristics;

3 (a) the label must give the prescribed nutrition labelling and may have additional relevant information;

   (b) when sold to the ultimate consumer, the food must be prepacked and completely enclosed by its packaging.

Reduced or low energy value claims

That is, a claim that a food has a reduced or low energy value, except that the presence of the words 'low calorie' for a soft drink and in accordance with the requirements below on misleading descriptions does not constitute such a claim:

1 foods that claim to have a reduced energy value must have energy no more than three-quarters of a similar food with no such claim (unless the food is an intense sweetener either on its own or mixed with another food, but still significantly sweeter than sucrose);

2 (a & b) foods that claim to have a low energy value should usually have a maximum energy of 167 kJ (40 kcal) per 100 g (or 100 ml) and per

normal serving (unless the food is an intense sweetener either on its own or mixed with another food, but still significantly sweeter than sucrose);

(c) in the case of an uncooked food, the claim must be in the form 'a low energy or calorie or Joule food'.

Protein claims

That is, a claim that a food, other than one intended for babies or young children is a source of protein:

1   a reasonable daily consumption of the food must contribute at least 12 g of protein;

2   foods claimed to be a rich or excellent source of protein must have at least 20% of their energy value provided by protein and in other cases at least 12%;

3   the label must give the prescribed nutrition labelling.

Vitamin/mineral claims

That is, a claim that a food, other than one intended for babies or young children is a source of vitamins/minerals; a claim is not made when a name includes the name of one or more vitamins/minerals and the food consists solely of vitamins and/or minerals and certain other substances and when mineral claims are made relating to a low or reduced level of minerals:

• claims may only be made with respect to vitamins or minerals in the table set out in Sched 6;

• where (a) the claim is not confined to named vitamins or minerals then, if the food is claimed to be a rich or excellent source of vitamins or minerals, it must contain at least one-half of the recommended daily amount (RDA) of two or more of the vitamins or minerals listed in the quantity reasonably expected to be consumed in one day or, otherwise, at least one-sixth;

• where (b) the claim is confined to named vitamins or minerals, the conditions of (a) must apply to each named vitamin or mineral;

• for foods to which nutrition labelling relates, the label must carry a statement of the % RDA of any vitamin or mineral involved in the claim in a quantified serving of the food or per portion (if number of portions in pack is stated);

• for food supplements or waters other than natural mineral waters, the label must carry a statement of the % RDA of any vitamin or mineral involved in the claim in either a quantified serving of the food or, if prepacked, per portion, and, if prepacked, the number of portions in the pack is to be stated).

Cholesterol claims

That is, a claim relating to the presence or absence of cholesterol:

- the food must have a maximum of 0.005% cholesterol except that if it is higher than this figure a claim may be made if the claim relates to the removal of cholesterol from, or its reduction in, the food if the claim is made (a) as part of an indication of the true nature of the food, (b) as part of an indication of the treatment of the food, within the list of ingredients, or (c) as a footnote in respect of a prescribed nutrition labelling; the claim must not include any suggestion of benefit to health because of its level of cholesterol;
- the food shall be marked or labelled with the prescribed nutrition labelling.

Nutrition claims

That is, a claim not dealt with above:

1   the food must be capable of fulfilling the claim;
2   the food shall be marked or labelled with the prescribed nutrition labelling.

Claims which depend on another food

That is, a claim that a food has a particular value or confers a particular benefit:

- the value or benefit must not be derived wholly or partly from another food intended to be consumed with the food.

The rules on nutrition labelling are contained in Sched 7 and set down specific requirements as to presentation and content.

Contents of nutrition labelling

(1) Except where (2) applies, prescribed nutrition labelling shall give the following:
   (a) it shall include either:
      (i) energy, protein, carbohydrates and fat, or
      (ii) energy, protein, carbohydrates, sugars, fat, saturates, fibre and sodium;
   (b) if a claim is made for any of sugars, saturates, fibre or sodium, then it shall be given according to (a)(ii);
   (c) where a nutrition claim is made relating to polyols, starch, monounsaturates, polyunsaturates, cholesterol, vitamins or minerals, the relevant amount shall be given except that, in the case of vitamins or minerals, the amount present must be a significant amount (15% of the RDA – see above);

(d) the items in (c) may be given even if no claim is made, but the restriction relating to vitamins or minerals also applies;

(e) if the labelling is presented in the form (a)(i) above, but includes monounsaturates, polyunsaturates, and/or cholesterol, the amount of saturates must also be given;

(f) where a nutrition claim is made relating to any substance which belongs to, or is a component of, one of the nutrients already required (or permitted) to be included, the name and amount of that substance shall be given.

(2) For food which is not prepacked and which is either sold to the ultimate consumer other than at a catering establishment, to the ultimate consumer from a vending machine, or to a catering establishment, prescribed nutrition labelling shall give any data relevant to any nutrition claim which is made and may include shown above under presentation.

THE LABELLING OF ADDITIVES

The Food Labelling Regulations specify certain requirements in respect of additives used as ingredients in foodstuffs. Additives need not be listed in the ingredients if their presence in a particular foodstuff is due only to the fact that they are contained in one of the other ingredients and provided that they serve no technological function in the finished product. Additives used in prepacked foods which do serve a technological function in the finished product must always be labelled. They must be declared on the label by the appropriate category name of the function. This must be followed by their specific name or serial number. The categories are:

Acid	Flour treatment agent
Acidity regulator	Gelling agent
Anti-caking agent	Glazing agent
Anti-foaming agent	Humectant
Antioxidant	Modified starch
Bulking agent	Preservative
Colour	Propellant gas
Emulsifier	Raising agent
Emulsifying salts	Stabiliser
Firming agent	Sweetener
Flavour enhancer	Thickener

Flavourings may be declared either by their name alone or by a more specific name. In the case of acids, if the specific name includes the word 'acid', the category name may be omitted. In the case of modified starches, neither the specific name nor the serial number need be indicated.

If an additive serves more than one function in a food, the category name which represents its principal function must be used to describe it. Where no category name is available for the function performed by an additive in a food, the additive must be declared in the ingredients list by its specific name. A serial number cannot be used on its own.

Foods which are not prepackaged and foods which are prepackaged on the premises where they are sold are exempt from the above requirements. Exceptions to this exemption are that any additive used in the food to perform the function of an antioxidant, artificial sweeteners, colour, flavour enhancer, or preservative must be indicated next to the name of the food or on a ticket or notice displayed in immediate proximity to the food using the category name. However, in the case of edible ices and flour confectionery, there need only be an indication that these additives may be present on a notice displayed near the food.

THE LABELLING OF GENETICALLY MODIFIED PRODUCTS

Article 8(1) of the EC Novel Foods and Novel Food Ingredients Regulation (258/97) applies labelling requirements to novel (including GM) foods approved in future. Food requires labelling if there are any health or ethical concerns or if it contains a live GMO.

EC Regulation 1139/98 on the labelling of GM soya and maize (as amended by EC Regulation 49/2000 – see below) applies labelling requirements for one GM herbicide tolerant soya and one GM insect protected maize approved and placed on the market before the introduction of the Novel Foods Regulation. This EC Regulation requires all foods or food ingredients containing GM soya or maize to be clearly labelled to indicate that the product contains GM material; for example, in the list of ingredients, the words 'produced from genetically modified [soya] [maize]' must appear next to (or linked to) the relevant ingredient.

EC Regulation 49/2000/EC came into force in April 2000 and amends EC Regulation 1139/98 by extending the requirements to foods sold to mass caterers and setting a *de minimis* threshold of 1% for the adventitious contamination of non-GM material. For such ingredients, there is no need to label them as GM if they contain less than 1% GM material. The threshold applies only to ingredients obtained from non-GM sources; this flexibility does not apply to supplies obtained from sources of unknown origin. Companies also need to demonstrate that their ingredients are of non-GM origin, and it is possible that the use of documented and audited identity preservation systems could satisfy this requirement. Steps should also be taken to keep the level of adventitious contamination in non-GM supplies to a minimum. Although the level agreed for the threshold is 1%, in practice, the need to provide proof that ingredients are of non-GM origin should ensure that actual levels are kept well below this figure. It is also important to realise that, because the limit operates at the level of each individual ingredient, the actual amount in the final foodstuff will be much lower.

EC Regulation 50/2000 also came into force in April 2000 and requires the labelling of foods and food ingredients containing additives and flavourings which contain GM material. The labelling requirements are the same as for Regulation 1139/98 (as amended) above. The Commission has undertaken to bring forward a *de minimis* threshold proposal for additives and flavourings in due course. The Regulation does not apply to additives and flavourings sold as such.

The requirements of the current labelling rules are triggered by the presence of novel DNA or protein in the final food. This approach to the labelling of GM foods was agreed unanimously by EU Member States and endorsed by the European Parliament. Ingredients obtained from GM crops, but which do not themselves contain novel DNA or protein, do not have to be labelled, as they are indistinguishable from those obtained from conventional crops.

The labelling of GM foods is governed in England by the Genetically Modified and Novel Foods (Labelling) (England) Regulations 2000, and by equivalent legislation in Scotland, Wales and Northern Ireland. These domestic Regulations consolidate all the national provisions on GM labelling and provide for the enforcement of the following EC rules on novel and GM food labelling.

The UK has led the way in Europe by applying the requirements of the EC Regulations to restaurants, cafés, takeaways, bakeries and delicatessens as well as food sold in supermarkets. It is not always possible for some establishments to provide actual labelling for foods which are not prepacked or are prepacked for direct sale, for example, food sold in restaurants, bakeries, delicatessens, etc. The domestic Regulations, therefore, offer a certain amount of flexibility for conveying information on the presence of GM material in food sold in this way.

Businesses selling foods to the ultimate consumer loose or prepacked for direct sale may provide the labelling information to customers verbally via the staff rather than having always to include details on menus, etc. This flexibility is only available in those establishments which have procedures in place for ensuring staff are aware of ingredients used. Those establishments must draw the customer's attention by way of an easily seen notice to the fact that information on the GM content is available on request. The requirement that catering establishments provide information relating to the GM content of the food they sell came into effect on 19 September 1999.

Businesses selling foods to catering establishments loose or prepacked for direct sale may provide the labelling information by a label attached to the food, a ticket or notice which the purchaser can see at the place where he/she chooses the food, or in commercial documents which either accompany the food, or are sent to the purchaser before or at the same time as the delivery of the food.

CHAPTER 6

GENETICALLY MODIFIED AND NOVEL FOODS

INTRODUCTION

Biotechnology is not a new science. For centuries people have been using various technological processes and selected breeding of plants and animals to develop new and better foods, to increase yields and to confer resistance to disease.

Foods such as cheese, wine, beer and bread are made using what are considered to be 'traditional biotechnology' such as fermentation and the use of bacteria. In simple terms genetic modification involves the identification of the gene coding of a particular characteristic and the moving of that gene from one living thing where it occurs naturally to another living thing where it does not occur naturally but in which that characteristic is required.

All plants and animals are made up of millions of cells. Every cell has a nucleus inside which there are strands of DNA, arranged into structures called chromosomes. Normally every cell will contain a double set of chromosome one set inherited from each parent. The cell formed after fertilisation divides into two identical copies, each of which inherits this unique new combination of chromosomes. These embryonic cells then continue to divide. The inherited genetic material, carried in the chromosomes, is therefore identical in every new cell.

No individual gene works alone. The sequences of DNA function in complex networks that are tightly regulated so that processes can occur in the right place and at the right time. Environmental factors are also important. According to Barbara McClintock, who won the Nobel Prize in 1983 for her pioneering work in the field of genetics, the functioning of genes is 'totally dependent on the environment in which they find themselves'. Traditional methods of breeding, achieved variety by selecting from the many genetic characteristics that already exist within the gene pool of a species. In nature, genetic diversity is created within certain limits. Plants may breed with other plants but a plant would never breed with an animal. Even species that may seem to be closely related will usually only produce infertile offspring. The integrity of species is thereby preserved. By contrast genetic engineering involves taking genes from one species and inserting them into another in order to transfer a desired trait or characteristic. One of the examples often cited is that of the insertion of a gene, taken from an arctic fish, which causes the production of a chemical with antifreeze properties, into a tomato to make it resistant to frost.

Those who are supporters of genetic engineering argue that because humans have been selectively breeding plants and animals for many years, genetic engineering is simply an extension of traditional breeding practices. Those who are against genetic engineering would argue that, while it is probably true that the food crops produced and consumed today do not bear much resemblance to the wild plants from which they originated, this new biotechnology modifies organisms in a fundamentally different way.

The difference between the traditional methods and the modern approach to biotechnology lies in the way in which humans can now influence the processes of growth, development and yield in both animals and plants. The laboratory processes that are used in modern genetic engineering have been likened to 'cutting and pasting'[1] where strands of DNA are 'cut' out and then 'pasted' into the nucleus of another living organism. The use of these advanced techniques makes modern genetic engineering different from the traditional methods in two basic ways. First, modern genetic engineering enables single well defined genes to be isolated and transferred whereas with traditional methods many thousands of genes are transferred at any one time. Secondly, genetic modification allows genes to be transferred from one plant species to another and even from animals and micro-organisms.

GM foods have been defined in the following way:

Genetically engineered foodstuffs are food organisms that have been genetically engineered, foodstuffs that contain an ingredient of a genetically engineered organism or foodstuffs that have been produced using a processing aid made with the use of genetic engineering.[2]

Some GM foods that have been developed are whole plants or parts of organisms that are eaten raw such as tomatoes and fresh chicory. GM yeasts have been produced for use in brewing beer and baking yeasts have been developed to allow better digestion of sugars obtained from the starch in flour to give a better texture. These yeasts are not yet being used commercially. Many crop plants that are used to produce food ingredients are now being genetically modified such as soya and maize. Some ingredients such as vegetable oils, which are derived from crop plants are very highly refined and the refining process destroys and removes any genetic material and protein that might be present in the food ingredient. The end product that goes into food is therefore not itself modified and cannot be distinguished from its traditionally produced counterpart. No genetically modified animals have yet been approved for food use. Genetically modified animals used to produce pharmaceutical products are not put into the food chain.

---

1   Donaldson and May, *Health Implications of Genetically Modified Food*, 1999, London, HMSO.

2   FAO/WHO, *Joint FAO/WHO Expert Consultation on Biotechnology and Food Safety*, Rome, 1995.

There are two main issues which trouble people with regard to GM crops. On the one hand there is concern for the environment, for the possibility that GM seed will travel and contaminate non GM crops. This is particularly a problem for organic farmers and growers of organic crops because they risk losing their organic status if their crops cannot be classified as GM free. The risk of environmental pollution and the contamination of other people's crops is of great concern, particularly following the discovery that GM seeds had got into normal oil seed rape seed and had consequently contaminated many thousands of acres of crops. This raises the issue of liability and compensation. The other issue of particular concern for the purposes of this book is the question of whether GM foods are safe. In the light of the way in which BSE developed, following government and scientific reassurances about the safety of beef consumers are understandably reluctant to trust scientists and governments when they suggest that there is not evidence that GM foods are detrimental to health. The truth is that they simply do not know. Very often the detrimental effects do not become apparent until some time in the future as in the case of BSE.

This raises ethical as well as legal issue s. If people wish to avoid eating GM products they should have the choice but if there is a risk that normal crops will be contaminated with GMOs, this removes the right of the consumer to choose. In effect, people are being forced to consume something they do not wish to. People are concerned about the possibility of unpredictable effects of genetic modification. Current understanding of the way in which genes are regulated is limited and there is concern that any change to the DNA of an organism might have effects that are impossible to predict or control.

There is concern that the random insertion of a foreign gene could disrupt the tightly controlled network of DNA in an organism and, for example, alter chemical reactions within the cell or disturb cell functions which could lead to instability, the creation of new toxins or allergens, and changes in nutritional value .

When a gene is inserted into an organism, a piece of DNA taken from a virus or bacterium (called a 'promoter') is inserted at the same time in order to 'switch on' the gene in its new host. Promoters, which often force genes to be produced at 10 to 1,000 times normal levels, also have the potential to influence neighbouring genes.[3] The promoter might, for example, stimulate a plant to produce higher levels of a substance which is harmless at low levels but which becomes toxic when present in higher concentrations.

As well as concern as to the possible future effects of genetic engineering, there are also other concerns expressed by the public and consumer and interest groups. One concern is the issue of choice – consumers should be able

---

3   Steinbrecher, R and Ho, M, *Fatal Flaws in Food Safety Assessment: Critique of the Joint FAO/WHO Biotechnology and Food Safety Report*, 1996.

to choose whether or not they eat food which has been genetically modified; another concern is the possibility of long term health effects. In the wake of the BSE crisis, people are no longer content to be reassured by statements to the effect that there is no evidence that GM foods cause any harm. People want proof that GM foods are safe. There are those who believe that the question of whether GM food is safe is irrelevant and that the idea of genetic engineering is morally and ethically unjustifiable in that it fundamentally distorts the relationship between humanity and nature.

There is concern that international trading agreements are increasing the power of multi-national corporations and that governments are increasingly being influenced by people who are unelected and unaccountable.

As far as determining the safety of GM foods is concerned, the concept of 'substantial equivalence' has been developed at international level to deal with the issues surrounding the testing of GM foods. There are those who argue that GM foods should be subject to the same rigorous testing as new pharmaceutical products. But the doctrine of 'substantial equivalence' means that if a food is regarded as substantially equivalent to a food which is already being produced and consumed then it will be approved with only limited assessment. If it is not substantially equivalent, then a more rigorous testing procedure will be required. This concept was adopted by the OECD in 1993 in a publication[4] produced by some 60 experts from 19 OECD countries who had spent more than two years discussing how to assess the safety of GM foods.

In 1996, participants at an expert FAO/WHO[5] conference on biotechnology and food safety recommended that safety assessment based upon the concept of substantial equivalence be applied in establishing the safety of food and food components derived from genetically modified organisms.

Substantial equivalence is not a substitute for a safety assessment but a part of the assessment process. Underlying the concept is the requirement that any safety assessment should show that a GM variety is as safe as its traditional counterpart through a consideration of both the intended and unintended effects of the product. This involves the consideration of a wide range of information, including agronomic properties and compositional data on nutrients and toxicants. In applying the concept of substantial equivalence, equivalent components are considered on the basis of the long history of safe use in the traditional counterpart and any differences are identified. The identified differences are than the subject of safety assessment which could include nutritional, toxicological and immunological testing, as appropriate. Since the concept of substantial equivalence was first adopted, many new foods have come onto the market and the international organisations continue

---

4   OECD, *Safety Evaluation of Foods Derived Through Modern Biotechnology: Concepts and Principles*, Paris, 1993.

5   See above, fn 2.

to keep the adequacy of the concept in its role in food safety assessment under review. The OECD's Task Force on the Safety of Novel Foods and Feeds keeps the application of the concept under review. This includes work on assessment methodologies when substantial equivalence cannot be applied, where differences have been identified or where no comparator exists. It also includes efforts to identify the critical nutrients and toxicants in crop plants that are relevant for the demonstration of substantial equivalence. Critical nutrients and toxicants are those components of a particular crop that are known to be relevant to human health through knowledge of the traditional, unmodified crop. Comparative assessment of these components and their potential for change as a result of genetic modification, together with a wide range of information allows an assessment of the likelihood of unintended effects in a modified crop.

Consumers are also concerned about the risk of developing food allergies. Many people have allergies to certain foods, particularly nuts, gluten, shellfish and cheese. It is well known that virtually all known allergens are proteins. There is a danger that the problem of food allergies could be made worse by genetic engineering.

Antibiotic resistance is another concern which arises in relation to GM foods. In 1996 the Advisory Committee on Novel Foods and Processes (ACNFP) in the UK recommended that antibiotic resistant genes should not be used in genetically engineered micro-organisms that are consumed alive, such as in yogurt. For all other foodstuffs containing genetically modified genes the ACNFP recommended that the safety of these genes should be demonstrated as well as the need for using such genes.

REPORT ON THE HEALTH IMPLICATIONS OF GM FOODS

In May 1999, Professor Liam Donaldson and Sir Robert May produced a report,[6] at the invitation of the Ministerial Group on Biotechnology, on the health implications of genetically modified food, in which they addressed the issues mentioned above. In the paper, they examine the process involved in genetic modification of food, the areas of human health which could be affected, the existing safety and regulatory mechanisms and the need for further research. The purpose of the paper was to address only those issues relating to the safety of food obtained by genetic modification processes and issues relating to human health. The paper considered the theoretical ways in which genetic modification could affect human health and the likelihood of those theoretical ways actually resulting in harm to human health. They described some of the theoretical health implications that could arise from the use of new technologies used to manipulate genetic material. These are:

---

6   *Op cit*, Donaldson and May, fn 1.

- the inserted gene may itself have adverse effects;
- the inserted gene may code for protein that is toxic to human beings or produces an allergic reaction;
- the inserted gene may alter the way existing genes in a plant or animal express themselves, which may in turn increase the production of existing toxins or switch on the production of previously silent genes;
- the inserted gene may alter the behaviour of a micro-organism which is carrying it to make it potentially harmful;
- the inserted gene may be transferred from a micro-organism which is carrying it to other micro-organisms, in the human gut or respiratory tract or to animals or humans;
- the consumption of a GM micro-organism may alter the balance of existing micro-organisms in the human gut.

In examining the likelihood of such events affecting human health, the paper observes that people are constantly exposed to foreign DNA from the food they eat and from the environment and those living on their skin and in their digestive and respiratory tracts. DNA itself is not a toxic chemical, and consuming it, therefore, will not have a direct effect. They also point out that genetic modification results in the transfer of only single genes or small groups of genes which are well characterised and whose function is understood. They point out that plants typically contain 20,000–40,000 genes and the functions of most of them are not yet understood. Traditional plant breeding methods increase the exposure of humans to some of the products of these genes in a random way that does not first involve the isolation and definition of those genes. The paper argues that the random nature of conventional plant breeding has produced potentially harmful products on a number of occasions (para 27).

The report makes the point that it has been very difficult to introduce genes into human cells, for example, to replace defective genes which they argue would tend to support the view that DNA from GM foods is unlikely to enter human cells (para 28). The report goes on to explain that 'the human intestinal tract is an effective digestive system and DNA is rapidly broken down under normal conditions into pieces too small to be functional', which would seem to indicate that foreign DNA is not thought to be available for transfer into human cells. However, the report does acknowledge that there is 'a remote possibility that DNA fragments may be taken up by bacteria in the gut' (para 29). The report admits that there is evidence to support exchange of genes between bacteria in the environment either by direct transformation or via natural vectors such as plasmids and that there is also evidence to support the transfer of free DNA (for example, in soil as a result of the breakdown of plant material) into bacteria in the environment. They also admit that there is recent evidence that marker genes used in genetically modified sugar beet have transferred into other plants. However, the report makes clear that this kind of transfer is extremely difficult to achieve and that the success of DNA transfer and of survival of the recipient bacteria is highly dependent on environmental conditions such as temperature, pH and any selection pressures and that there are many natural factors that reduce the chances of successful gene transfer (paras 30 and 31).

The paper observes that non GM micro-organisms have been used in agriculture for many years in pathogen control and as a means of increasing nitrogen fixation with no apparent adverse effects on human health, and that data from field releases of GM micro-organisms have not shown any evidence of transfer of selective marker genes from modified bacteria to bacteria in the environment. The paper does acknowledge, however, that there is evidence to support transfer of DNA from plasmids under laboratory conditions, but points out that the rate of transfer of inserted marker genes from GM plants into soil micro-organisms is extremely small (para 32).

The paper acknowledges that some of the issues in connection with GM foods are equally applicable to foods produced by conventional means and there are a number of examples of health concerns arising from traditional plant breeding (para 33). It considers some of the possible health concerns relating to communicable and non-communicable diseases, including foetal abnormalities, nutritional imbalances and the potential of altered immune responses.

The findings of the report were as follows:

In seeking to assess possible hazards to human health arising from GM foods the main issues which need to be considered are:

- whether there are any inherent hazards in the genetic modification process itself;
- whether the products (that is, the food itself) might be harmful; and
- whether GM food given to animals which are then eaten by people could pose a hazard to human health.

The report acknowledged that there was also the question of whether GM technology could lead to environmental change which could give a secondary effect on human health, but stated that this issue was beyond the scope of the paper, which considered the possibility of direct effects on human health. It identifies the main measures to provide safeguards against any real or hypothetical risks as: '... rigorous pre-market assessment of safety, research to improve understanding of the science of genetic modification of food and health surveillance to provide resistance against any unexpected adverse effects on health.'

The main conclusions of the report are as follows:

- Many of the issues raised by foods resulting from genetic modification are equally applicable to foods produced by conventional means, for example, potential nutritional imbalances or allergic effects could occur from either type of food.

- There is no current evidence to suggest that the GM technologies used to protect food are inherently harmful.

- We are reassured by the precautionary nature and rigor of the current procedures used to assess the safety of individual GM foods. This process could be strengthened by the development of a health surveillance system.

- Nevertheless, nothing can be absolutely certain in a field of rapid scientific and technological development. Genetic modification is a young science and there is a need to keep a close watch on developments and to continue to find research to improve scientific understanding in this area.

- We welcome the recent moves to improve the openness of the regulatory procedures to public scrutiny and would encourage further such moves to help to inform public debate on the issues relating to the health implications of GM foods [Executive Summary, para 7].

The report makes certain recommendations. In relation to tracking research and acting on new evidence, it recommends that government advisory bodies should continue to closely monitor developments in scientific knowledge and regulation on an international basis and provide advice on any fresh action which they consider necessary.

The report recommends the promoting high standards of regulation. It states that the United Kingdom's current system of regulation of GM food technology and other novel foods is rigorous. 'We propose that the Government should offer its expertise and use its influence to promote high standards of regulation internationally.'

The report identifies the need for a continuing research strategy and recommends that the Government should continue to fund research to improve scientific understanding and to fill gaps in current knowledge. 'We propose that the Government should invite the Medical Research Council and other major research bodies to participate in the future development of this research strategy. We propose that before any new research is acted upon by Government it must have been through the standard peer review process to ensure that it has scientific credibility. Government's own response to new data should be made in line with the *Guidelines on the Use of Scientific Advice in Policy Making* to allow the full scientific merits of new research to be assessed.'

The report also states that the development of population health surveillance in relation to the consumption of GM and other novel foods is essential to ensure that Government is able to respond rapidly should any unexpected effects occur. The ACNFP and the Medical Research Council are already discussing how this might be done. As part of this, consideration also needs to be given to the establishment of a national surveillance unit to monitor population health aspects of genetically modified and other novel foods. Surveillance could be used to examine trends over time to detect any early changes in the incidence of adverse health outcomes, whilst recognising the difficulties in establishing causal relationships.

A great deal of concern has been expressed about the use of antibiotic resistance marker genes and the report makes clear that the use of alternatives to antibiotic resistant genes as part of the GM process is already stated good practice by the ACNFP. The authors of the report recommend that those who are developing food using genetic modification should be encouraged to phase out the use of antibiotic resistance marker genes as soon as is feasible.

EC LEGISLATION

Even as early as 1985, the Commission acknowledged the need to take account of 'food from biotechnology' by including a reference to it in the White Paper on the completion of the internal market on foodstuffs. The first priority for legislation, however, was to control genetically modified crops, that is, organisms that have been 'deliberately released' into the environment rather than being grown in a controlled situation.

Micro-organisms

Directive 90/219/EEC regulates the continued use of genetically modified micro-organisms for research and industrial purposes.

Deliberate release controls

Directive 90/220[7] was adopted in 1990 to deal with both the deliberate release into the environment of genetically modified organisms for research and development and also with the issue of the placing on the market of these organisms for subsequent research and development. This Directive covers 'genetically modified organisms' which are defined as organisms in which the genetic material has been altered in a way that does not occur naturally by mating and/or recombination. The Directive was introduced to protect consumers and the environment from the possible risks of the deliberate release into the environment of genetically modified organisms and also to facilitate the proper functioning of the internal market. The Directive was also introduced to establish a Community-wide authorisation procedure for the

---

7   Council Directive 90/220/EEC (OJ 1990 L117/15) on the deliberate release into the environment of genetically modified organisms.

placing on the market of products containing or consisting of genetically modified organisms (GMOs) which would be deliberately released into the environment.

The Directive lays down the procedure to be adopted for giving approval for the release of such organisms into the environment or for placing GM products on the market. Annex 2 to the Directive contains full details of the information that is required for both a notification of a deliberate release into the environment and for the placing on the market of a GM product. Article 4(2) provides that before releasing GMOs into the environment, a company is required to submit a notification to the relevant competent authority in each Member State. A technical dossier must be submitted to the authority so that it can evaluate any foreseeable risks to human health and the environment which might be caused by the release of the relevant GMOs. In the case of a deliberate release into the environment, the competent national authority will, upon receipt of the notification, examine it for compliance with the Directive, evaluate the risks posed by the release, record its conclusions in writing and carry out any tests or inspections as may be necessary for control purposes. Having considered all the required factors and taken account of the views of the other Member States, the authority will make its decision known to the applicant within 90 days. In the case of placing a product on the market, Art 11 provides that the manufacturer or importer into the EC must submit a notification to the competent authority of the Member State in which the product is to be placed on the market for the first time. The notification will include a technical dossier specified in Annex 2. On receipt of the notification, the competent national authority must examine it for compliance with the Directive, paying special attention to the risk assessment and recommended precautions for the safe use of the product. Within 90 days, the authority must either forward the information to the Commission with a favourable opinion or inform the applicant that the product does not comply with the requirements of the Directive and is therefore rejected.

Upon receipt of a favourable opinion, the Commission must immediately inform the competent national authorities of all the other Member States and seek their views. Having obtained their views, the Commission will make the final decision as to whether to allow the GM product on to the market of the Member State concerned. If the product is allowed on to the market, this will, of course, mean that it can be circulated throughout the Community, within the internal market, under the rule of free movement of goods.

Article 16 of the Directive does, however, provide that a Member State may temporarily prohibit a particular GM product from circulation within its territory, even where the product has been properly notified and has received written consent from the Commission, if the State concerned has justifiable reasons to consider that the product 'constitutes a risk to human health or the environment'.

The Member State concerned must inform the Commission immediately and the Commission will make a decision within three months as to whether to continue to allow the prohibition.

Repeal and replacement of Directive 90/220

In February 1998, the Commission adopted a proposal for a Directive to amend Directive 90/220/EEC. The proposal sought to increase the transparency and efficiency of the decision making process to promote the harmonisation of risk assessment and to introduce clear labelling requirements for all GMOs that are to be placed on the market.

In February 1999, the European Parliament adopted its first reading with 78 amendments. In December 1999 the Council of Ministers adopted its Common Position (political agreement). In April 2000, at its second reading the European Parliament adopted 29 amendments. In September 2000, the Council formally notified the Parliament that it could not accept those amendments. A Conciliation Committee was therefore convened and a joint text was agreed on 20 December 2000. On 14 February 2001, the Parliament voted in favour of this compromise. The following specific issues are worth noting.

Pharmaceuticals

At its second reading, the European Parliament had wanted to exclude genetically modified pharmaceutical products for human use from the scope of the Directive. The compromise provides that the Directive will not apply to genetically modified medicinal substances and compounds for human use. If they are to be used for research purposes, the Directive will apply and certain conditions will need to be met, including a risk assessment, consent prior to release, surveillance plan and the provision of information.

Public registers

At second reading the European Parliament had wanted the establishment of public registers for GMOs released both for research purposes and for commercial application. This was a difficult issue to resolve, but in the compromise it was agreed that GMOs released in the trial period should be registered and details made available to the public. As regards GMOs released for commercial purposes, their locations will need to be notified to the competent authorities and made known to the public in a manner deemed to be appropriate by those authorities.

Antibiotic resistance

In GM research, antibiotic resistance 'marker genes' are often used. A timetable for the gradual elimination of the use of antibiotic resistant marker genes has been introduced. The deadlines are the end of 2002 for commercial releases and the end of 2008 for research purposes.

Labelling and traceability of GMOs

The Directive contains general rules on the labelling and traceability of GMOs. The Commission has also announced its intention to bring forward a proposal on the labelling and traceability of GMOs throughout the food chain and on GM animal feed.

Environmental liability

The Commission has also undertaken to bring forward a proposal for legislation on environmental liability which will include liability for damage resulting from GMOs. The proposal is due before the end of 2001.

Since the entry into force of the original Directive 90/220, approval has been given for 18 authorisations for the commercial release of GMOs. The majority of these consents were granted following a qualified majority vote in the Regulatory Committee composed of Member States. However, no authorisations have been approved since October 1998 and, at the time of writing, there are 14 applications pending approval at various stages in the procedure.

Genetically modified soya and maize

Two types of crop were evaluated using the EC system: genetically modified soya, produced by Monsanto, and genetically modified maize, produced by CibAGeigy, and these subsequently received approval in two further Directives.[8]

Neither Directive 90/220 nor the Directives made under it, which gave approval for the growing of GM crops, included any provisions for the labelling of these products. In effect, these products could be sold without being specifically identified or segregated as they were regarded as being equivalent to their traditional counterparts and, therefore, not requiring any additional labelling.

Although there are labelling requirements laid down in Art 8 of the Novel Foods Regulation, these do not cover either GM soya or GM maize because both these products were approved before the adoption of the Regulation. With the increasing concern expressed by consumers about GM crops and the growing demand for consumer choice, Regulation 1813/97[9] was adopted in

---

8   Directive 96/281/EC gave approval to GM soya and Directive 97/98/EC gave approval to GM maize.

9   Commission Regulation 1813/97/EC (OJ 1997 L257/77).

an attempt to define the labelling requirements for GM soya and maize by making an amendment to Art 4(2) of the framework labelling Directive (79/112). Regulation 1813/97 was repealed by Regulation 1139/98 (see below).[10]

Regulation 258/97 on novel foods and novel food ingredients

In 1997, following several years of discussions of the issue of novel foods, Regulation 258/97[11] on Novel Foods was adopted. The Regulation was adopted on 27 January 1997 and came into effect on 15 May 1997. This was after the approval had been given to both GM soya and GM maize. It introduced a pre-market approval system for all novel foods. This Regulation sets out rules for the authorisation and labelling of GMO derived food products and other novel foods.

Art 1 of the Regulation defines those foods that are to be considered as 'novel' and to which the provisions of the Regulation apply. It states that 'This Regulation concerns the placing on the market within the Community of novel foods or novel food ingredients' (Art 1(1)). The article continues:

> This Regulation shall apply to the placing on the market within the Community of foods and food ingredients which have not hitherto been used for human consumption to a significant degree within the Community and which fall under the following categories:
>
> (a) foods and food ingredients containing or consisting of genetically modified organisms within the meaning of Directive 90/220/EEC;
>
> (b) foods and food ingredients produced from, but not containing, genetically modified organisms;
>
> (c) foods and food ingredients with a new or intentionally modified primary molecular structure;
>
> (d) foods and food ingredients consisting of or isolated from micro-organisms, fungi or algae;
>
> (e) foods and food ingredients consisting of or isolated from plants and food ingredients isolated from animals, except for food and food ingredients obtained by traditional propagating or breeding practices and having a history of safe food use;
>
> (f) foods and food ingredients to which has been applied a production process not currently used, where that process gives rise to significant changes in the composition or structure of the food or food ingredients which affect their nutritional value, metabolism or level of undesirable substances.
>
> ...

---

10 Council Regulation 1139/98/EC (OJ 1998 L159/4).

11 European Parliament and Council Regulation 258/97/EC concerning novel foods and novel food ingredients (OJ 1997 L43/1).

Where necessary, it may be determined in accordance with the procedure laid down in Art 13 whether a type of food or food ingredient falls within the scope of para 2 of this Article.

Article 2 provides that the Regulation shall not apply to:

(a) food additives falling within the scope of Council Directive 89/107/EEC of 21 December 1988 on the approximation of the laws of the Member States concerning food additives authorised for use in foodstuffs intended for human consumption;

(b) flavourings for use in foodstuffs, falling within the scope of Council Directive 88/388/EEC of 22 June 1988 on the approximation of the laws of the Member States relating to flavourings for use in foodstuffs and to source materials for their production;

(c) extraction solvents used in the production of foodstuffs, falling within the scope of Council Directive 88/344/EEC of 13 June 1988 on the approximation of the laws of the Member States on extraction solvents used in the production of foodstuffs and food ingredients ...

The exclusions from the scope of this Regulation referred to in para 1, indents (a) to (c) shall only apply for so long as the safety levels laid down in Directives 89/107/EEC, 88/388/EEC and 88/344/EEC correspond to the safety level of this Regulation.

The authorisation procedures for GMOs are slightly different from the procedure under Directive 90/220, but the basic rule is similar. In general, the authorisation of GMOs is a one step process if all other Member States agree to the initial assessment of one of the Member States and a two step process if one or more of the Member States objects.

The first step is an assessment by the Member State where the food is to be placed on the market for the first time. In the event of a favourable opinion, the Member State informs the Commission, which then informs all the other Member States. If there are no objections, the first Member State can give authorisation for the whole of the EU and the product can circulate freely. If there are objections, then the second step has to be taken. The Commission must consult with the Scientific Committees and reach a decision.

Art 3(1) establishes the general principle of the control and, in Art 3(2), the requirement for a full EU safety assessment is specified:

1 Foods and food ingredients falling within the scope of this Regulation must not:

- present a danger for the consumer,
- mislead the consumer,
- differ from foods or food ingredients which they are intended to replace to such an extent that their normal consumption would be nutritionally disadvantageous for the consumer.

2   For the purpose of placing the foods and food ingredients falling within the scope of this Regulation on the market within the Community, the procedures laid down in Arts 4, 6, 7 and 8 shall apply on the basis of the criteria defined in para 1 of this Article and the other relevant factors referred to in those Articles.

However, in the case of foods and food ingredients referred to in this Regulation derived from plant varieties subject to Directives 70/457/EEC and 70/458/EEC, the authorisation decision referred to in Art 7 of this Regulation shall be taken in accordance with the procedures provided for in those Directives, provided they take account of the assessment principles laid down in this Regulation and the criteria set out in para 1 of this Article, with the exception of the provisions relating to the labelling of such foods or food ingredients, which shall be established, pursuant to Art 8, in accordance with the procedure laid down in Art 13.

3   Paragraph 2 shall not apply to the foods or food ingredients referred to in Art 1(2) (b) where the genetically modified organism used in the production of the food or food ingredient has been placed on the market in accordance with this Regulation.

Article 3(4) contains a derogation from the full authorisation procedure and contains the concept of 'substantial equivalence' under which foods are exempted from the testing required under Art 3(2). The assessment of whether a food is 'substantially equivalent' is carried out by a competent body within a Member State and, if considered to be substantially equivalent at this stage, then this view is passed on to other Member States (as specified in Art 5).

Article 3(4) provides that:

By way of derogation from para 2, the procedure laid down in Art 5 shall apply to foods or food ingredients referred to in Art 1(2)(b), (d) and (e) which, on the basis of the scientific evidence available and generally recognised, or on the basis of an opinion delivered by one of the competent bodies referred to in Art 4(3), are substantially equivalent to existing foods or food ingredients as regards their composition, nutritional value, metabolism, intended use and level of undesirable substances contained therein.

Where necessary, it may be determined in accordance with the procedure laid down in Art 13 whether a type of food or food ingredient falls under this paragraph.

Article 8 sets down additional labelling requirements for the products covered by the Regulation:

1 Without prejudice to the other requirements of Community law concerning the labelling of foodstuffs, the following additional specific labelling requirements shall apply to foodstuffs in order to ensure that the final consumer is informed of (a) any characteristic or food property such as composition, nutritional value or nutritional effects ... intended use of the food, which renders a novel food or food ingredient no longer equivalent to an existing food or food ingredient.

A novel food or food ingredient shall be deemed to be no longer equivalent for the purpose of this Article if scientific assessment, based upon an appropriate analysis of existing data, can demonstrate that the characteristics assessed are different in comparison with a conventional food or food ingredient, having regard to the accepted limits of natural variations for such characteristics. In this case, the labelling must indicate the characteristics or properties modified, together with the method by which that characteristic or property was obtained; (b) the presence in the novel food or food ingredient of material which is not present in an existing equivalent foodstuff and which may have implications for the health of certain sections of the population; (c) the presence in the novel food or food ingredient of material which is not present in an existing equivalent foodstuff and which gives rise to ethical concerns; (d) the presence of an organism genetically modified by techniques of genetic modification, the non-exhaustive list of which is laid down in Annex I A, Part 1 of Directive 90/220/EEC.

2   In the absence of an existing equivalent food or food ingredient, appropriate provisions shall be adopted where necessary in order to ensure that consumers are adequately informed of the nature of the food or food ingredient.

3   Any detailed rules for implementing this Article shall be adopted in accordance with the procedure laid down in Art 13.

Regulation 1139/98 on the labelling of GM foods

This Regulation provides for the indication of certain information, other than that required by the framework labelling Directive 79/112, on the labels of foodstuffs produced from genetically modified organisms.

Article 2 sets out the additional specific labelling requirements. Article 2(2) exempts products in which there is no protein or DNA from the requirements of the Directive. For all other products produced from GM organisms, the requirements are set down in Art 2(3):

1   The specified foodstuffs shall be subject to the specific labelling requirements laid down in para 3.

2   However, the specified foodstuffs in which neither protein nor DNA resulting from genetic modification is present shall not be subject to the said additional specific labelling requirements.

A list of products not subject to the additional specific labelling requirements shall be drawn up under the procedure laid down in Art 17 of Directive 79/112/EEC, taking account of technical developments, the opinion of the Scientific Committee on Food and any other relevant scientific advice.

The additional specific labelling requirements shall be the following: where the food consists of more than one ingredient, the words 'produced from genetically modified soya' or 'produced from genetically modified maize', as appropriate, shall appear in the list of ingredients provided for in Art 6 of Directive 79/112/EEC in parentheses immediately after the name of the ingredient concerned. Alternatively, these words may appear in a prominently displayed footnote to the list of ingredients, related by means of an asterisk (*) to the ingredient concerned. Where an ingredient is already listed as being produced from soya or maize the words 'produced from genetically modified' may be abbreviated to 'genetically modified'; if the abbreviated form of words is used as a footnote, the asterisk shall be directly attached to the word 'soya' or 'maize'. Where either form of words is used as a footnote, it shall have a typeface of at least the same size as the list of ingredients itself.

In the case of products for which no list of ingredients exists, the words 'produced from genetically modified soya' or 'produced from genetically modified maize', as appropriate, shall appear clearly on the labelling of the food.

Where in accordance with the provisions of the first indent of Art 6(5)(b) of Directive 79/112/EEC an ingredient is designated by the name of a category, that designation shall be completed by the words 'contains ... (*) produced from genetically modified soya/genetically modified maize (*) (ingredients to be specified as appropriate).

Where an ingredient of a compound ingredient is derived from the specified foodstuffs, it shall be mentioned on the labelling of the final product, with the addition of the wording set out in point (b):

3   This Article shall be without prejudice to the other requirements of Community law concerning the labelling of foodstuffs.

The Regulation also provides for a *de minimis* threshold for the presence of DNA or protein from GM sources as a result of unavoidable adventitious contamination and for the formulation of a negative list of products that would not require labelling (that is, those not containing novel protein and DNA). Regulation 1139/98 came into force on 1 September 1998.

The Commission also adopted Directive 97/35,[12] which makes labelling compulsory for all new agricultural products containing or consisting of GMOs and which have been notified under Directive 90/220. They must include in a label or accompanying document an indication that the product contains or consists of GMOs. If the products to be placed on the market are going to be mixed with non-GM products, then information on the possibility that GMOs might be present in the product must be indicated.

The issue of the contamination of non-GM ingredients with small amounts of GM ingredients has been dealt with by the adoption of the *de minimis* threshold, where a manufacturer who has tried to obtain GM free ingredients might obtain a supply which has a small amount of contamination.

Regulation 49/2000[13] came into force on 10 April 2000. This Regulation amends EC Regulation 1139/98 (on the labelling of foods containing GM soya

12   Commission Directive 97/35/EC (OJ 1997 L169/72).
13   Regulation 49/2000/EC.

and maize) to widen the scope of the labelling requirements to include foods sold to catering establishments, and to establish a 1% *de minimis* threshold for the adventitious contamination of non-GM produce, below which it will not require labelling. Therefore, a product may be called 'GM free' even if it might contain up to 1% of GM ingredients. EC Regulation 50/2000[14] also came into force on 10 April 2000. The Regulation requires the labelling of foods and food ingredients using additives and flavourings which contain GM material. EC Regulation 1139/98, requiring the labelling of foods containing GM soya or maize, came into force on 1 September 1998, but food additives and flavourings were not included in the main novel food legislation.

Legislation on seeds

There are various pieces of legislation that deal with seeds. Once there has been notification of acceptance in a national catalogue, the Commission will examine whether acceptance is in accordance with the provisions of the seed legislation, based on the information provided by the relevant Member State. If the Commission confirms the acceptance, the seed varieties will be published in the Official Journal under the title 'Common Catalogue of Varieties of Agricultural Plant Species'. The legislation also requires that GM seed varieties must be authorised in accordance with Directive 90/220 before they can be included in the catalogue and become commercially available within the EU. If the seeds are going to be used for food production, they also have to be authorised under the procedure laid down in the Novel Foods Regulation (248/87). The intention is that, eventually, the necessary authorisation can be carried out under the seed legislation and there is a provision in the White Paper for a proposal on this issue to be put forward by June 2001. Up to now, only two GM seed varieties have been included in the Common Catalogue which can be marketed in the EU. They received prior authorisation under Directive 90/220. There are, at the time of writing, three more GM varieties awaiting authorisation for inclusion in the Catalogue.

Animal feed

There is currently no specific Community legislation on GM derived animal feed. However, eight GMOs have been authorised under Directive 90/220 for use in feed. They are four maize varieties, three rape varieties and one soya variety.

---

14   Regulation 50/2000/EC.

REGULATION IN THE UK

The Genetically Modified Organisms (Deliberate Release) Regulations 1992 (as amended)[15] implement Regulation 90/220/EEC on the deliberate release into the environment of GMOs.

The Novel Foods and Novel Food Ingredients Regulations 1997[16] made provision for the enforcement of the Novel Foods Regulation 258/97 and designates the Minister of Agriculture and the Secretary of State for Health as the competent food assessment body.

The Food Labelling (Amendment) Regulations 1999[17] came into force in Great Britain on 19 March 1999. They provide the means for local authorities to be able to enforce EC Regulation 1139/98 on the labelling of foodstuffs containing genetically modified soya or maize. Guidance notes were also issued.[18] The Genetically Modified and Novel Food (Labelling) (England) Regulations 2000[19] now draw together all the current domestic rules on GM food labelling in England. The Regulations provide for the enforcement in England of existing rules (EC Regulation 1139/98 and Art 8(1) of the EC Novel Foods Regulation), as well as providing for the enforcement in England of EC Regulations 49 and 50/2000. The domestic Regulations also provide flexible labelling arrangements for appropriate businesses, and penalties for non-compliance. In Scotland, the Genetically Modified and Novel and Novel Foods (Labelling) (Scotland) Regulations 2000 (SSI 2000/83) apply.

Advisory Committee on Novel Foods and Processes

UK Government ministers are advised on all novel foods, including those produced using genetic modification, by an independent committee of experts, the ACNFP. This committee carries out safety assessments of individual novel foods as part of the pre-market approval scheme controlled by the EC Novel Food and Novel Food Ingredient Regulation. In carrying out such assessments, the ACNFP can seek specialist advice from other Government advisory committees, such as the Committee on Toxicity of

---

15 SI 1992/3280, as amended by the Genetically Modified Organisms (Deliberate Release) Regulations 1993 (SI 1993/152); the Genetically Modified Organisms (Deliberate Release) Regulations 1995 (SI 1995/304); the Genetically Modified Organisms (Risk Assessment) (Records and Exemptions) Regulations 1996 (SI 1996/1106); the Genetically Modified Organisms (Deliberate Release and Risk Assessment Amendments) Regulations 1997 (SI 1997/1900).

16 SI 1997/1335.

17 Food Labelling (Amendment) Regulations 1999 (SI 1999/747).

18 *Labelling of Foods Containing Genetically Modified Soya and Maize*, PB 4447, 1999, London: MAFF, and *Novel Foods and Novel Food Ingredients*, PB 4520, 1999, London: MAFF.

19 SI 2000/768.

Chemicals in Food, Consumer Products and the Environment or the Committee on Medical Aspects of Food and Nutrition Policy. ACNFP can also seek advice from the Food Advisory Committee on the labelling of GM foods and on any general issues arising from individual applications. The ACNFP holds joint meetings with these other committees and the wider scientific community to discuss more general technical issues, as the need arises. The ACNFP itself consists of 14 members with expertise in areas such as genetic modification, toxicology, nutrition, microbiology, biotechnology and food processing, as well as an ethicist and a consumer representative. Its job is not only to assess individual applications in as rigorous a manner as possible, but to keep up to date with the emerging science in this rapidly growing area and to advise on changes to the assessment procedure in the light of this.

All the agendas and minutes of the committee meetings are published on the internet. The individual assessment reports produced by ACNFP are also published, as well as being brought together in an annual report. Companies making applications are encouraged to deposit as much of the supporting data as possible in the British Library, where it can be inspected by anyone with an interest.

In May 2000, reports came out revealing that a small proportion of oilseed rape, grown in the UK and other European Union countries for the past year, contained low levels of a genetically modified variety. The chairman of the UK Food Standards Agency announced that this posed no added risk to public health. The seeds were produced in Canada in 1998, and around 1% of them could be affected:

> The variety of oilseed rape in question, Monsanto's RT73, was fully assessed for safety by the Advisory Committee on Novel Foods and Processes in 1995 and cleared for food use in 1996. The Committee concluded that the oil was as safe for food use as that obtained from conventional crops. The oil was subsequently notified under the EC Novel Foods Regulations and drew no objections from other Member States. The oil can consequently be freely traded within the European Community.

> The oil from the GM variety, which is indistinguishable from oil obtained from non-modified oilseed rape, does not require labelling since neither DNA or protein will be present in the refined oil. Nevertheless, when consumers buy a product which is described as coming from GM-free sources, they need to have complete confidence that the claims made by manufacturers are true. Anything less will undermine consumer choice. I therefore welcome steps being taken to ensure seed purity and monitor standards.

The Government announced a package of new steps relating to seed purity. These include pressing for concerted international action to seek new legal standards for seed purity, testing of seed imports and working with the industry on a Code of Practice. The ACNFP assessment of Monsanto's RT73 (or GT73) oilseed rape oil was published in their 1995 annual report. Data supporting the application to the ACNFP have been deposited in the British

Library.[20] The RT73 line had been approved in the UK for experimental field trials (Part B consent under EC Directive 90/220). The seed stocks in question were produced in Canada in 1998, and appear to have been affected by growing too close to Monsanto Roundup Ready rape seed.

Around 9,000 hectares were sown with the affected stocks in the UK in 1999, and around 4,700 ha have been sown in spring 2000. Around 500,000 hectares of oilseed rape are grown annually in this country.

A study has been set up by MAFF on seed sourcing, and the risk that GM presence may occur in other seed supplies. The Department of the Environment, Transport and the Regions (DETR) officials have introduced testing of seed imports under the Environmental Protection Act 1990. MAFF and the DETR met the UK seeds sector and urged them to take industry-wide voluntary action to check sources of seed and monitor GM content. DETR referred the information to the Advisory Committee on Releases to the Environment, which considered that there was no risk to environmental safety.

INTERNATIONAL ORGANISATIONS AND BIOTECHNOLOGY

All the major international organisations described in Chapter 1 are involved in discussing and developing policies on genetically modified organisms and foods derived from biotechnology. The issue of GM foods is of such crucial importance in so many ways that it is being addressed at the highest international level. As well as the moral and ethical issue mentioned at the beginning of this chapter and the fundamental issue of freedom of choice for the consumer, the GM debate goes to the heart of world trade. The core principle of free trade upon which the World Trade Organisation is based is being called into question where the principle conflicts with issues of safety and choice. The GM debate has brought into the open the concerns that many have been expressing for some time about the globalisation of the world economy and the increasing power and influence of the multi-national biotechnology companies.

This chapter will now examine the work being undertaken on genetic modification by some of the major international organisations.

---

20   BL SUP 11097.

The Biosafety Protocol

The UN Convention on Biological Diversity defines biotechnology as 'any technological application that uses biological systems, living organisms, or derivatives thereof, to make or modify products or processes for specific use'.

After nearly five years of negotiations, parties to the United Nations Convention on Biological Diversity (CBD) finally reached agreement on a Biosafety Protocol to the CBD on 29 January 2000. The agreement, the Cartagena Protocol on Biosafety, will enable importing countries to limit imports of genetically modified foods and to use the precautionary principle. The Protocol was finally agreed after difficult negotiations during which GM exporting countries, namely the US, Canada, Argentina and their associates Australia, Chile and Uruguay (the so called 'Miami Group') tried to obstruct the agreement.

One of the most contentious issues during the negotiations concerned the relationship between the Protocol and other international agreements, particularly the WTO agreements. While environmental agreements are premised on the precautionary principle, which allows potentially dangerous activities to be restricted or prohibited even before there is any scientific proof that they cause damage, trade law requires 'sufficient scientific evidence'. The agreement states that the Protocol and the WTO agreements should be mutually supportive, but it does not override the rights and obligations contained in the multilateral WTO agreements.

Benedikt Haerlin of Greenpeace described the agreement as 'a historic step towards protecting the environment and consumers from the dangers of genetic engineering'. Greenpeace has urged all countries to ratify the agreement so that it can enter into force at the latest by the 10th anniversary of the Rio Earth Summit in 2002. Until the Protocol comes into force, Greenpeace wants to see the export of GMOs prohibited.

The objective of the protocol is:

> ... to contribute to ensuring an adequate level of protection in the field of the safe transfer, handling and use of living modified organisms resulting from modern biotechnology that may have adverse effects on the conservation and sustainable use of biological diversity, taking also into account risks to human health, and specifically focusing on transboundary movements [Art 1].

The Protocol applies to 'the transboundary movement, transit, handling and use of all living modified organisms that may have adverse effects on the conservation and sustainable use of biological diversity, taking also into account risks to human health' (Art 4). Living modified organisms (LMOs) are defined as 'any living organism that possesses a novel combination of genetic material obtained through the use of modern biotechnology' (Art 3). The Protocol covers LMOs which are intended to be introduced into the environment, such as seeds, animals and micro-organisms. It also contains provisions covering LMOs intended for use in food, animal feed or processing. The Protocol stipulates that LMOs intended for food, feed or processing must be identified as such when they cross national boundaries. The Protocol does not cover products which are derived from LMOs, nor does it cover pharmaceutical products for human use that are covered by other international agreements (Art 5).

The precautionary principle will underpin decision making under the Protocol. References to the precautionary principle are contained in Preamble 4 and Art 1. Articles 10(6) and 11(8) state:

> Lack of scientific certainty due to insufficient relevant scientific information and knowledge regarding the extent of the potential adverse effects of a living modified organism on the conservation and sustainable use of biological diversity in the Party of import, taking also into account risks to human health, shall not prevent that Party from taking a decision, as appropriate, with regard to the import of the living modified organism in question as referred to in para 3 above, in order to avoid or minimize such potential adverse effects.

The Protocol sets out international procedures for advanced informed agreement (AIA) for *transboundary movements* of living modified organisms. The AIA procedures do not apply to the *transit* of LMOs (Art 6(1)), nor do they apply to LMOs for contained use (Art 6(2)). These issues must be regulated by national measures. The Protocol contains two different approaches for AIA procedures: one procedure for LMOs that are intended for intentional release into the environment (Arts 7–10) and another procedure for LMOs that are intended for food, feed or for processing (Art 11). There will not necessarily always be a clear distinction between the two categories.

With regard to LMOs for intentional release into the environment, Art 10 contains provisions for full notification to the party of import of information about the LMO and its potential impacts. The party of export must ensure that there is in place a legal requirement regarding the accuracy of the information supplied by the exporter. There must be explicit consent from the party of import before the transboundary movement can take place.

Under Art 11, which deals with LMOs intended for direct use in food, feed or for processing, there is a much less direct and detailed procedure for notifying the party of import. This is largely due to pressure exerted by the Miami Group. The party of export is only obliged to provide information about their domestic use to the Biodiversity Clearing House. They also have to send written copies of the information to the national focal point of each party that has informed the Secretariat in advance that it does not have access to the Clearing House (Art 11(1)).

The Protocol states that any party may take a decision on the import of LMOs intended for direct use as food, feed or for processing under its own domestic regulatory framework so long as it is consistent with the objectives of the Protocol (Art 11(4)).

For parties that are developing countries or countries whose economy is in transition, the Protocol provides a basic decision making process for LMOs intended for food, feed or for processing (Art 11(6)). Failure by a party to communicate its decision will not imply consent or refusal to imports and this means that transboundary movements of these types of LMO should not take place until the explicit consent of the party of import has been obtained.

There are provisions in the Protocol for dealing with risk assessment, risk management and the unintentional transboundary movement of LMOs and emergency procedures (Arts 15, 16, 17).

The Protocol sets down international rules for the handling, transport, packaging and identification of LMOs (Art 18). There are differentiated rules for the identification of LMOs intended for direct use in food, feed, or processing, LMOs intended for intentional release into the environment and LMOs intended for contained use. Identification is intended to ensure traceability and includes labelling and segregation. As a result of pressure from the Miami Group, the rules on the identification of living modified organisms intended for direct use as food, feed or for processing were not as rigorous as many had hoped they would be. They now only require parties of export to identify shipments of transgenic commodities as 'may contain' LMOs. Final decisions on the identification of these types of LMO will be taken by parties to the Protocol within two years of the entry into force of the Protocol.

Under the Protocol, trade with third parties is only permitted if it is consistent with the objectives of the Protocol. Parties can enter into specific bilateral, regional or multilateral agreements with non-parties provided that these agreements do not result in a lower level of protection than under the Protocol.

Article 26 of the Protocol makes reference to socio-economic considerations:

1 The Parties, in reaching a decision on import under this Protocol or under its domestic measures implementing the Protocol, may take into account, consistent with their international obligations, socio-economic considerations arising from the impact of living modified organisms on the conservation and sustainable use of biological diversity, especially with regard to the value of biological diversity to indigenous and local communities.

2 The Parties are encouraged to cooperate on research and information exchange on any socio-economic impacts of living modified organisms, especially on indigenous and local communities.

The Protocol also contains obligations for parties to develop international rules on liability and redress for any damage that might be caused by the transboundary movement of LMOs, within four years of the entry into force of the Protocol (Art 27).

The Protocol will enter into force once 50 countries which are already parties to the Convention on Biological Diversity have signed and ratified the

Protocol. It is expected that this will have happened by 2002 or 2003. In the meantime, it is expected that those parties who signed the agreement in Montreal will adhere to the spirit and objectives of the Protocol.

OECD Task Force

The OECD Task Force is also involved in considering the issue of biotechnology and food safety. A Task Force for the Safety of Novel Foods and Feeds is held under the auspices of the Environment Directorate. The OECD also held a Conference on the Scientific and Health Aspects of Genetically Modified Foods in Edinburgh in 1999. The conference formed part of the ongoing work at the OECD on biotechnology. Its conclusions were fed into a report submitted by the OECD, following a request from the G8 leaders at their summit in Cologne in June 1999 that the OECD 'undertake a study of the implications of biotechnology and other aspects of food safety' and an earlier endorsement by OECD ministers in May 1999 of the OECD's biotechnology programme.

The conference, entitled *GM Foods: Facts, Uncertainties and Assessments*, brought together 400 participants from over 25 countries representing governments, industry and interest groups. The focus of the conference was the safety of the GM crops currently in use for food. The issues of environmental impact, trade and developmental effects or ethical and societal concerns were not addressed at length, but obviously they could not be entirely disregarded or separated from the issue of safety.

The conference considered the different approaches to the assessment of the risks and benefits of GM food and, as the rapporteurs' report acknowledges, a strong feeling emerged that there was a need to restore trust between the various parties involved. In their summary, the rapporteurs identify a significant number of points on which there was general agreement amongst most, if not all, the participants. There were also, of course, areas of disagreement and issues about which there was insufficient knowledge.

The conference focused on GM food safety and human health. The chairman of the conference acknowledged that this was only one part of the debate about GM technology in food and agriculture, which in turn was only one part of the debate about the future of biotechnology.

The conference also focused on the science (including the social science of consumer attitudes) of GM food safety.

The conference was not aimed at producing a simple consensus, but rather at identifying areas of greater agreement, of divergence of opinion, and of uncertainty due to lack of knowledge. Even the very basic question of whether or not GM technology is fundamentally different from genetic modification through conventional breeding was one on which there was not a consensus amongst the participants.

The conference was divided into three sections:

(a) What is the science of GM and its potential risks and benefits for food and agriculture?

(b) What is the science of assessment of food safety, and what, if any, are the special problems posed by GM foods?

(c) What are the regulatory systems worldwide, and do these require adjusting because of special features of GM foods?

The principal conclusions, outlined in the chairman's report, are as follows:

Food safety

8   Worldwide, many people are eating GM foods (especially in North America and China) with no adverse affects on human health having been reported in the peer-reviewed scientific literature.

9   There could, in theory, be long-term effects on human health that have not yet been detected because GM foods have been available for less than ten years.

Decision making, assessment and choice

10 In the future, policy decisions about GM food, as well as the assessment of their safety, should be more inclusive and open than has typically been the case in the past. People want to know how decisions have been reached and to be consulted. This process will help to remove suspicion.

11 Having said this, there was no clear conclusion on how attitudes and beliefs that might become apparent as a result of consultation should be incorporated into the assessment and communication of GM food safety. For many, safety assessment remains an essentially technical and scientific process.

12 Consumers should be allowed to choose. Labelling of GM foods is important, although there was no agreement on how far this should extend (for example, to GM derivatives? To animals fed on GM?). It is important also to note that the labelling applies to the process by which organisms are created and not the food product, which in many cases is identical to its conventional counterpart.

The assessment of GM food safety

13 The assessment of the safety of any novel food, including GM food, involves a variety of kinds of evidence. One commonly used tool is the concept of 'substantial equivalence'. The essence of this idea is that a comparison between the novel food and one already in the diet provides the basis for asking questions about the safety of the novel product. Substantial equivalence is not a quantitative criterion or a hurdle, but a framework for thinking. It is continually modified and updated, but it is timely now, after six years of using the tool, to undertake a more detailed review.

14 On two more technical issues: (a) there is no clear agreement about the importance of animal feeding trials (other than toxicity trials) in assessing the safety of novel foods, including GM foods; (b) the methods for testing toxicity and allergenicity of GM foods need re-examination.

15 Existing international bodies are working to achieve consistent standards and criteria for the assessment of food safety, and this is to be applauded. The precautionary principle is now beginning to be discussed internationally in relation to food safety, but it has not yet been translated into an agreed operational form.

GM technology in developing and developed countries

16 The majority of speakers from developing countries stressed the crucial importance of GM technology as part of the armoury for feeding their population in the future. In China, with 20% of the world's population and 7% of the land surface, GM is already playing a major role in food production, and its importance was also emphasised by speakers from Africa and Latin America. However, the view was also expressed that the future application of GM technology in developing countries should be more explicitly tuned to the needs of local people rather than of multi-national corporations.

17 In light of this last comment, GM technology for the developing world should be carried forward through a mixture of public and private funding.

18 Whilst it is essential that standards of safety assessment should be consistent and high throughout the world, the strongly expressed demand for GM technology in developing countries casts substantial doubt on proposals for a worldwide moratorium made by some participants.

19 The first generation of GM crops and foods are perceived as having brought little direct benefit to consumers in developed countries, but this may well change as new products appear with direct quality, health or price benefits.

Concerns about GM other than food safety

20 The principal concerns of the opponents of GM related less to food safety than to the broader question of why GM food is being produced at all. Most developing country speakers argued forcefully that GM technology is an essential part of their future food production (see para 16), but this was rejected by some NGO speakers from Europe and North America. They argued, instead, for solving world food shortage by redistribution, better prevention of loss during storage and so on. They also pointed out, as did some developing country participants, that citizen engagement in decision-making and discussion (see para 10) should be improved in developing countries.

21 A second concern about GM agriculture was the potential environmental impact. Although there have been many field trials and, in some parts of the world, large-scale commercial planting of GM crops, there has been insufficient work to fully assess environmental impacts, especially in the biodiversity-rich tropics.

The report observes that the most significant aspect of the Edinburgh Conference was that it included all sides of the debate surrounding GM foods and nevertheless identified certain areas of agreement. It also succeeded in identifying issues in which there is disagreement or uncertainty due to lack of knowledge, and in separating out issues which are subject to scientific analysis and those which are related to political factors, beliefs and values. Further detail is available in the rapporteurs' report.

The conference represents a new start in the global debate about GM food and agriculture: a more inclusive approach in which the protagonists discussed some of the key issues with each other. There was support for continuation of this process to deal with other parts of the debate.

The chairman therefore recommended that an international forum be set up to continue the process started in Edinburgh. The aim of such a forum would be to provide governments with a state of the art assessment of scientific knowledge about GM technology, and to set this assessment in the context of broader concerns of society. It was suggested that such a global assessment could be modelled on the Intergovernmental Panel on Climate Change (IPCC). This Panel allows governments to draw on worldwide expertise in climate science. It informs, but does not make policy, and it acknowledges the minority scientific views as well as the current majority view. It also updates its reports at intervals (paras 24 and 25).

The forum proposed by the chairman would have similarities to the IPCC, but it would include not only scientists, but also other stakeholders, and the following suggestions were made as to how the forum might be developed:

(a) It should build on and interact with, rather than duplicate or replace, the work of existing international groups such as Codex Alimentarius.

(b) It should be global in scope and not restricted to G8 countries or a subset thereof. In particular, a key message of the Edinburgh conference was the role of developing countries where application of the technology is proceeding rapidly.

(c) It should be led by the world's best scientific experts, but include a wider range of expertise and opinion than scientists.

(d) Two initial themes for the forum would be food safety and environmental safety of GM in agriculture and food production.

(e) There would be two kinds of outputs: (1) scientific assessments in the form of reports that inform policy; (2) an inclusive and global debate about the relationship between GM technology and society. It will be essential that governments take ownership of the forum and its reports.

(f) The reports should be produced in a timely way so as to facilitate the assessment of rapidly emerging technologies.

In his summary of the proposal, the chairman observed that the proposed forum could serve two important functions by enabling a global debate and assessment of GM technology in food and agriculture. First, it would allow the best scientific analysis of the risks and benefits of the new technology, as it develops, to be carried out in order to provide governments worldwide with appropriate expert advice. This advice will acknowledge the range of scientific opinion and uncertainties, as well as indicating the current majority opinion and, secondly, it could create a better understanding of the relationship between technological developments, policy, and the concerns and aspirations of citizens. This would be achieved by widening the forum beyond purely scientific analysis. It is acknowledged that there is more than one way of achieving these twin objectives. One approach would be to have an expert panel, led by scientists but including other stakeholders, to carry out the scientific assessments. Draft reports of this expert panel could be used as the basis for discussion by a broader forum, along the lines of the Edinburgh meeting, in which the non-science issues are brought into the debate. The expert panel might choose to revise its report in light of this broader discussion.

In July 2000, the G8 met at a summit in Okinawa. One of the agenda items they considered was 'Biotechnology/Food Safety', having requested a report on this subject from the OECD. In the Communique released by the G8 following their summit, they acknowledged the OECD report as a 'useful step' in the direction towards policy dialogue (para. 57 of the communique). The G8 acknowledge the need for open and transparent consultation with the involvement of all stakeholders'. Their observations on biotechnology and food safety were as follows:

55 Maintenance of effective national food safety systems and public confidence in them assumes critical importance in public policy. We are committed to continued efforts to make systems responsive to the growing public awareness of food safety issues, the potential risks associated with food, the accelerating pace of developments in biotechnology, and the increasing cross-border movement of food and agricultural products.

56 Commitment to a science based rule based approach remains a key principle underlying these endeavours. The ongoing work in international for a to develop and refine such an approach need to be accelerated. In particular, we attach strong importance to the work of the Codex Alimentarius Commission (CAC), the principle standard setting body in food safety, and encourage its Ad Hoc Intergovernmental Task Force on Food Derived from Biotechnology to produce a substantial interim report before completion of its mandate in 2003. We also support the efforts of the CAC's Committee on General Principles to achieve greater global consensus on how precaution should be applied to food safety in circumstances where available scientific information is incomplete or contradictory.

57 Policy dialogue, engaging all stakeholders and including both developed and developing countries, must be intensified to advance health protection, facilitate trade, ensure the sound development of biotechnology, and foster consumer confidence and public acceptance. The report by the OECD Ad

Hoc Group on Food safety and the work of the Task Force for the Safety of Novel Foods and Feeds and the Working Group on Harmonisation of Regulatory Oversight of Biotechnology represent a useful step in this direction. We welcome the further work agreed by OECD ministers. We note with approval that the OECD will continue to undertake analytical work and to play an effective role in international policy dialogue on food safety, maintaining its engagement with civil society and seeking to share its work in this area with countries outside the organisation's membership. Drawing on its comparative advantages, the work of the OECD will effectively compliment the activities of other international organisations, in particular the FAO and WHO. We also encourage the FAO and WHO to organise periodic international meetings of food safety regulators to advance the process of science based public consultations.

58 In pursuing this dialogue we will pay particular attention to the needs, opportunities and constraints in developing countries. We will work to strengthen our support for their capacity building to harness the potentials of biotechnology, and encourage research and development as well as data and Information sharing in technologies, including those that address global food security, health, nutritional and environmental challenges and are adapted to specific conditions in theses countries.

59 Open and transparent consultation with and involvement of all stakeholder, including representatives of civil society, supported by shared scientific understanding is a key component of a credible food and crop safety system. We note the proposal to establish an independent international panel put forward at the recent OECD Edinburgh conference. Building on the success of that conference we will explore, in consultation with international organisations and interested bodies, including scientific academies, the way to integrate the best scientific knowledge available into the global process of consensus building on biotechnology and other aspects of food and crop safety.[21]

FAO Statement on Biotechnology

In March 2000, the FAO issued its first statement on biotechnology, reported in a press release.[22] The FAO acknowledged that 'Biotechnology provides powerful tools for the sustainable development of agriculture, fisheries and forestry, as well as the food industry' and 'can be of significant help in meeting the food needs of a growing and increasingly urbanised population'.

It acknowledges that there are a wide range of 'biotechnologies' with different techniques and applications. The FAO statement acknowledges that this definition can be interpreted in two ways.

---

21 G8 Communique Okinawa 2000, available at www.oecd.org/subject/biotech/okinawareport.htm.

22 FAO Press Release, 15 March 2000.

Interpreted broadly, the definition would cover many of the tools and techniques that are already commonly used in agriculture and food production. Interpreted narrowly, considering only the new DNA techniques, molecular biology and reproductive technological applications, the definition would cover different technologies such as gene manipulation and gene transfer, DNA typing and the cloning of plants and animals.

Whilst acknowledging that many aspects of biotechnology and its application cause little controversy, the FAO statement recognises that GMOs 'become the target of a very intensive and, at times, emotionally charged debate'.

In the case of GMOs, the FAO called for 'a cautious case by case approach to determine the benefits and risks of each individual GMO' and for the 'legitimate concerns for the biosafety of each product and process prior to its release' to be addressed.

The statement identifies the benefits of genetic engineering, such as the potential to increase yields on marginal lands in countries that cannot at present grow enough food to feed their populations; the development of new vaccines against human and animal diseases; the genetic engineering of rice to contain pro-vitamin A (beta carotene) and iron which could improve the health of poor communities; drought resistant crops; improved root systems.

There are two broad, but overlapping areas of concern: the threat of environmental damage, and the threat to human and animal health.

The statement observes that current investment in biotechnological research tends to be concentrated in the private sector and oriented towards agriculture. The FAO takes the view that, in view of the potential contribution of biotechnologies for increasing food supply and overcoming food insecurity and vulnerability, efforts should be made to ensure that developing countries in general and resource-poor farmers in particular, benefit more from biotechnological research. They should, however, also continue to have access to a variety of sources of genetic material. These concerns could be addressed by increasing public funding and ensuring dialogue between the public and private sector.

The statement was published on the occasion of the meeting of the Codex Alimentarius Ad Hoc Intergovernmental Task Force on Foods Derived from Biotechnologies. The Task Force will develop standards, guidelines or recommendations for food derived by biotechnology or which contains traits introduced into it by biotechnological methods.

The FAO itself has a Commission on Genetic Resources for Food and Agriculture, a permanent intergovernmental forum in which countries are developing a Code of Conduct on Biotechnology with a view to maximising the benefits and minimising the risks of modern biotechnologies.

The code will be based on scientific considerations and will take account of the environmental, ethical and socio-economic implications of biotechnology. The FAO is also working towards the establishment of an international expert committee on food and agriculture. This reflects the importance of ethical considerations in these areas just as in the area of medicinal products.

Codex Ad Hoc Intergovernmental Task Force

The Joint FAO/WHO Food Standard Programme and Codex Alimentarius Commission have established the Codex Ad Hoc Intergovernmental Task Force on Foods Derived from Biotechnologies. The Task Force will develop standards, guidelines or recommendations for food derived by biotechnology or which contains traits introduced into it by biotechnological methods.

The first session of the Codex Ad Hoc Intergovernmental Task Force on Foods Derived from Biotechnology took place in March 2000.

In its summary and conclusion, the Report outlined certain 'Matters for Consideration by the Executive Committee and/or the Codex Alimentarius Commission'. The Task Force agreed to report to the Executive Committee for approval the following work plan:

(a) Elaboration of major texts, namely:
  - A set of broad general principle for risk analysis of foods derived from biotechnology (precise title still to be determined);
  - Specific guidance on the risk assessment of foods derived from biotechnology (precise title still to be determined) [para 27].

(b) Preparation of a list of available analytical methods including those for the detection or identification of foods or food ingredients derived from biotechnology [para 32].

The Task Force also decided to establish two open-ended Ad Hoc Working Groups, namely:
- Ad Hoc Working Group, to be chaired by Japan, to develop texts mentioned in (a) above [para 35]; and
- Ad Hoc Working Group, to be chaired by Germany, to compile a list of analytical methods mentioned in (b) above [para 36].

The Task Force welcomed the initiative of the FAO and WHO to convene an expert consultation to support the scientific aspects of its work and agreed upon five specific questions for which scientific advice of the expert consultation would be sought (paras 37, 38; Appendix III).

In the Report, attention was drawn to the recommendation of the 1996 FAO/WHO Expert Consultation that developing countries should be provided with assistance and education regarding approaches to the safety assessment of foods and food components produced by genetic modification.

The Task Force noted that the representatives of FAO and WHO reaffirmed the support of these organisations for technical assistance to developing countries (para 9).

The Task Force considered the Biosafety Protocol:

It was noted that the objective of the protocol was in accordance with the precautionary approach contained in Principle 15 of the Rio Declaration on Environment and Development to contribute to ensuring an adequate level of protection in the field of the safe transfer, handling and use of living modified organisms resulting from modern biotechnology that may have adverse effects on the conservation and sustainable use of biological diversity, taking also into account risks to human health and specifically focusing on transboundary movements [para 11].

The Task Force noted that interpretation of the provisions of the Protocol was beyond the mandate of the Commission. It also noted that the Protocol formed part of the international regulatory framework within which the development, adoption, acceptance and use of Codex standards had to be undertaken. The objective and provisions of the Protocol would therefore need to be taken into account during the development of appropriate Codex texts by the Task Force.

Consideration was given to the elaboration of standards, guidelines or other principles for foods derived from biotechnology.

Member countries and observer organisations were invited to express their views on identification of area of the work of the Task Force, work priorities, and key concepts and definitions to be developed by the Task Force [para 13]:

Many delegations and observer organizations identified safety and nutrition assessment of foods derived from biotechnology as the main priority area of the work. While recognizing that the concept of the substantial equivalence was being used in safety assessment, several delegations and observer organizations stressed the need for further review of the concept and its applicability to safety assessment. Several delegations stated that risk management and especially pre-market approval were fundamental aspects of risk analysis in relation to foods derived from biotechnology. The Task Force noted the necessity to study marker genes and the potential for non-intentional and long-term health effects. Some delegations expressed the view that it would be useful to establish an international expert body that would be responsible for risk assessment [para 14].

With regard to legitimate factors other than science that were relevant to the health of consumers and the promotion of fair trade practice, several delegations and the observer from the European Commission proposed to develop a specific guideline to take into account those factors. Several other delegations were of the opinion that since the Codex Committee on General Principles (CCGP) was currently working on this issue the development of a guideline specific to the Task Force was not an immediate priority. Some of the delegations identified the following factors were mentioned by some delegations as potential other legitimate factors: ethical/religious/cultural considerations, consumer concerns/interests, food security, enforcement capacity and environmental risk (para 15).

Many delegations and observers also pointed out the need for addressing precautionary principles or approaches to be recommended by the Task Force. Several other delegations stressed that the issue of precaution should first be discussed at the Codex Committee on General Principles (CCGP).

It was also proposed that the concept of 'familiarity' used in environmental risk assessment should be considered. It was noted that this concept had not previously been used by Codex and that further clarification would be needed (para 17).

The development of a guideline for the monitoring and traceability of the foods derived from biotechnology was identified as a priority by many delegations and observers who indicated that these issues were not related only to consumer information but to consumer health protection. Other delegations and observers stated that the concept of 'traceability' was new to Codex and required further clarification and explanation including the implications for developing countries. It was also noted that the concept might not be exclusive to foods derived from biotechnology and might need to be considered at a more general level (para 18).

Some delegations also pointed out the need to consider the methods of analysis, including the detection methods of genetically modified foods and several delegations were of the view that these issues also required the involvement of the Codex Committee on Food Labelling (CCFL) or the Codex Committee on Method of Analysis and Sampling (CCMAS) (para 19).

Many delegations and observer organisations emphasised the need to develop a specific guideline on transparency and involvement of all stakeholders particularly consumers in the decision making process (para 20).

Many delegations emphasised the need to establish clear definitions on several key words. The definitions of 'modern biotechnology' and 'substantial equivalence' were identified by many delegations and it was suggested that the Task Force refer to definitions established or to be established by other organisations (para 21).

Genetically modified foods derived from plants, microorganism and animals were identified as among the various food categories that may come within the scope of the Task Force. Animal feed and food additives were also identified. It was noted that animal feed would be covered by the Codex Ad Hoc Intergovernmental Task Force on Animal Feeding to be held in Denmark in June 2000 (para 22).

The Task Force produced a list of subjects potentially to be dealt with in its work by summarising the proposals made by delegations which is reproduced as Appendix II to the report. The Task Force recognised that the time frame prescribed in its terms of reference meant that it was necessary to prioritise its work. It also noted that many of the proposed subjects were covered by other Codex Committees or other international organisations. According to its terms of reference, the Task Force should coordinate and collaborate closely with the appropriate Codex Committees and take full account of existing work carried out by other international organisations. It agreed to identify those subjects that were already under discussion by other Codex subsidiary bodies or other international organisations and which therefore would not need to be considered in detail in the priority areas of the work of the Task Force. It noted that the issue of labelling was covered by the Codex Committee on Food Labelling (CCFL) and agreed that the precautionary approach/principle should be dealt with as a matter of priority by the Codex Committee on General Principles (CCGP). The Task Force further agreed that the environmental risk was addressed by other instruments or bodies such as the Cartagena Biosafety Protocol under the Convention on Biological Diversity, the International Plant Protection Convention (IPPC) and the Commission on Genetic Resources for Food and Agriculture (CGRFA) (para 24).

The Task Force outlined a Programme of Work and, taking account of the priorities discussed, the Task Force decided that it would proceed with the elaboration of two major texts, namely:

1 A set of broad general principles for risk analysis of foods derived from biotechnology including matters such as:

  • science-based decision-making;

  • pre-market assessment;

  • transparency;

  • post-market monitoring [including traceability]; and

  • other legitimate factors as appropriate.

2 Specific guidance on the risk assessment of foods derived from biotechnology including such matters as:

  • food safety and nutrition;

  • 'substantial equivalence';

  • potential long-term health effects; and

  • non-intentional effects [para 27].

The Task Force agreed that in preparing these texts preference should be given to guidance that was applicable to all foods derived from biotechnology. If it proved necessary to prioritise the work it was agreed that first priority should be given to foods of plant origin, followed by micro-organisms used directly in foods and then foods of animal origin. It was noted, however, that early attention might have to be given to fish (para 28).

The Task Force also agreed that consideration should be given to the development of guidelines for transparency in decision making and the participation of all stakeholders in the decision making process. It was noted that the approach of establishing over-arching general principles would allow the development of further, detailed explanatory guidelines on specific issues if these were required and if time allowed (para 29).

It was agreed that careful attention should be paid to the development of adequate and appropriate definitions, drawing on definitions already developed and agreed to in other texts (such as the Cartagena Protocol) or by other bodies (such as the Codex Committee on Food Labelling) (para 30).

With regard to the issues of Traceability and Familiarity, the Task Force noted that a better understanding of these concepts and their implications was required before they could be included definitively in either of the main texts to be developed. It therefore agreed that discussion papers should be prepared on these issues as soon as possible (para 31).

The Task Force agreed that a list of available analytical methods including those for the detection or identification of foods or food ingredients derived from biotechnology should be prepared, and that this list should indicate the performance criteria and status of the validation of each method. It was further agreed that the list of methods, once finalised, should be transmitted to the Codex Committee on Methods of Analysis and Sampling for endorsement (para 32).

There was a general consensus that the above issues had the highest priority and should be achievable within the time frame allowed. The Task Force noted that finalisation of its work programme would require the resolution of questions regarding labelling, the application and use of precautionary approaches, and consideration of legitimate factors other than science in decision making. It therefore called upon the Codex Committees on Food Labelling and on General Principles for an early resolution of these matters.

The Task Force welcomed the initiative of the FAO and WHO to convene an Expert Consultation to support the scientific aspects of its work. In support of the programme of work outlined above, it requested advice on the five specific questions as contained in Appendix III to this report. It requested the FAO and WHO to make the results of the Consultation available as soon as possible to all interested parties.

PATENTS

A further controversial issue affecting food production is the increasing proliferation of patent applications for seeds and plants.

Patents are a form of intellectual property protection and give monopoly rights over an invention to its creator for up to 20 years. The rationale of intellectual property protection of any kind is that the creator of something,, whether it is artistic or commercial, should be able to benefit from and, to a certain extent, control the future exploitation of their invention or creation. A patentable invention can be either a product invention or a process invention. To be patentable it must be novel; there must be an 'inventive step' and it must be capable of industrial application Naturally occurring life forms cannot be patented but genetically engineered plants and animals can. Naturally occurring substances such as genes and hormones can also be patented so long as the 'inventor' can demonstrate a specific use for them. The holder of a patent for a human, animal or plant gene thus acquires control over the future commercial exploitation of that gene. With regard to food there is real concern that in this way the large biotechnology companies will gain considerable control over food production and supply.

CONCLUSION

It is clear from the above that there is a great deal of activity going on at international level with regard to the question of the safety of food derived from biotechnology. This is a reflection of the increasing concerns expressed by consumers and the refusal of many people to either grow or eat genetically modified products.

The increasing power of the global, multi-national companies to determine the trading rules for the world is making it increasingly difficult for individual nations or even groups of nations to maintain their own rules on food safety and composition where those rules appear to interfere with free trade. The whole issue of genetically modified and novel foods is inextricably bound up with the ongoing debate on free trade versus individual choice in food and agriculture.

CHAPTER 7

THE CHEMICAL SAFETY OF FOOD

INTRODUCTION

Food products contain a number of different substances. There will be the constituent *ingredients* and possibly also *additives* and *contaminants*. Ingredients are things that can be regarded as foodstuffs in their own right such as flour, sugar, butter and eggs used in a cake. Additives are substances which are included in the recipe but which are not foodstuffs in their own right and are there to serve a particular purpose such as flavourings, colourings, antioxidants etc. Contaminants are undesirable substances that are accidentally present in some foodstuffs. They can be present as a result of environmental pollution (for example, dioxins), as a result of an agricultural process (for example, pesticides) or as a result of microbiological growth (for example, aflatoxins). Food might also become contaminated by residues of veterinary medicines such as antibiotics or growth promoting hormones. In recent years consumers have also become all too aware that foods for human consumption can also become contaminated as a result of what the animals they eat are fed on.

ADDITIVES

In the European Union, different rules on additives in the different Member States constituted barriers to the free movement of goods. Accordingly, Directive 89/107 was introduced to regulate the situation.[1]

The Directive established lists of categories of food additives, contained in Annex I, which were to be authorised in food processing and manufacturing, based on agreed scientific and technological criteria. Annex I to the Directive lists 24 types of additive to which the Directive applies, these being substances that are 'used or intended to be used as ingredients during the manufacture or preparation of a foodstuff and are still present in the final product, even if in an altered form (Art 1(1)).

For the purposes of the Directive, 'food additive' is defined in line with the Codex Alimentarius definition:

---

1) Council Directive 89/107/EEC on the approximation of the laws of the Member States concerning food additives authorised for use in foodstuffs intended for human consumption (OJ 1989 L40/27).

> ... any substance not normally consumed as a food in itself and not normally used as a characteristic ingredient of food whether or not it has nutritive value, the intentional addition of which to food for a technological purpose in the manufacturing, processing, preparation, treatment, packaging, transport or storage of such food results, or may be reasonably expected to result in it or its by-products becoming directly or indirectly a component of such food [Art 1(2)].

Only those food additives which are included in the lists in Annex I may be used in the manufacture or preparation of foodstuffs and only under the conditions of use specified in the Annex. Additives are placed in the appropriate category according to their principal function. Additives can be authorised for a number of different functions, in which case they will be listed in a number of categories in Annex I.

The general criteria for listing in Annex I are contained in Annex II, which states that food additives can be approved only if:

(a) a reasonable technological need for their use can be demonstrated, which cannot be achieved by any other means which are economically and technologically practicable;

(b) they present no hazard to the health of the consumer at the level of use proposed, so far as can be judged on the available scientific evidence;

(c) they do not mislead the consumer.

Paragraph 2 of Annex II goes on to stress that 'The use of food additives may only be considered where there is evidence that the proposed use of the additive would have demonstrable advantages to the benefit of the consumer'. In other words, it is necessary to establish the case for what is commonly referred to as 'need'.

The use of a food additive should serve one or more of the following purposes:

(a) to preserve the nutritional quality of the food;

(b) to provide necessary ingredients or constituents for food manufactured for groups of consumers having special dietary needs;

(c) to enhance the keeping quality or stability of a food product;

(d) to assist in the manufacture, processing, preparation, treatment, packing, transport or storage of food provided that the additive is not used to disguise the effects of the use of faulty raw materials or of undesirable practices.

The Directive requires food additives to be subjected to appropriate toxicological testing and evaluation and to be kept under constant observation. They must be re-evaluated whenever necessary in the light of changing conditions of use and new scientific information.

Approval for food additives must:

198

(a) specify the foodstuffs to which these additives may be added and the conditions under which they may be added;

(b) be limited to the lowest level of use necessary to achieve the desired effect;

(c) take into account any acceptable daily intake (ADI) or equivalent assessment established for that food additive.

Under Art 4, Member States may derogate from the provisions of the Directive if new scientific evidence is produced or there is a re-evaluation of existing evidence which indicates that there might be a risk to human health from the use of a particular additive. In these circumstances, Member States may suspend the use of a particular additive.

Member States may also 'provisionally' authorise (for up to two years) a food additive within its territory, even if the additive is not included in one of the Annex I categories (Art 5).

In both the above situations, the Commission, having consulted the Standing Committee on Foodstuffs, will present a proposal to the Council for approval, as to whether to allow either the derogation or the provisional authorisation.

There are specific labelling requirements for food additives set down in the Directive, in Art 7 for additives not intended for sale to the ultimate consumer, and Art 8 for additives which are intended for sale to the ultimate consumer. The information must include the name under which the additive is sold, special conditions regarding storage and use, directions for use, a mark which will identify the batch or lot, the name or business name and address of the manufacturer, net quantity, and date of durability within the meaning of the framework Directive on food labelling.[2] This information must be presented in a language which can be understood by the purchaser. The Directive has been amended by Directive 94/34/EC[3] to permit certain specific exemptions to the harmonisation of the authorisation for all foodstuffs throughout the EU. Article 3 of the 1989 Directive has been amended to provide for certain derogations to the normal authorisation procedure for additives. Member States would be permitted to ban the use of certain food additives in the production of certain foodstuffs regarded as 'traditional' if the prohibition was already in place on 1 January 1992 and if the Member States allowed the production and sale within their territory of all foodstuffs not regarded as 'traditional' which comply with the rules contained in Art 3 of the 1989 Directive. The Member States had until 1 July 1994 to notify the Commission of their 'traditional' foods. Following this deadline, the Commission put forward proposals in June 1995[4] on the maintenance of national laws

---

2   Directive 79/112.

3   European Parliament and Council Directive 94/34/EC (OJ 1994 L237/1).

4   Commission Proposal for European Parliament and Council Directive COM 95(126) (OJ 1995 C134/20).

prohibiting the use of certain additives in the production of certain foodstuffs. An Annex to the proposal listed eight foodstuffs for which the Member States concerned could continue to prohibit the use of certain or all food additives. In December 1996, the European Parliament and the Council adopted a Decision[5] which allows Member States listed in the attached Annex to continue to prohibit the use of certain categories of additive in the production of certain foodstuffs.

In addition to the 1989 framework Directive, as amended, there are three other Directives dealing with the authorisation and conditions of use for specific types of additive. These are Directive 94/35 on sweeteners, Directive 94/36 on colours in foodstuffs and Directive 95/2 on other food additives. They were all introduced as measures to prevent barriers to the free movement of goods and to facilitate free trade. All three Directives acknowledge that the overriding concerns when making rules on additives must be the protection of the consumer and the avoidance of any harm to human health.

Directive 94/35 on sweeteners[6]

This Directive applies to food additives known as sweeteners which are used either in the manufacture of foodstuffs or which are added to food or drink at the table. Only sweeteners listed in the Annex to the Directive may be placed on the market and, in the case of sweeteners used in manufacturing foodstuffs, they may only be used in the manufacture of the foodstuffs listed in the Annex and under the conditions for use specified therein. The Annex also indicates the maximum usable dose for every sweetener used in food manufacturing. Some sweeteners may be used to the level known as *quantum satis*. This has been defined in Directive 96/83/EC[7] as indicating a dosage level not higher than is necessary to achieve the intended purpose, provided that the consumer is not misled.

The labelling requirements for foodstuffs containing sweeteners were introduced by Directive 96/21 EC,[8] which provides that foodstuffs containing a sweetener must indicate on the label 'with sweetener' together with the name under which the product is sold as required by the 1979 framework labelling Directive. Foodstuffs which contain added sugars should be labelled in the same way. For foodstuffs which contain aspartame, the label should state 'contains a source of phenylalanine'. For foodstuffs containing more than

---

5   European Parliament and Council Decision 292/97.

6   European Parliament and Council Directive 94/35 on sweeteners for use in foodstuffs.

7   European Parliament and Council Directive 96/83/EC (OJ 1997 L48/16) amending Directive 94/35/EC.

8   Council Directive 96/21/EC (OJ 1996 L88) which amended Commission Directive 94/54/EC (OJ 1994 L300/14) on labelling of food products which have been treated by packaging gases to prolong their shelf life.

10% added polyols, the label must state 'excessive consumption may produce laxative effects'.

Directive 94/35 was amended by Directive 96/83, mentioned above, which contained additions to the Annex.

Directive 94/36 on colours in foodstuffs[9]

The Directive acknowledges that the main concern for measures dealing with food additives such as colours should be the need to protect the consumer and avoid any harm to human health. The original framework Directive provides that food additives should only be used where it is technologically necessary and where the necessary safeguards are in place. Colours are usually used to make the food look more attractive to the consumer, particularly where the natural colour of the product might have been impaired during processing. Colour is also often used in conjunction with flavour, to make the appearance of the food match the flavour.

Under the Directive, colours are defined as 'substances which add or restore colour in a food, and include natural constituents of foodstuffs and natural sources which are normally not consumed as foodstuffs as such and not normally used as characteristic ingredients of food'.

As in the case of the Directive on sweeteners, only those substances listed in Annex I of the Directive may be used in foodstuffs. The list identifies specific permitted colours. Annex II lists foodstuffs in which colours may not be used, except in limited circumstances. Annexes III–V lay down the conditions for use of these specified colours, including the maximum amounts to be used. In some cases, as with the sweeteners Directive, there is no specified maximum and the *quantum satis* rule applies. The Directive does state, however, that colours should be used according to good manufacturing practice and at a level no higher than necessary to achieve the intended purpose, and that they must not mislead the consumer.

Commission Directive 95/45/EC[10] lays down specific criteria or purity concerning colours for use in foodstuffs.

Directive 95/2 on other food additives[11]

This Directive covers 23 different categories of additive including preservatives, antioxidants, modified starches, gelling agents, emulsifiers,

---

9   European Parliament and Council Directive on colours in foodstuffs (OJ 1994 L237/13).
10 OJ 1995 L226/1.
11 European Parliament and Council Directive 95/1/EC on food additives other than colours or sweeteners (OJ 1995 L61/1).

stabilisers, acids and anti-caking agents. All the additives are defined in Art 1(3). Annex I lists those additives in the 23 categories defined in Art 1(3) that may be used in foodstuffs. Annexes II–V list the additives which are permitted in certain foodstuffs and the maximum permitted levels.

Member States may apply to the Commission if they wish to have an additive added to one of the annexes in the additives Directive. If the Commission takes the view that the substance is appropriate, it will ask for the relevant scientific data from the applicant and will forward it to the EU Scientific Committee for Food (SCF) which will evaluate the safety of the substance. If the SCF approves the substance, the Commission will initiate the process to amend the relevant legislation. Only when the legislative process is complete will it be permissible to use the new substance in the manufacture of certain foodstuffs.

In 1999, the Commission issued a draft proposal for a third amendment to Directive 95/2, which contained the following aims:

- to allow certain additives which had previously been authorised on a national basis to be used at Community level;[12]

- to take account of the views of the Scientific Committee on Food (SCF) which had evaluated the use of hydrogen and found its use as a packaging gas to be toxicologically acceptable and considered that the establishment of an Acceptable Daily Intake (ADI) level was unnecessary;

- to allow some already authorised food additives[13] to be used in certain new applications;

- to allocate an E number to the authorised food additive Propane–1.2-diol (propylene glycol).

Two requests from the UK for new additive uses were contained in the proposal. The first was that hydrogen should be added to the list of additives in Annex I (food additives generally permitted for use in foodstuffs) and the second was that an entry to allow the use of the propellants butane, iso-butane and propane in vegetable oil pan sprays (for professional use only) and water-based emulsion sprays in *quantum satis* levels be included in Annex IV (other permitted additives). The use of water-based emulsion sprays had been permitted in the UK under a temporary UK national authorisation which expired at the end of December 1997. The Commission proposal would now permit the use of these propellants on an EU-wide basis.

There has been considerable controversy over the request by a French company for the inclusion of E401 Sodium alignate in Annex II (foodstuffs in

---

12 Ethyl hydroxyethyl cellulose; butane; iso-butane and propane.

13 Sodium alignate; E445 glycerol esters of wood rosin (requested by a German spirit drinks company in order to make some of its products cloudy), to be consistent with what is already allowed in soft drinks; E650 zinc acetate which had received a favourable opinion from the SCF on its safe use as a flavour enhancer in chewing gum.

which a limited number of additives from Annex I may be used) in order to improve the texture of prepacked, ready to eat carrots.

Adding additives to the list

The procedure for requesting a new additive to be listed is to contact the EU Commission. If DG III believes that the substance is appropriate, it will request the necessary scientific data from the applicant. Once submitted, the data will be forwarded to the EU Scientific Committee for Food for safety evaluation. Evaluation may take several months. If approved by the SCF, the Commission will then initiate the process to amend the legislation so as to add the substance to the appropriate directive. This can take a further 12–18 months. Only when the legislation has been passed will the substance then be permitted.

The Directives allow a Member State to grant temporary authorisation for products marketed on their territory. The maximum authorisation is two years after which, if the substance has not been added to the directive, sales must cease.

The law in the UK

The Directives have been implemented into UK legislation by the following Regulations which came into effect on 1 January 1996:

(a) the Sweeteners in Food Regulations 1995;[14]

(b) the Colours in Food Regulations 1995;[15] and

(c) the Miscellaneous Food Additives Regulations 1995.[16]

All these Regulations have been amended on a number of occasions.

Sweeteners

The Sweeteners in Food Regulations 1995 implement European Parliament and Council Directive 94/35/EC and Commission Directive 95/31/EC[17] laying down specific criteria concerning sweeteners for use in foodstuffs. The Regulations define 'food additive' and 'sweetener'; list the permitted sweeteners and, by cross-reference, the purity criteria with which they must comply; set down conditions of use for sweeteners in food; control the sale of sweeteners direct to the public (table top sweeteners) and specify additional

---

14   SI 1995/3123.
15   SI 1995/3124.
16   SI 1995/3187.
17   OJ 1995 L178/1.

labelling requirements for these products; and prohibit the sale and use of sweeteners and the sale of food containing sweeteners which do not comply with these provisions.

The Regulations are amended by the Sweeteners in Food (Amendment) Regulations 1996[18] and the Sweeteners in Food (Amendment) Regulations 1997.[19] The 1997 Regulations implemented EC Directive 96/83/EC, which amended Directive 94/35/EC. The Regulations extend the use of sweeteners to certain additional categories of food and add certain technical provisions to bring the 1995 Regulations in line with two other Great Britain Regulations on colours and miscellaneous additives. They also amend the title of the food category 'vitamins and dietary preparations' to reflect more closely the needs of the market.

The Sweeteners in Food (Amendment) Regulations 1999 came into force on 22 April 1999 to implement Directive 98/66/EC. They amend the Sweeteners in Food Regulations 1995 by updating a reference to Directive 95/31/EC on specific purity criteria to deal with its amendment by Directive 98/66/EC, which changed the specification for isomalt. The new Regulations also update the references to the 1995 Regulations contained in other Regulations.

Miscellaneous additives

The Miscellaneous Food Additives Regulations 1995 implemented European Parliament and Council Directive 95/2/EC on food additives other than colours and sweeteners ('miscellaneous additives'), together with various directives governing purity criteria. The Regulations define each class of miscellaneous food additives and list those which are permitted; specify the purity criteria with which they must comply; set conditions on their use; control their sale direct to the public; and prohibit the sale and use of miscellaneous additives, and the sale of food containing them, which do not comply with these provisions. The Miscellaneous Additives (Amendment) Regulations 1997[20] implemented EC Directives 96/85/EC[21] amending Directive 95/2/EC and 96/77/EC[22] laying down specific purity criteria on food additives other than colours and sweeteners. The Regulations also amend the 1995 Regulations to authorise a variation to the existing two year national authorisation to permit propane, butane and iso-butane to be used in water-based emulsion sprays until December 1997. In addition, they amend the Fruit Juices and Nectars Regulation 1977[23] to reflect an EC prohibition on

18 SI 1996/1477.
19 SI 1997/814.
20 SI 1997/1413.
21 OJ 1996 L86.
22 OJ 1996 L339.
23 SI 1997/927.

the simultaneous use of added acids and added sugar in fruit juices and make minor amendments to bring the text of the 1995 Regulations more closely in line with the wording used in Directive 95/2/EC.

The Miscellaneous Food Additives (Amendment) Regulations 1999[24] came into force on 28 May 1999 and amend the Miscellaneous Food Additives Regulations of 1995 for the second time. The 1999 Regulations implement EC Directives 98/72[25] and 98/86[26] in Great Britain. There are equivalent Regulations which cover Northern Ireland. The main provisions of the Regulations relating to the use of food additives are:

(a) to add flour treatment agents, currently regulated at national level, to the list of harmonised additives categories controlled under the provisions on miscellaneous additives;

(b) to add four new additives to the list of miscellaneous additives that are generally permitted for use in most foods;

(c) to provide for additional uses for additives in various foods;

(d) to add a number of new substances to the list of permitted carriers and carrier solvents;

(e) to provide for additional uses of certain additives in specified foods for infants and young children, including such foods for special medical purposes; and

(f) to place additional restrictions on the use of additives in plain pasteurised cream, and to reduce the level of sulphur dioxide permitted in certain sugars.

Colours

The Colours in Food Regulations 1995[27] implement European Parliament and Council Directive 94/36/EC and Commission Directive 95/45/EC. The Regulations define 'food additive' and 'colour'; list the permitted colours and, by cross-reference, the purity criteria with which they must comply; set down conditions of use for colours in food; control the sale of colours direct to the public, and prohibit the sale and use of colours and the sale of food containing colours which do not comply with these provisions.

---

24 SI 1999/1136.

25 European Parliament and Council Directive 98/72/EC, which amended Directive 95/2 on food additives other than colours or sweeteners.

26 Commission Directive 98/86, amending Commission Directive 96/77/EC which sets down specific purity criteria on food additives other than sweeteners.

27 SI 1995/3124.

The Colours in Food (Amendment) (England) Regulations 2000[28]amend the 1995 Colours in Food Regulations and implement Commission Directive 99/75/EC.[29]

The Food Additives Labelling Regulations of 1992[30] implement certain provisions of the 1989 Directive. The Regulations define food additives and lay down labelling requirements at retail and wholesale level for additives sold as such. These Regulations have been emended by the above mentioned Regulations[31] which implemented the specific EC Directives on sweeteners, colours and miscellaneous additives.

Flavourings

Council Directive 88/388/EEC[32] on the approximation on the laws of Member States relating to flavourings for use in foodstuffs and to source materials for their production is the framework flavourings Directive. It has been amended by Directive 91/71/EEC.[33]

In the UK, the Flavourings in Food Regulations 1992[34] implemented certain provisions of the above Directives. The Regulations define categories of flavourings to be controlled, lay down limits for certain undesirable substances that are present in some flavourings and should therefore be restricted. The Regulations prohibit the sale or importation of food having in it or on it any flavouring which is not a permitted flavouring (that is, one that does not comply with the general provisions). The Regulations also set down labelling requirements for business and consumer sales of flavourings sold as such. The Regulations were amended by the Flavourings in Food (Amendment) Regulations 1994.[35]

The European Commission has a Working Group on Flavourings which keeps the register of permitted flavourings under review. There is also an ongoing evaluation programme.

---

28 SI 2000/481.

29 Commission Directive 99/75/EC (OJ 1999 L286/19) which changed the specification for 'E160a(i) mixed carotenes'.

30 SI 1992/1978.

31 Sweeteners in Food Regulations 1995 (SI 1995/3123); Colours in Food Regulations 1995 (SI 1995/3124); Miscellaneous Food Additives Regulations 1995 (SI 1995/3187); Food Labelling Regulations 1996 (SI 1996/1499); Miscellaneous Food Additives (Amendment) Regulations 1999 (SI 1999/1136).

32 Council Directive 88/388/EEC on the approximation of the laws of Member States relating to flavouring for use in foodstuffs and to source materials for their production (OJ 1988 L184/61).

33 Commission Directive 91/71/EEC (OJ 1991 L42/25).

34 SI 1992/1971.

35 SI 1994/1486.

In July 1999, the Working Group on Flavourings met and, amongst other things, confirmed that so called 'precursor flavourings' (substances which do not in themselves have significant flavouring properties, but which react with other food components during processing to create flavour in the final food product) would be dealt with separately and would not be covered by the register.

A task group has been established by the Scientific Committee on Food (SCF) to consider the way in which the evaluation of flavourings should be carried out. The task group decided that the SCF should use the evaluation procedures adopted by the joint FAO/WHO Expert Committee on Food Additives (JECFA) with certain modifications relating to how exposure is estimated.

CONTAMINANTS

Unlike additives which are deliberately added to foods, contaminants are usually present unintentionally, although there can be deliberate or negligent contamination of foods. It has been argued that the presence of naturally occurring contaminants poses a greater threat to human health than the presence of synthetic substances.[36]

The Codex Alimentarius defines a contaminant as 'any substance mot intentionally added to food, which is present in such food as a result of the production (including operations carried out in crop husbandry, animal husbandry and veterinary medicine), manufacture, processing, preparation, treatment, packing, packaging, transport or holding of such food or as a result of environmental contamination. The term does not include insect fragments, rodent hairs and other extraneous matter'.

Regulation 315/93 EC deals with contaminants in foods. Under the Regulation, any foodstuff containing an unacceptable amount of a contaminant, as far as human health is concerned, will not be allowed to enter the market.

Mycotoxins

Mycotoxins are chemicals which are naturally produced by certain moulds in some foods. They are usually found in warm, damp conditions and occur mainly in foods imported into the UK or where dampness has affected storage. Foods which can be infected include nuts (particularly peanuts), cereal grains, dried fruit, spices and coffee. Laboratory studies have shown

---

36 Diggle, 'Risk assessment and natural toxins' (1992) 1 Natural Toxins 71.

Products at retail sale must comply with a maximum limit of 4 micrograms per kilogram.

3-MCPD[39]

3-MCPD is a chemical formed during processing of some foods. It is found in foods such as hydrolysed vegetable protein (HVP), dark speciality malts and malt extract (used as ingredients for dark beers), salami, toasted cereal products (such as toasted bread and crackers), some cooked foods and soy sauce. Laboratory studies have shown that 3-MCPD is carcinogenic and genotoxic (that is, it can cause damage to DNA).

Dioxins and PCBs[40]

Dioxins and PCBs are persistent organic chemical pollutants which do not break down easily and concentrate in fatty tissues. Dioxins are produced during most combustion processes, such as waste incineration. They are the unwanted by-products of some industrial processes. PCBs were manufactured for a wide range of uses, including use in lubricants and sealants in electrical appliances. The manufacture and general use of PCBs is now prohibited in the UK.

In May 1999, in Belgium, contaminated animal feed resulted in the contamination of animal products with dioxins and PCBs.

On 16 and 17 June 1999, an emergency joint meeting of the European Parliament's Agriculture Committee and its Environment and Consumer Protection Committee was called to consider the Belgian food contamination crisis. There were calls for the newly elected Parliament to take action against the guilty parties.

Demanding a radical rethink of the European Union's approach to food, MEPs called for a new food policy for Europe based on the integrated control of the whole food chain 'from stable to table'. The lessons of BSE, it was felt, had not been learned. One demand was for the establishment of an authoritative new parliamentary committee of inquiry – along the lines of the recent BSE committee of inquiry – to examine and propose solutions to the crisis sparked by the contamination, with cancer-causing dioxins, of feed for poultry, pigs and cattle in Belgium.

One possibility put forward by MEPs would be the creation of an autonomous body modelled on the US Food and Drugs Administration. Other demands were for improved consumer information; an end to cover-ups; government transparency; financial compensation for farmers; the establishment of food quality labelling and certification; and a ban on the

---

39 3-monochloropropane 1, 2-diol.
40 Polychlorinatedbiphenyls.

recycling of 'exhausted' fats and on the use of meat and bone meal in animal feed.

Economic interests should not prevail over food quality, it was said, and there was strong criticism of the Agenda 2000 decisions on this score. Some MEPs took the view that the profit motive was gaining a stranglehold over farm production in Europe at the expense of food safety.

The Belgian Ministers for Agriculture and Health who spoke at the meeting were given a hostile reception. They defended the action taken by Belgium in response to the crisis, admitting that mistakes had been made, but pointing out that vast numbers of checks were being carried out. They stressed that the original source of the contamination was still unknown and maintained that the problem was a 'one-off'.

However, the Consumer Protection and Agriculture Commissioners severely criticised the Belgian Government for its 'chaotic' handling of the crisis and suggested that the Belgian authorities had behaved much as the UK Government had when the BSE crisis broke. They had delayed reporting the contamination to the Commission until late May, although it had first caused poultry to fall sick in February, and had been traced in April to the presence of dioxins in supplies of fat used in the production of animal feedingstuffs.

Some MEPs voiced 'lurking suspicions' of systematic fraud and concerns about a black market, with 'mafiosi involvement', in suspect or banned products, with polluted waste material apparently being recycled back into the food chain.

The Council representative regretted that the Belgian authorities had left their own population and that of their European partners in the dark about the problem for weeks. The Council and the Commission were agreed that the rules on feed products had to be strengthened. The Commission considered that, in not informing the Commission and the other Member States immediately that dioxin had been found in foodstuffs and in animal feed, Belgium had failed to fulfil its obligations under Directive 89/662/EEC[41] and Directive 90/425/EEC.[42] The Commission also considered that Belgium had not fulfilled its obligations under certain Directives and Decisions in conjunction with Art 10 of the Treaty. Belgium had failed to fulfil its obligations by not taking steps to prohibit the marketing, distribution to the final consumer, trade within the Community and export to third countries of the products mentioned in Commission Decision 1999/389/EC (on protective measures with regard to contamination by dioxins of products intended for human consumption derived from bovine animals and pigs from establishments placed under veterinary supervision, in particular pigmeat,

---

41 Concerning veterinary checks in intra-Community trade with a view to the completion of the internal market.

42 Concerning veterinary and zootechnical checks applicable in intra-Community trade in certain live animals and products with a view to the completion of the internal market.

beef and veal, certain meat products, raw milk, heat-treated milk and milk products other than butter). For the above reasons, the Commission initiated infringement proceedings against Belgium under Art 226 of the Treaty.

Sewage sludge in French animal feed

On 10 June 1999, a Reuters report alleging contamination of French animal feed with waste was received by the Joint Food Safety and Standards Group (JFSSG) of the Ministry of Agriculture, Fisheries and Food and the Department of Health. JFSSG officials received oral assurances from their French counterparts on 15 June that these were isolated incidents and remedial action had been taken. The Commission, in the wake of the Belgian dioxin scandal, formally raised the issue with the French Government in mid-August and sent in a team of veterinary inspectors. Ministers in the UK were then advised by JFSSG that there was no basis for consumers to do other than continue with normal hygiene precautions in relation to the handling, storing and cooking of meat.

JFSSG acknowledged that the practice of using sewage sludge is both unacceptable from the consumer's point of view and illegal under European law. It had also kept under review whether this practice would cause any health risks to consumers of meat, milk or eggs obtained from animals fed sludge-containing feedingstuffs.

Food safety considerations

The use of sewage sludge in animal feed raises concerns about the potential microbiological and chemical safety of meat and other animal products. JFSSG made a careful assessment of these potential risks using its own in-house expertise as well as consulting external experts, including the chairmen of three independent advisory committees.

The term 'sewage sludge' is used in this context to describe the materials recovered from the treatment of waste water produced by plants processing animal waste into products such as gelatine and tallow. The term includes the solid waste removed by filters, material resulting from chemical/physical processing of the waste water (for example, using fat traps) and residues resulting from the biological treatment of the waste waters. In some plants, waste water from septic tanks handling human sewage from the plant was mixed with waste processing water which would have led to human waste being incorporated into the sewage sludge. The Commission is seeking to ensure that the provisions of Commission Decision 91/516/EEC which prohibit the use of sludge covers all three types of material. The Decision has been fully transposed into UK legislation. Domestic legislation in some Member States including France currently allows the first and second types of waste to be used in animal feed. Where sewage sludge has been used in this way, it has been mixed with other waste materials and heat-treated to produce meat meal for incorporation into animal feed. The sewage sludge concerned is stated to have been derived on site and there has been no suggestion that the output from municipal sewage plants might be involved.

The following assessments were made of the potential risks to consumer safety.

Microbiological safety

The sewage sludge would be mixed with other raw materials and subjected to heat treatment as part of the process used in the manufacture of meat meal. Pathogenic micro-organisms that might be present in the waste are sensitive to heat and would be effectively killed by the heat treatment. The Commission report states that the French authorities confirmed that the feed material is heat-treated and would not present any microbiological risks.

Chemical safety

A wide range of chemicals could potentially have contaminated the sewage sludge, including heavy metals, organochlorine compounds (for example, dioxins, PCBs), residues of veterinary medicines, disinfectants and detergents. The French authorities were only able to provide analytical data on certain heavy metals. These data gave rise to no food safety concerns. Organic chemicals, such as dioxins and PCBs, are widespread in the environment. Although they would be expected to be present in these materials at the normal background levels, there is no reason to expect that the sludge used in animal feed would contain unusually elevated levels. All Member States undertake statutory surveillance programmes for veterinary residues such as hormones and antibiotics and the results of this programme for France do not give rise to any particular concerns. It is possible that residues of detergents and disinfectants used in the plant might occur in sewage sludge, but these compounds are of low toxicity and are unlikely to occur at levels of concern. In general, any sewage sludge would not have been a major input into feedingstuffs and any chemical contaminants present would be further diluted by other materials.

The report produced by the Commission's veterinary inspectors stated that waste from the biological treatment of waste water is no longer incorporated into animal feed. This change produces an additional reassurance that French animal products do not pose any unacceptable food safety risk. Overall, it was concluded that chemical contaminants were unlikely to pose immediate health concerns.

Conclusion and JFSSG advice

The practice of adding sewage sludge to animal feed is repugnant to consumers and illegal under Community law. The UK has fully supported the action being taken by the Commission to ensure that Community rules are properly enforced. JFSSG advise strongly that the UK should continue to press for compliance with this law in France and other Member States.

JFSSG advised on the basis set out above that there was no immediate public health risk and therefore no basis for seeking a ban on French products either at a Community level, or unilaterally. JFSSG continues to monitor the situation.

Food contact materials and articles

The Materials and Articles in Contact with Food Regulations 1987[43] re-enact the Materials and Articles in Contact with Food Regulations 1978, as amended, and implement Council Directive 83/229/EEC.[44] These Regulations set out the general requirement that all food contact materials and articles should not transfer their constituents to the food with which they have contact in quantities which could endanger human health or make the food otherwise unacceptable to consumers. The Regulations also lay down requirements for labelling materials and articles as suitable for food contact use. A restriction is imposed on the use of vinyl chloride monomer (VCM) in the manufacture of food contact plastics, by setting a residual limit of one milligram VCM per kilogram of material or article and a migration limit of 0.01 milligrams VCM per kilogram of food, and laying down the laboratory methods for testing compliance with these restrictions. The Regulations place controls on food contact with regenerated cellulose film (RCF), by establishing a 'positive list' of substances that can be used in the manufacture of coated and uncoated RCF, and setting migration limits for some substances.

The 1978 Regulations implemented the framework Council Directive 76/893/EEC, which was replaced by Council Directive 89/109/EEC.[45] The 1987 Regulations, which re-enact the 1978 Regulations, did not require amendment to implement 89/109/EEC.

The Regulations are amended by a number of later Regulations.[46]

---

43 SI 1987/1523.

44 OJ 1983 L123, as amended by Commission Directive 86/388/EEC (OJ L128, 14.8.86).

45 OJ 1989 L40/38.

46 Food Safety Act 1990 (Consequential Modifications) (No 2) (Great Britain) Order 1990 (SI 1990/2487); Food Safety (Exports) Regulations 1991 (SI 1991/1476), which implements Council Directive 89/397/EEC (OJ L186, 30.6.89), Arts 2 and 3; Materials and Articles in Contact with Food (Amendment) Regulations 1994 (SI 1994/979), which implement Commission Directive 93/10/EEC (OJ L94, 17.4.93), as amended by Commission Directive 93/111/EEC (OJ L310, 14.12.93) and Commission Directive 92/15/EEC (OJ L102, 16.4.92), amending Council Directive 83/229/EEC (OJ L123, 11.5.83).

Pesticides

The use of pesticides in the growing of crops is an issue of concern for consumers because of fears about the levels of residues that are found in food products. In September 2000 the UK Working Party on Pesticide Residues (now known as the Pesticide Residues Committee) published its 1999 Report in which it indicated that almost all pesticide residues levels were well within the safety levels set by independent experts. Of the 2,500 food samples tested, using 85,000 different tests, only two[47] presented any possible health risk to the public and appropriate action was swiftly taken to deal with the problem.

Consumers are also concerned about the possibility of multiple residues in foodstuffs (the so called 'cocktail' effect) and this has been recognised by the Chairman of the Food Standards Agency who indicated that expert advice was being sought from a working group of the Committee on Toxicity of Chemicals in Food, Consumer Products and the Environment.[48]

On 9 February 2001, the Food Standards Agency issued a statement on its approach to the acceptability of residues of pesticides and veterinary medicines in food.

In the UK there are a number of statutory instruments, implementing various EC measures which set limits on the maximum residues levels permitted in specific foodstuffs.

The Pesticides (Maximum Residue Levels in Crops, Food and Feeding Stuffs) Regulations 1994[49] implement the provisions of Council Directives 90/642/EEC (OJ L350, 14.12.90), 93/57 (OJ L211, 23.8.93) and 93/58/EEC (OJ L211, 23.8.93) setting maximum residue levels (MRLs) for fruit and vegetables, cereals and animal products. They also introduce some national MRLs pending the adoption of Community provisions.

The Pesticides (Maximum Residue Levels in Crops, Food and Feeding Stuffs) (Amendment) Regulations 1995[50] implement EC Directives 94/29/EC[51] and 94/30/EC[52] setting further MRLs for fruit and vegetables, cereals and animal products.

The Pesticides (Maximum Residue Levels in Crops, Food and Feedingstuffs) (Amendment) Regulations 1996[53] implement EC Directives

---

47 Chlormequat in a pear sample and Methamidophos in a sweet pepper.
48 FSA Press Release (2000/0040), 19 September 2000.
49 SI 1994/1985.
50 SI 1995/1483.
51 OJ 1994 L189.
52 OJ 1994 L189.
53 SI 1996/1487.

95/38/EC[54] and 95/39/EC[55] setting further MRLs for fruit and vegetables, cereals and animal products. They also implement Directive 95/61/EC[56] by establishing MRLs for certain 'open positions' set in Directive 93/58/EC.

The Pesticides (Maximum Residue Levels in Crops, Food and Feeding Stuffs) (Amendment) Regulations 1997[57] implement EC Directives 96/32/EC[58] and 96/33/EC[59] setting further MRLs for fruit and vegetables, cereals and animal products.

Irradiation

Commercial food irradiation is normally carried out using electron beams generated by machines or gamma rays emitted from the element Cobalt–60. When food is exposed to ionising radiation, charged molecules called ions are produced along with short-lived molecules, known as free radicals. These molecules kill many micro-organisms and also interact with the food itself. It is the action of these molecules, rather than the radiation itself, that is responsible for the preservative effects of food irradiation.

Food irradiation can be used to kill pathogenic organisms in a range of foods including herbs and spices, poultry meat and shellfish. It can also be used to reduce spoilage, to delay ripening in fruit, and to prevent sprouting in vegetables such as potatoes and onions.

On the basis of scientific studies, the Food and Agriculture Organisation, the International Atomic Energy Agency and the World Health Organisation (FAO/IAEA/WHO) concluded in 1980 that the irradiation of any food up to a maximum dose of 10 kGy is considered to be safe. In fact, WHO encourages the use of the irradiation process in order to reduce the incidence of food-borne diseases caused by micro-organisms.

Building upon the work of the FAO, the IAEA and the WHO, the EU Scientific Committee on Food (SCF) expressed opinions on irradiated foods in 1986, 1992 and 1998. It gave favourable opinions on irradiation of a number of foodstuffs (fruit, vegetables, cereals, starchy tubers, spices and condiments, fish, shellfish, fresh meats, poultry, camembert from raw milk, frogs' legs, gum arabic, casein/caseinates, egg white, cereal flakes, rice flour and blood products). The SCF emphasised that food irradiation must not be used to cover negligence in handling foodstuffs or to mask their unsuitability for use as food.

---

54 OJ 1995 L197.
55 OJ 1995 L197.
56 OJ 1995 L292.
57 SI 1997/567.
58 OJ 1996 L144.
59 OJ 1996 L144.

In 1999, the FAO/IAEA/WHO published the report of a study group on the wholesomeness of food irradiated with doses above 10 kGy. This study group concluded that food irradiated with any dose appropriate to achieve the intended technological objective is both safe to consume and nutritionally adequate.

Detection methods are available for most of the foods which can be irradiated. These methods are validated and either already standardised by the European Committee for Standardisation (CEN) or in the process of CEN standardisation. Thus, analytical control of whether irradiated foods are correctly labelled is possible in most cases, even at the level of the final products. In the few remaining cases, documentary control is an alternative.

As far as the application of irradiation is concerned, it is the case that, although existing authorisations in certain Member States allow the irradiation of a number of foods and food ingredients, in practice very few of them are actually irradiated. The total amount of a particular food which is treated by ionising radiation is, in most cases, small in comparison to the untreated amounts.

The main application of irradiation is the reduction of micro-organisms in food ingredients intended for the production of industrially produced compound foodstuffs in order to extend the shelf life of the final products. This is especially the case for ingredients which are added to products for which the production process does not involve heating, such as yoghurt containing flakes of cereals or white cheese containing herbs and spices. Certain foodstuffs intended for the direct use of the consumer may be contaminated with Salmonella, Listeria or other harmful micro-organisms which can affect the health of the consumers (for example, chicken and red meat, eggs, cheese from raw milk). Some of these products, especially frogs' legs and shrimps, are often insufficiently heated during preparation to destroy these harmful micro-organisms or even ingested without further heat treatment. Health hazards may also arise from cross-infection of utensils and other foodstuffs at the place of culinary preparation. Since irradiation is a suitable method for decontamination, these products are often treated by ionising radiation in countries in which this is authorised.

In February 1999, the European Council and the European Parliament published two EC Directives on foods and food ingredients treated with ionising radiation in the Official Journal of the European Communities.

The framework Directive 1999/2/EC[60] on the approximation of the laws of Member States concerning foods and food ingredients treated with ionising radiation, covers general and technical aspects for carrying out the process, labelling of irradiated foods and conditions for authorising food irradiation. The Directive lays down the general provisions such as the conditions for

---

60 European Parliament and Council Directive 199/2/EC (OJ 1999 L399/2).

treatment, the rules governing the approval and control of irradiation and the labelling of foodstuffs that have been treated with ionising radiation.

The framework Directive requires or provides specifically that:

(a) food irradiation may only be authorised if:
   - there is a reasonable technological need;
   - it presents no health hazard and is carried out under the conditions proposed;
   - it is of benefit to the consumer;
   - it is not used as a substitute for hygiene and health practices or for good manufacturing or agricultural practice;

(b) any food irradiated as such or containing irradiated food ingredients has to be labelled;

(c) a favourable opinion of the Scientific Committee on Food (SCF) is needed to place a food on the positive list;

(d) national authorisations of Member States which allow the irradiation of certain foods can be maintained until the completed positive list enters into force;

(e) until the completed positive list enters into force, Member States may also maintain restrictions or bans of irradiated foods, in compliance with the Treaty;

(f) Member States shall ensure that the analytical methods used to detect irradiated foods are validated or standardised;

(g) foodstuffs, including those imported from third countries, may only be irradiated in approved irradiation facilities.

The implementing Directive 1999/3/EC on the establishment of a Community list of food and food ingredients authorised for treatment with ionising radiation makes provision for a 'positive list' of foods to be authorised throughout the EU for irradiation treatment. So far, this positive list contains only a single food category: 'dried aromatic herbs, spices and vegetable seasonings'.

The food irradiation Directives 1999/2/EC and 1999/3/EC became applicable on 20 September 2000. However the issue of which foodstuffs should be allowed to be treated by ionising radiation has still to be resolved.

A requirement was introduced in Directive 1999/2/EC that the Commission should forward a proposal by 31 December 2000 to complete the Community positive list of foodstuffs authorised for irradiation. Until this positive list is completed, Member States can maintain existing national authorisations for irradiation of certain foodstuffs and can continue to apply existing national restrictions or bans. This situation is confusing for consumers and detrimental to the functioning of the internal market. It is to be hoped that, in the interests of consumers and to achieve a degree of certainty in this area, agreement on a Community list will be reached soon.

ANTIBIOTICS AND HORMONES

One of the most disturbing features of modern food production is the use of hormones and antibiotics. There are two separate issues in respect of these products: there is the use of growth promoting hormones and there is the regular use of antibiotics either for growth promotion or for prophylactic reasons. These issues raise concerns not only about the potential risks to human health, but also about the moral and ethical questions about the health and welfare of animals. As consumers demand more and cheaper food, there is a risk that there might be long term harm caused to human health as well as to the health of animals. It appears to be very difficult to justify the regular use of antibiotics not to cure disease, but to promote growth in animals – to make them bigger and fatter – or to prevent them from contracting disease. Is it ethically acceptable for animals to be treated in this way just so that consumers can have cheaper meat?

The use of antibiotics

There is growing concern that the global use of antibiotics is increasing in human medicines and in animal husbandry. Resistance to antibiotics is also increasing and has occurred in all classes of antibiotics currently developed, and multiple drug resistance is becoming more common.

In order to understand how the use of antibiotics in UK agriculture had become such a contentious issue, it is helpful to consider briefly the historical development of their use and attempts to control their use.

The Penicillin Act 1947 restricted the use of penicillin, streptomycin and chlortetracycline to that prescribed by a doctor, vet or dentist. In 1953, the Therapeutic Substances (Prevention of Misuse) Bill was introduced. This Bill extended the restrictions which applied to penicillin, streptomycin and chlortetracycline to new antibiotics which were then coming onto the market. But, the Bill also allowed penicillin and chlortetracycline (marketed as Aureomucin) to be made available to farmers and feed compounders, without veterinary prescription, to add to pig and poultry feed in small amounts to make the animals grow faster.

In Parliament, only one MP expressed his opposition to the Bill. Colonel Gomme-Duncan said: 'May I ask whether we have all gone mad to give penicillin to pigs to fatten them? Why not give them good food as God meant them to have?' This expression of incredulity must surely be on the lips of many people today when they realise the full extent of the use on antibiotics for purposes other than curing disease.

Although some MPs asked about the possibility of residues and resistance, they were reassured by Sir Thomas Dugdale, Minister for Agriculture, Fisheries and Food and Ian MacLeod, the Minister of Health, who said: 'I am assured by the Medical Research Council ... that there will be no adverse effect whatever on human beings.'

MPs were told that by adding small amounts of these antibiotics to pig and poultry feed, the animals would grow faster and, thereby, increase the supply of cheap meat, a tempting thought after the very recent shortages caused by the Second World War.

Further legislation in 1956 dealt with new antibiotics, but did not include tylosin, which was already being used for growth promotion in pigs. As a result of its omission, tylosin remained an unscheduled medicine until 1971.

Scientists were already aware in 1953 that some bacteria were resistant to penicillin and, in 1959, the Japanese scientist, Watanabe, had discovered that antibiotic resistance could be transferred from one type of bacteria to another. In the light of this evidence, in 1960, the Agricultural and Medical Research Councils established a joint committee (the Nettlethorpe Committee) to examine the consequences of feeding antibiotics to animals. Its terms of reference were limited. Its main conclusion was that the practice was quite safe. It recommended that the use of growth promoting antibiotics could be extended to calves up to three months of age. This recommendation was implemented in 1971.

As a result of public concern following the outbreak of multi-drug-resistant Salmonella food poisoning in the 1960s, an independent advisory committee was established in 1968 – the Swann Committee. Its remit was to examine the issue of transferable antibiotic resistance and the possible consequences for human and animal health arising from the use of antibiotics for growth promotion and in veterinary medicine. The Committee reported in 1969.[61] Its main recommendation was that permission to supply and use drugs without prescription in animal feed should be restricted to antibiotics which are of economic value in livestock production under UK farming conditions, have little or no application as therapeutic agents in man or animals, and will not impair the efficacy of a prescribed therapeutic drug or drugs through the development of resistant strains of organisms.

The Swann Report specifically mentioned penicillin, the tetracyclines and tylosin as antibiotics which did not satisfy the three criteria and which should, therefore, not be sold without prescription. The report also recommended that

---

61 Swann, MM, Blaxler, KL, Field, HI, Howie, JW, Lucas, AIM, Miller, ELM, Murdock, JC, Parsons, JH and White, EG, *Report of the Joint Committee on the Use of Antibiotics in Animal Husbandry and Veterinary Medicine*, Cmnd 4190, 1969, London: HMSO.

a single, permanent committee should be established with 'responsibility for the whole field of use of antibiotics and related substances, whether in man, animals, food preservation or for other purposes' to oversee medical and veterinary use of antibiotics. The committee would also be responsible for monitoring trends in antibiotic use and resistance. The report also recommended that this committee 'should review periodically existing antibiotics and their use to ascertain whether changing circumstances justify either greater relaxation or more restrictive control'.

The Swann Committee was dealing with an issue where many commercial interests were involved. There was great resistance to the idea of restricting the use of antibiotics for growth promotion and following the publication of the report there was a concerted campaign against it by the farming and pharmaceutical industries. Probably partly as a result of this negative campaign, the incoming administration in 1970 either ignored or failed to implement fully many of the main recommendations of the report and successive governments have failed to implement the report in full. Penicillin and the tetracyclines continued to be prescribed for growth promotion by vets following the Swann Report, despite its recommendations.

In 1973, the government established a Joint Sub-Committee on Antimicrobial Substances (JCAMS). It did not have many powers and was made responsible to both the Veterinary Products Committee and the Committee on Safety of Medicines. The Committee did not have the powers the Swann Report had recommended and one of the areas in which the Committee's members felt particularly impotent was in relation to the review of existing antibiotics. This was of particular importance at that time, the early 1970s, as the UK had just joined the European Communities and a range of antibiotics which were permitted in various EEC Member States were under consideration for scheduling as non-prescription food additives for growth promotion under Directive 70/524.

It appears that the VPC would not allow the sub-committee to undertake a review of existing antibiotics or to obtain data on the use of antibiotics or to monitor resistance. The committee discussed the issues in detail and eventually the chairman, Sir James Howie, wrote to the Minister of Agriculture, Fisheries and Food and the Minister of Health explaining their concerns and requesting increased powers. The ministers refused even to discuss the issues and immediately abolished the Sub-Committee.[62]

Although two microbiologists were appointed to the VPC following the abolition of the Sub-Committee, the VPC has had no committee to advise it on antibiotic resistance since that time.

---

62 Howie, J, 'The situation in the UK – then and now', in *Ten Years on from Swann*, 1981, London: The Association of Veterinarians in Industry, Royal College of Physicians, pp 3–7.

Despite the potential threat to human health caused by the prophylactic or inappropriate use of antibiotics, as well as their use for growth promotion, the Swann Committee concluded that 'it would in any case be difficult to frame or enforce legislation to allow the prescription of antibiotics for some purposes but not for others. We recommend, therefore, that no change should be made to the law which allows the supply of antibiotics on veterinary prescription'.

In 1997, a World Health Organisation report[63] drew attention to the problem of antibiotic resistance in farm animals and passing to humans. It concluded that 'the magnitude of the medical and public health impact of antimicrobial use in food animal production is not known'.

This is a frightening thought, and explains why, increasingly, the countries of the EU are adopting a more 'precautionary' approach to the use of antibiotics. In the light of the increasing evidence of resistance and the horrors of BSE, it appears that people are increasingly taking the view that, while the risks of the use of a particular substance or product remain unknown, the best approach is one of caution.

In April 1998, the House of Lords' Science and Technology Select Committee produced a report on the subject of antibiotic resistance[64] and warned of the 'dire prospect of revisiting the pre-antibiotic era'.[65]

In July 1999, the EU suspended the use of four of the antibiotic growth promoters which had been included in the feed of most poultry and pigs and in the farming of some cattle.

In August 1999, in the UK, the Advisory Committee on the Microbiological Safety of Food (ACMSF) published its report on antibiotic resistance.[66] The report examines the role of food in the transfer of antibiotic-resistant bacteria from animals to humans. The report makes a number of wide ranging recommendations which include the collection of data on the use of antibiotics in animals, increased monitoring and surveillance for resistant micro-organisms, the development of standard methodologies to improve comparability of data between laboratories investigating clinical diseases in human beings and animals, the development of Codes of Practice for the veterinary profession in the use of antimicrobial products and improvement of on-farm animal husbandry practices. The report also calls for a considerable amount of research to be done into the subject of antibiotic resistance.

The Soil Association has produced two reports on the subject under the heading 'The use and misuse of antibiotics in UK agriculture'. The first

---

63 WHO, *The Medical Impact of the Use of Antibiotics in Food Animals: Report of a WHO Meeting*, Berlin, 13–17 October 1997.

64 House of Lords, *Resistance to Antibiotics and Other Antimicrobial Agents*, 1998, London: HMSO.

65 House of Lords, 'Lords lead fight against killer bugs', press information, 23 April 1998.

66 Advisory Committee on the Microbiological Safety of Food, *Report on Microbial Antibiotic Resistance in Relation to Food Safety*, 1999, London: HMSO.

report[67] dealt with the current usage of antibiotics and the second[68] dealt with antibiotic resistance and human health.

The reports form part of the Soil Association's campaign against the excessive use of antibiotics and, as such, obviously represent a particular viewpoint. Nevertheless, they contain factual information and statistics which demonstrate the level of antibiotic use and highlight the potential risks to human health.

The first part on current usage contains the first detailed statistics for 30 years on the tonnage of antibiotics used on farms, and highlights the extent to which the use of antibiotics in intensive livestock production has continued to increase despite previous attempts to restrict it.

The key findings of the report are summarised on p 3 of the report and are quoted below:

> tetracycline use has increased by 1,500% in 30 years when it was supposed to fall;
>
> Penicillin-type drug use has increased by 600% over the same period;
>
> comparing industry estimates with published figures from the Department of Health suggests that about 1,225 tonnes of antibiotics are used annually in the UK in the following proportions: farm animals, 37%; pets and horses, 25%; medical use, 38%;
>
> inclusion of the ionophones – a major class of in-feed antibiotics, which the industry leaves out of its tables on a technicality – would give a considerably higher percentage for farm use;
>
> the Ministry of Agriculture, Fisheries and Food does not collect data on antibiotic use on farms, despite this being a recommendation of several independent committees;
>
> as many as 12,000 farmers in the UK may be illegally top dressing livestock feed with antibiotics;
>
> there is a major disagreement between the British Veterinary Association and the pharmaceutical industry over the advertising of prescription-only medicines directly to farmers;
>
> virtually all growing pigs and broiler chickens receive antibiotics in their feed throughout their lives up to and the day of slaughter;
>
> most intensively reared cattle are fed antibiotics routinely in replacement milk powders, compounded feed and feed blocks;
>
> banning individual antibiotics will not stop the problem continuing to get worse. A complete change in the way animals are reared is required.

---

67 Harvey, J and Mason, L, 'The use and misuse of antibiotics in UK agriculture', Part 1: Current Usage, The Soil Association, December 1998.

68 Young, R, Cowe, A, Nunan, C, Harvey, J and Mason, L, 'The use and misuse of antibiotics in UK agriculture,' Part 2: Antibiotic Resistance and Human Health, The Soil Association, October 1999 (amended).

The Soil Association calls for:

> a ban on all non-medical use of antibiotics in agriculture;

> the prophylactic use of therapeutic medicines to be restricted to cases of genuine need and only made available as part of a planned disease reduction programme involving changes in housing, feeding and management practice;

> co-ordination of all Government departments, agencies and other bodies with a statutory involvement in the regulation of antibiotic use on farms to be undertaken by the proposed Food Standards Agency;

> responsibility for the safety evaluation of veterinary medicines to pass to the Food Standards Agency as proposed in the Green Paper;

> the establishment by Government of a surveillance system for antimicrobial resistance comparable with that for anti-microbial residues;

> the central annual collection of data on the use of antimicrobial agents on farms, in order to monitor trends in usage;

> livestock products imported into the European Union to be subject to routine surveillance for bacteria carrying antibiotic resistance and subject to the same controls in relation to permitted antibiotics as those produced within the EU;

> a ban on the advertising of antibiotics directly to farmers.

The Soil Association further recommended that:

> veterinary surgeons should charge directly for advice and recoup a smaller percentage of their income from the sale of drugs;

> veterinary and agricultural colleges should place greater emphasis on the teaching of drug-free preventative medicine.

In Part 2 of the Soil Association report, 'Antibiotic resistance and human health', the paradox that lies at the heart of the problem of antibiotic use is outlined. To bring a new antibiotic on to the market in the US costs, it has been estimated, between \$100 m and \$350 m.[69] Drug companies which invest such large amounts of money will want to see a return on their investment and that means they will want to sell as much of the product as possible. This is precisely where the problem lies. The drugs need to be developed, but then preferably not used. It has become clear recently that the use of antibiotics in human medicines has caused resistance to occur in many bacterial diseases. It is also suggested that resistance can pass from farm animals to humans.

Bacteria

Bacteria are the smallest, single cell, free-living organisms known. They are normal and essential organisms which exist in the intestines of humans and

---

69 Gold, HS and Moellering, Jr, MD, 'Anti-microbial drug resistance' (1996) 35 New England Journal of Medicine 1445.

animals and also on the skin, in the mouth and in the respiratory and genito-urinary tracts.

Bacteria multiply by cell division. A bacterial cell will divide into two cells, each of which will normally carry the same genetic information as the other. Bacteria multiply very quickly.

Antibiotics were originally fermented from natural micro-organisms but are now often produced synthetically. Antibiotics cure diseases either by killing the bacteria or by inhibiting their growth and multiplication. If the bacteria are resistant to the antibiotics used against them, the disease will not be cured; the bacteria survive and can go on to infect other people or animals.

There are a number of ways in which bacteria can become resistant to antibiotics. It can occur through competitive selection or through mutation. It can also occur through gene transfer. Gene transfer is where a resistant gene is transferred from one bacterium to another enabling resistance to spread from one species of bacteria to another (horizontal transmission).

As the Soil Association report points out, horizontal transmission has been recognised as a major cause of increasing antibiotic resistance and it is the process of horizontal transmission 'pushed well beyond its natural limits' which is used by scientists to create genetically modified plants and animals.[70] Antibiotic-resistant genes are widely used in genetic engineering, and some scientists believe that this might contribute to the resistance problem.[71]

Most antibiotics used for animals are the same as, or related to, those used in humans. Resistance can pass from animals to humans in a number of ways: by direct contact with an infected animal, by eating contaminated meat, by consuming contaminated eggs or milk, by eating food containing antibiotic residues, by eating contaminated fruit or vegetables or by eating food containing antibiotics used as food preservatives.

Plants can carry bacteria and transfer them to people. Plants can become contaminated by animal bacteria when fresh manure is used. They can also become contaminated through being sprayed with antibiotics to prevent bacterial diseases.

Normally, bacteria are beneficial, but some of them cause disease. The development of antibiotic resistance is an inevitable consequence of the use of antibiotics. When the appropriate antibiotics are used selectively and in full therapeutic doses for short periods in individual people or animals, there should not be any problems. Any resistant strains that might develop will usually not last long and will be replaced by sensitive strains quite quickly. Where antibiotics are used continually, and where there is little or no exposure to sensitive strains to compete with the resistant strains, then resistance can

---

70 *Op cit*, fn 61, p 19.
71 *Op cit*, fn 61, Appendix III.

become established. This is what occurs, for example, in intensive livestock rearing and in places such as hospitals.

There is now a considerable body of evidence to show that, in the case of food poisoning, bacteria resistance to the tetracyclines is almost entirely due to the use of the antibiotics in farm animals. Multi-drug resistance is an increasing problem.

Hormones

As well as the problem of using antibiotics for growth promotion, certain hormones are also used in some countries. The use of hormonal growth promoters has been banned in the EC since 1988. Third countries which allow the use of such products are required to guarantee that no animal or meat coming from an animal treated with these hormones is exported to the EC.

There has been a great deal of controversy over the use of growth promoting hormones in cattle. The EU and the US have been involved in a protracted legal dispute over the issue of the EU ban on these hormones. The US believes that the ban is a breach of the EU's obligations under the World Trade Organisation Agreements.

In 1996, the US and Canada held formal consultations in the framework of the WTO dispute settlement mechanism with the EU regarding its legislation covering the ban on hormones (17 beta-oestradiol, progesterone, testosterone, zeranol, trenbolone and melengestrol acetate) for growth promoting purposes in livestock. Following requests from the two countries, WTO panels were set up to assess the conformity of the EU measures with its WTO obligations. The reports from these panels were delivered in August 1997. The EU measures were found to be in breach of a number of WTO rules. The EU objected to the conclusions of the panels in September 1997, which were consequently submitted for review to the Appellate Body.

On 13 February 1998, the report of the Appellate Body was adopted which, in particular, found that the Community had provided:

> ... general studies which do indeed show the existence of a general risk of cancer; but they do not focus on and do not address the particular kind of risk at stake here – the carcinogenic or genotoxic potential of the residues of those hormones found in meat derived from cattle to which the hormones had been administered for growth promotion purposes ... those general studies are in other words relevant, but do not appear to be sufficiently specific to the case at hand.

The Appellate Body clarified, however, that a WTO member:

(a) has the right to choose the level of health protection it deems appropriate;

(b) is not obliged to assess risk in a quantitative form in order to be able to take measures;

(c) is not obliged to follow majority and mainstream scientific views – minority views can also be taken into account.

It also overruled the earlier Panel ruling that the EC had not been consistent in the level of protection it had set for hormones used for growth promotion on the one hand and naturally occurring hormones on the other.

The report mentioned Art 5.7, which deals with measures taken when scientific information is insufficient. This article permits members to take measures, but they must be provisional and based on pertinent information. Members are obliged to seek the additional information necessary for a more objective assessment of risk and to review the measures within a reasonable period of time.

The Appellate Body recommended that the EC bring its measures into conformity with its obligations under the SPS Agreement. On 29 May 1998, the Arbitrator granted the Community a 'reasonable period' of 15 months from the adoption of the recommendations to implement those recommendations – that is, until 13 May 1999.

Following the indications of the WTO Appellate Body, in early 1998 the Commission launched a series of 17 studies concerning the issues the Appellate Body indicated as relevant to improve and complement current knowledge. They concern toxicological aspects, residue analysis, abuse and control aspects and environmental aspects.

In response to the WTO Appellate Body's main concern about the need for a comprehensive risk assessment, the Commission mandated the Scientific Committee of Veterinary measures relating to Public Health (SCVPH) at the end of 1998 to deliver an assessment of the risk to human health arising from the use of the six hormones as growth promoters, in particular from residues in meat and meat products.

The SCVPH adopted its opinion in April 1999, concluding that for all six hormones, endocrine, developmental, immunological, neurobiological, immunotoxic and carcinogenic effects could be envisaged.

On 17 May 1999, the Commission issued two press releases highlighting the findings of the Scientific Committee for Veterinary Measures relating to Public Health (SCVPH). In one of them[72] it was stated that the main finding of the SCVPH was that 'the use of six growth hormones for growth promotion in cattle poses a risk to the consumers but with different levels of conclusive evidence'.[73]

The independent scientists had concluded that there is substantial recent evidence that the natural hormone 17-oestradiol has to be considered as a

---

72 Health and Consumer Protection Directorate, General Press Release, 'Growth hormones in meat pose risk to consumers – different levels of evidence'.

73 The six growth hormones were 17-oestradiol, progesterone, testosterone, xeranol, trenbolone, and melengesterol acetate (NGA).

complete carcinogen and that it exerts both tumour initiating and tumour promoting effects. This means that even small additional doses of residues of this hormone in meat, arising from its use as a growth promoter in cattle, carry an inherent risk of causing cancer. The data available did not allow a quantitative estimate of the risk. For the other five hormones, the available information was also considered to be inadequate for a quantitative assessment. With respect to all six hormones, the report envisaged the possibility of 'endocrine, developmental, immunological, neurological, immunotoxic, genotoxic and carcinogenic effects', but the available data did not enable a quantitative assessment of the risk. The Committee stressed that exposure even to small amounts of residues in meat and meat products carries a risk and that no threshold levels could be established for any of the substances. Prepubertal children were the risk group which gave greatest concern.

In the other press release,[74] it was acknowledged that there was 'evidence that the abusive use of six growth hormones for growth promotion purposes creates a significant increase in risk'.

This was the main conclusion of the report by the SCVPH and a draft report on the assessment of risks of hormonal growth promoters in cattle arising from abusive use and difficulties of control. Both reports were made public and sent to the US and Canada for comment.

The press release went on to say:

Human exposure and risk are in particular increased by the fact that regulatory controls over residues of hormones in meat placed on the market are deficient in the USA and are insufficient in Canada. There is a clear potential for adverse effects on human health arising especially from the presence of residues of these hormones in undetected implantation sites following the misplacement of implants.

'Abusive use' could include the misplacement of approved implants, off-label uses of hormonal growth promoters, the use of multiple implants either simultaneously or within very short intervals of time and the use of unapproved substances obtained on the black market.

The main deficiencies highlighted in the report were:

... in the USA and Canada, hormonal growth promoters are freely available over the counter. They can be obtained without veterinary prescription and used without supervision by a vet;

although there are regulations which requires that implants be used only on the animal's ear, there is proof that implantations are made or injections given on other parts of the animal's body;

---

74 Health and Consumer Protection Directorate, General Press Release, 27 May 1999, 'Abusive use and difficulties of control of growth hormones increase risks', http://europa.eu.int/comm/dg24/library/ptrss/press25_eu.html

when implantation sites (that is, the parts of the animal's body that have had a hormone implant inserted into them) enter the food chain, the risk to human health increases. The example is given that a single implantation site can contaminate 4,000 glasses of baby food to such an extent that consuming even one glass would result in a dose to a baby of up to 33 times of what would be acceptable consumption for one day;

although hormonal growth promoters are not approved for use in veal calves recent Canadian surveys showed residues of the synthetic hormone trenbolone in 32–40% of liver samples from veal calves;

melengestrol acetate, which is approved for use in heifers only, has been proven to be used in male animals too;

in the USA and Canada, repeated treatment of animals is common;

unapproved hormonal substances are available on the black market;

neither the US nor the Canadian meat inspection regulations provide for regular checks of animal carcasses for misplaced implants, even though in 1986 the US meat inspection service reported widespread misuse of hormone implants;

within the framework of the US National Residue Program, the residue testing is either non-existent or deficient;[75]

the lack or insufficiency of residue control programmes and/or their insufficient enforcement increases the probability of not detecting misplaced implants, off-label uses and the use of black market substances;

the lack of adequate residue control programmes increases the probability of human exposure and risk;

each of the documented scenarios is cumulative and the effects may be additive.

As far as the risks of misuse were concerned, the SCVPH concluded that higher doses and more frequent applications will obviously result in higher residue concentrations in the tissues of treated animals. One of the concerns which was acknowledged in the press release was that there is a potential risk of extremely high residue levels, if implants are misplaced, particularly if the total content of an implant is present in a single portion of minced meat or in a batch of meat products.

As indicated above, the SCVPH concluded that, for 17-oestradiol, there is a substantial body of evidence suggesting that it has to be considered a complete carcinogen, but it was not possible to quantify the risk. For the other five hormones, the available information was incomplete and did not allow a

---

75 No tests have ever been performed on four of the substances: three of the hormones (17-estradiol, progesterone and testosterone) and trenbolone acetate. No residue tests have been performed for zeranol since 1989 and for melengestrol acetate, no tests have been performed since 1990. No residue testing has ever been performed as part of that programme for illegal hormonal growth promoters other than DES.

quantitative estimate of the risk, however, a risk to consumers was identified. Of particular relevance to the SCVPH is that even exposure to small traces in meat carries risks. No threshold levels can be defined for any of the six substances. Of the various susceptible risk groups, prepubertal children is the group of greatest concern.

The opinion of the SCVPH was elaborated in full awareness of the 17 ongoing studies and with direct scientific feedback from the experts involved. However, the SCVPH was not involved in the setting up and management of the studies. The Commission intends to allow completion of the few still ongoing from the 17 scientific studies, and will keep the SCVPH fully informed of progress and results. It is important to note that, in the meantime, the SCVPH has concluded that very significant gaps in current knowledge exist.

The results of the 17 studies were made available to the scientific community and have since been made publicly available by the scientists concerned through presentations and publication in scientific journals following the normal peer review process, which may take several months.

The US had, on 17 May 1999, requested the Dispute Settlement Body of the WTO to authorise the suspension of the application to the EC and its Member States of tariff concessions covering trade in an amount of US $202 m per year. A similar request was made by Canada on 20 May 1999 for an amount of CDN $75 m per year. The EC objected to the level of suspension proposed by the US and Canada, and, on 12 July 1999, the WTO Arbitrator determined that the level of nullification or impairment suffered by the US and Canada was US $116.8 m per year, and CDN $11.3 m per year, respectively.

The US suspended the application of tariff concessions by imposing a 100% *ad valorem* rate of duty on mainly agricultural products from 29 July 1999. On 1 August 1999, Canada also imposed 100% ad valorem tariffs on, in particular, beef and pork products.

Since adoption of the SCVPH opinion on 30 April 1999, some new reports have been published on this subject. In the light of this information, the Commission asked the SCVPH to either confirm that there is no recent scientific information that would lead it to revise its previous opinion, or to revise the relevant parts of the opinion as necessary. On 3 May 2000, the SCVPH delivered an opinion[76] that recent scientific reports did not provide convincing data and arguments requiring a revision of the conclusion drawn in their opinion of 30 April 1999.

---

76 Review of specific documents relating to the SCVPH opinion of 30 April 1999 on the potential risks to human health from hormone residues in bovine meat or meat products.

In the light of that opinion, the Commission concluded that it would not be appropriate to lift the existing ban on the use of growth promoting hormones for meat production. The Commission also took the view that the strength of the evidence as presented in the opinion of 30 April 1999 against 17-oestradiol is strong enough to justify a permanent ban on its use for any purposes for farm animals. For the other hormones, the SCVPH outlined areas where more information was required. For this reason, the Commission considered that a provisional ban would be in compliance with the ruling of the Appellate Body, while recognising the need to seek further information and to review the measures in the light of future evidence.

In reaching its opinion of 3 May 2000, the SCVPH reviewed a number of documents in deciding whether or not to depart from its decision of 30 April 1999.

The SCVPH examined the Committee on Veterinary Medicinal Products' opinions and summary reports on 17-oestradiol and progesterone for zootechnical and therapeutic purposes from December 1999, and the October 1999 report of the UK's Veterinary Products Committee sub-group on the SCVPH opinion of 30 April 1999. The SCVPH also considered other relevant literature, including a report by the FAO/WHO Joint Expert Committee on Food Additives (JECFA).

The SCVPH's comments and conclusions were as follows:

2.2 Comments

The advisory working group as well as SCVPH reviewed the above mentioned documents thoroughly and discussed all comments submitted. However, re-consideration of the previous opinion (SCVPH 1999) in light of these documents, leads the Committee to state again its concerns.

Briefly, these concerns were that an increased exposure to hormones can be associated with an increased risk of cancer and detrimental effects in development. Most of these effects have been demonstrated following high dose exposure in experimental animals, as well as human beings, at different stages of development (including adulthood). However, particularly in regard to the subject of estrogenic effects during development, there is no compelling evidence suggesting that these effects do not also occur at low doses. More importantly, if endogenous levels of hormones are associated with life-time risk of disease, for example, human breast cancer, then continuous additional exposure, even at low doses, is likely to add to this risk, but, as yet, cannot be quantified.

The SCVPH Committee's report of April 1999 identified several important considerations, linked to the use of hormones for growth promoting purposes in food producing animals. These include:

- the possible consequences of continuous daily exposure – even to low levels of hormones – to all segments of the human population, including at the most susceptible periods (*in utero* and prepubertal);

- the risk to the consumer posed by the use of synthetic hoffilones in implants, although the database for a comprehensive evaluation of these synthetic compounds is obviously incomplete;

- the risk posed by higher hormone doses that might be present in meat, when hormonal implants are inappropriately used. These implant residues may end up in the diet of either the population at large or an individual consumer.

The SCVPH opinion stated that hormones exert their effects differently, at different stages of life. Concerns have been expressed that the current state of the art does not allow a reliable quantitative risk assessment to be made with respect to the impact of hormones, and particularly 17-oestradiol, the most abundantly used hormone for growth promoting purposes. All segments of the human population, including the developing embryo, foetus and prepubertal children, are susceptible. New published data argue for low doses of natural and synthetic estrogens having a deleterious effect on the normal development of secondary sex organs in experimental settings.

Data from epidemiological and experimental studies provided strong evidence that 17-oestradiol exposure is the most consistent risk factor in breast cancer. Consequently, any added exposure through exogenous hormones is likely to increase the lifetime risk for these cancers, but as yet cannot be quantified.

Adequate exposure assessment requires, first, an inventory of the physiological variation in hormone production during the entire human life span – bearing in mind that these physiological levels have been associated with hormone-dependent cancers, and, secondly, the knowledge of hormone concentrations in food commodities. Novel techniques in chemical analysis allow for quantification of very low hormone levels, even below those levels considered at present to be physiological. It is expected that these more sensitive methods will be applied to measure thoroughly endogenous and environmental estrogens (including dietary ones) in different human populations. Therefore, additional time will be required to validate and apply this methodology in a reliable, accepted fashion before a re-evaluation of this issue can be conducted.

A large number of investigations have focused on elucidating the mechanisms by which hormones cause cancer. A relatively recent and unique aspect of this research concerns the genotoxic potential of these compounds, in particular 17-oestradiol. Studies showing a lack of correlation between the estrogenic and carcinogenic potencies of certain estrogens (and their metabolites) have led to the hypothesis that besides oestrogen-receptor mediated effects, DNA damage effects may contribute to carcinogenicity.

Whilst 17-oestradiol failed to show any direct and indirect effects in conventional mutagenicity assays, evidence is accumulating that 17-oestradiol and/or its metabolites are capable of directly damaging DNA. Considering these more recent data, the Joint FAO/WHO Expert Committee on Food Additives, which very recently published its toxicological evaluation of the natural hormones 17-oestradiol, progesterone and testosterone in animal production (WHO Food Additive Series, 43/2000), also concluded that oestradiol has a genotoxic potential. Concerning progesterone and testosterone, the data presented with this evaluation did not identify essentially new information.

Any disparities between the various evaluation reports are based on the different interpretation of individual research data. Some authors argue that the dietary exposure to residual amounts of oestradiol, progesterone and testosterone comprises an acceptable risk for the consumer, as these natural hormones (but not the synthetic hormones) occur naturally in meat. Others stress the fact that the new scientific evidence suggests an increased lifetime risk for certain forms of cancers and the possibility of detrimental developmental effects even at low dose of added dietary exposure. Thus, although the evaluation reports show a high degree of consensus, the degree of acceptance of the risk related to the use of hormones in animals is modulated by their intended use, that is, defined medicinal applications versus abundant use for growth promotion purposes, taking into account the resultant consumer exposure.

2.3 Conclusion

The reports of the UK's Veterinary Products Committee subgroup and of the Committee on Veterinary Medicinal Products presented for review to the Scientific Committee, as well as recent scientific information, did not provide convincing data and arguments demanding revision of the conclusions drawn in the opinion of the SCVPH of 30 April 1999 on the potential risks to human health from hormone residues in bovine meat and meat products.

The SCVPH discussed again the obvious gaps in the present knowledge on metabolism and residue disposition of the hormones under consideration, including the synthetic hormones. The SCVPH expects that the ongoing EU research programs will provide additional data on both topics.

On 24 May 2000, the Commission proposed revised legislation banning hormones as growth promoters. The Commission adopted a proposal to amend its existing legislation (Council Directive 96/22/EC) on the prohibition of the use of hormones as growth promoters. The decision was made in the light of the opinion of the SCVPH, quoted above and adopted on 3 May 2000. As can be seen, the SCVPH unanimously agreed to reiterate its opinion of April 1999 that the use of hormones as growth promoters in cattle poses a health risk to consumers. The Commission considered that the presentation of this proposal represented another step towards the implementation of the Community's international obligations under Art 51 of the WTO Sanitary and Phytosanitary Agreement, whilst maintaining its chosen high level of health protection. In light of the confirmation of the scientific opinion, the Commission proposed to ban definitively the use of 17-oestradiol and its ester-like derivatives in farm animals both for growth promotion and therapeutic purposes and zootechnical treatment. The Commission also proposed to maintain the current prohibition on the five other hormones on a provisional basis (testosterone, progesterone, trenbolone acetate, zeranol and melengestrol acetate) while it sought more complete scientific information.

These provisions will be kept under regular review. They will apply to Member States and imports from third countries alike. The revision of the Directive will be decided by the European Parliament and the Council in co-decision procedure as soon as possible. The proposal foresees entry into force of the revised legislation by 1 July 2001 at the latest.

Bovine somatotropin (BST)

BST is a hormone which is secreted by the pituitary gland in cattle which regulates body functions such as growth and milk production.

Studies showed that the cows which produced the most milk had higher levels of BST in their blood than those with a lower milk yield. Stock breeders tried to enhance this trait, and between 1954 and 1987 they managed to more than double milk production.

Scientists found that they could get between 10% and 25% more milk by injecting cows with BST and that the cows needed to eat between 10% and 20% more feed to keep up with the increased production.

The effects of BST have been known for many years, but the only source of it used to be the carcasses of slaughtered animals and, since the pituitary gland is very small, it was economically prohibitive to use BST commercially. Nowadays, through the use of biotechnology, BST can be produced cheaply.

A moratorium on the placing on the market and use of BST in dairy cows was introduced in the EC in 1990. It was extended by the Council in 1994 until 21 December 1999. In October 1999, the Commission put forward a proposal to ban outright the use and marketing of BST in dairy cattle in the EU with effect from 1 January 2000. The ban will not affect the import of meat or dairy products from third countries. Before putting forward its proposal, the Commission had requested the opinions of two scientific committees, which were delivered in March 1999.

The Scientific Committee on Animal Health and Animal Welfare (SCAHAW) adopted its report, entitled Animal Welfare Aspects of the Use of Bovine Somatotrophin, on 10 March 1999. It stated that the use of BST increases the risk of clinical mastitis as well as the duration of treatment of mastitis. The report also stated that the use of BST increases the incidence of foot and leg disorders and that it can adversely affect reproduction and cause severe reactions at the site of the injection.

Directive 98/58[77] on the protection of animals kept for farming purposes states that no other substance with the exception of those given for therapeutic or prophylactic purposes shall be administered to an animal unless it has been demonstrated by scientific studies of animal welfare or established experience that the effect of the substance is not detrimental to the health or welfare of the animal. BST is not used in cattle for therapeutic purposes and it was the opinion of the SCAHAW that BST should not be used in dairy cows.

---

77 Council Directive 98/58/EC.

The Scientific Committee on Veterinary Measures Relating to Public Health (SCVPH), in its opinion of 16 March 1999, acknowledged that significant gaps existed in scientific knowledge on the possible effects of the use of BST on the health of the public, and requested further studies.

In December 1999, the European Parliament adopted a resolution supporting the Commission's proposal to convert the moratorium into a permanent ban.

In the UK, the Veterinary Products Committee (VPC), which provides expert advice to ministers on the quality, efficacy and safety of veterinary medicinal products, established a new working group on the safety on BST (recombinant bovine somatotropin) in 1999 to consider scientific information on the human and animal safety aspects of the use of BST. The work of the group forms the basis of the advice given by the VPC to Agriculture and Health Ministers.

CHAPTER 8

FOODS FOR PARTICULAR NUTRITIONAL PURPOSES[1]

Directive 89/398[2] is the framework Directive dealing with foodstuffs for particular nutritional uses. It covers foodstuffs whose composition and preparation must be specially designed to meet the particular nutritional need of the category of people for whom they are primarily intended. The Directive has been supplemented by later directives dealing with specific groups of nutritional foodstuffs.

Directive 89/398 defines foodstuffs for particular nutritional uses as foodstuffs which 'owing to their special composition of manufacturing process, are clearly distinguishable from foodstuffs for normal consumption, which are suitable for their claimed nutritional purposes and which are marketed in such a way as to indicate such suitability' (Art 1(2)(a)).

The particular nutritional use must satisfy one of the following requirements (Art 1(2)(b)):

- it must be prepared for certain persons whose digestive processes or metabolism are disturbed;
- it must be prepared for persons who are in a special physiological condition and who benefit from consuming such products; or
- it must be prepared for healthy infants and young children.

Under the Directive, foods which come within the first two categories are referred to as 'dietetic' or 'dietary' and may be labelled as such. No other foods, labelled under the framework labelling Directive 79/112, may use these terms unless they have been authorised under the procedure laid down in Directive 89/398. For other foodstuffs, an application must be made to the Commission and the Standing Committee for Foodstuffs to get permission to label them as 'suitable' for nutritional/dietary purposes. Specific labelling to that effect must follow the procedures laid down in Directive 89/198.

Under the Directive, nutrition claims are prohibited and, therefore, the labelling and advertising of these foodstuffs must not attribute to them or imply any ability to prevent, cure or treat diseases. An application may be made to the Commission and the Standing Committee on Foodstuffs for a derogation from this rule to allow a nutritional claim.

---

1 In the UK, 'foods for particular nutritional purposes' is abbreviated to 'PARNUTS'.
2 Council Directive 89/398/EEC on the approximation of the laws of the Member State relating to foodstuffs intended for particular nutritional uses (OJ 1989 L186/27) as amended by European Parliament and Council Directive 96/84/EC (OJ 1977 L48/20).

tuffs for particular nutritional uses must indicate on the label their
r nutritional characteristics. Foodstuffs for particular nutritional uses,
ch no specific Directive has been adopted, must also include the
following information on the label:

- qualitative or quantitative composition or the particular manufacturing process which gives the product its particular characteristics; and

- the energy value in kilojoules and kilocalories and the amount of protein, carbohydrate and fat per 100 grammes or 100 millilitres of the final product (Art 7(3)).

Where a nutritional product is placed on the market for the first time and is not covered by one of the specific directives, the manufacturer or importer must inform the competent authority in the relevant Member State and supply an example of the label it intends to use. The same information must be submitted to the competent authority of any other Member State where the product is to be placed on the market. The producer may also be required to provides the various competent national authorities with the scientific data that establishes the food's compliance with the provisions of Directive 89/398 (the framework Directive), especially the labelling provisions. Member States are not allowed to restrict trade in these foods if the foods comply with Directive 89/398. However, if a Member State is concerned that a particular product might pose a danger to health it may temporarily prohibit that product from entering its territory and suspend trade in that product. The Member State concerned must inform all other Member States and the Commission. The Commission will consider the issue in conjunction with the Standing Committee on Foodstuffs (SCF) and, if it believes that the national measure should be withdrawn, it will initiate proceedings, seeking an opinion from the SCF and ultimately a vote in the Council to overturn the national measure.

The Annex of the original Directive listed nine 'groups of foods for particular nutritional uses for which specific provisions will be laid down by specific directives'. The categories of products requiring specific provisions has now been reduced to five by Directive 99/41,[3] adopted in May 1999, following a meeting of the Conciliation Committee. The five categories are:

(a) infant formulae and follow on formulae;

(b) cereal-based foods and baby foods for infants and young children;

(c) foods intended for use in energy-restricted diets for weight loss;

(d) dietary foods for special medical purposes;

(e) foods intended to meet the expenditure of intense muscular effort, especially for sportsmen.

---

3   European Parliament and Council Directive 99/41/EC (OJ 1999 L172/38).

Directives have already been adopted for the first three categories. A decision on whether or not to introduce special provisions for foods intended for diabetics is due to be taken after a transition period during which there will be further consultations between the Commission and the Scientific Committee on Food. The decision must be taken by 8 July 2002.

The European Parliament had introduced an amendment to Directive 99/41 to ban any pesticide residues in foodstuffs for infants and young children. The amendment was withdrawn during the Conciliation Committee, after the Commission agreed to bring forward proposals on pesticide residues which will amend the specific Directives on Baby Foods (Directives 96/4 and 96/5).

Directive 99/41 also provides that low sodium and gluten free foods can be placed on the market once rules for the use of terms like 'reduced sodium content' and 'absence of gluten' are adopted in accordance with the procedure outlined in Art 13 of Directive 89/398.

SPECIFIC DIRECTIVES

Infant and follow-on formulae

Directive 91/321,[4] as amended by Directive 96/4,[5] contains compositional and labelling requirements for foods which are produced for babies and very young children. 'Infant formulae' are foods produced for the particular nutritional needs of infants during the first four to six months of life. 'Follow-on formulae' are foods intended for the particular nutritional needs of infants over the age of four months and which constitute the main liquid element in a diet which is becoming progressively diversified. Both infant and follow-on formulae must be manufactured from protein sources specified in Annexes to the Directive or from other food ingredients where their suitability for the particular nutritional use of infants has been established by generally accepted scientific evaluation.

The compositional requirements for both formulae are listed in the Annexes to the Directive. The Directive states that, to make the formulae ready to eat, only the addition of water should be necessary. Annex 3 lists the nutritional substances which may be added to the formulae in order that they satisfy those compositional requirements (vitamins, minerals, amino acids and other nitrogen compounds and certain other limited substances). In addition, there are certain mandatory labelling requirements. The labelling must include the following statements or information:

4   Council Directive 91/321/EEC (OJ 1991 L175/35).
5   Commission Directive 96/4/EC (OJ 1996 L49/12).

(a) that infant formula does not contain added iron;

(b) that infant formula is suitable for babies who are not being breast fed;

(c) that follow-on formula should form only part of a diversified diet;

(d) the energy value of the product;

(e) the average amount of every mineral substance in the product;

(f) information about the preparation for use of the product and warnings of the health risks if the product is not properly prepared.

The food label on infant formulae must include a statement specifying that breast feeding is to be preferred and must not include pictures of infants which might tend to idealise the product. Infant formulae may only be advertised in scientific publications and publications specialising in baby care. Member States are free to restrict further or prohibit the advertising of these products.

Processed cereal-based foods

Directive 96/5[6] covers processed cereal-based foods and baby foods for use by infants while they are being weaned and by young children as a supplement to their diet and /or for their progression onto ordinary food.

In the UK, the relevant Regulations are the Processed Cereal-based Foods and Baby Foods for Infants and Young Children Regulations 1997.[7] These Regulations came into force on 31 March 1999.

Definitions

Baby foods are defined as foods for particular nutritional use fulfilling the particular requirements of infants and young children in good health and intended for use by infants while they are being weaned, and by young children as a supplement to their diet or for their progressive adaptation to ordinary food other than processed cereal-based foods.

Processed cereal-based foods are defined as foods for particular nutritional use within specified categories (see list below) and fulfilling the particular requirements of infants and young children in good health and intended for use by infants while they are being weaned and by young children as a supplement to their diet or for their progressive adaptation to ordinary food.

Requirements

(1) No person shall sell any processed cereal-based food or baby food unless:

(a) it is labelled as specified below; and

---

6   Commission Directive 96/5/EC (OJ 1996 L49/17).

7   SI 1997/2042.

(b) it complies with the requirements as to manufacture and composition set out below.

(2) The Regulations do not apply to any baby food which is a milk intended for young children.

Categories of processed cereal-based foods

(1) Simple cereals which are or have to be reconstituted with milk or other appropriate nutritious liquids.

(2) Cereals with an added high protein food which are or have to be reconstituted with water or other protein-free liquid.

(3) Pastas which are to be used after cooking in boiling water or other appropriate liquids.

(4) Rusks and biscuits which are to be used either directly or after pulverisation with the addition of water, milk or other suitable liquids.

Composition of processed cereal-based foods

The following table gives the specified essential composition of processed cereal-based foods for infants and young children. The requirements concerning nutrients refer to the products ready for use, marketed as such or reconstituted as instructed by the manufacturer.

Composition of baby foods

There is a table which indicates the specified essential composition of baby foods for infants and young children. The requirements concerning nutrients refer to the products ready for use, marketed as such or reconstituted as instructed by the manufacturer.

Labelling

(1) Processed cereal-based food and baby food shall be labelled with the following particulars –

(a) a statement as to the appropriate age (not less than four months) from which the food may be used, regard being had to its composition, texture or other particular properties;

(b) information as to the presence or absence of gluten if the age stated according to a) is less than six months;

(c) the available energy value (expressed in kJ and kcal), and the protein, carbohydrate and fat content (expressed in numerical form, per 100 g or 100 ml of the food as sold and, where appropriate, per specified quantity of the food as proposed for consumption);

(d) the average quantity (expressed in numerical form, per 100 g or 100 ml of the food as sold and, where appropriate, per specified quantity of the food as proposed for consumption) of each mineral substance and of each vitamin in respect of which a maximum or a minimum compositional requirement is specified [in a table in the Regulations]; and

(e) if preparation of the food is necessary, appropriate instructions for preparation and a statement as to the importance of following those instructions.

(2) Subject to para 1(d) above, no person shall label processed cereal-based food or baby food with the average quantity of any nutrient specified in the Regulations (see list in Regulations) unless –

   (a) that average quantity is expressed in numerical form, per 100 g or 100 ml of the food as sold and, where appropriate, per specified quantity of the food as proposed for consumption; and

   (b) in the case of a mineral substance or vitamin, it is a mineral substance or vitamin other than one referred to in paragraph (1)(d) above.

(3) Where processed cereal-based food or baby food is labelled with the average quantity of any specified vitamin or mineral, the labelling of the food shall not express that average quantity as a percentage of the relevant specified reference value, given in the ... table, unless the quantity present is equal to 15% or more of the reference value.

In April 2000, the Commission issued draft amendments to Directives 96/5/EC (processed cereal-based foods) and 91/321/EEC (baby foods for infants and young children and infant formulae and follow-on formulae). The proposals fulfil European Commission obligations, laid down in Directives 99/50/EC and 99/39/EC, to draw up a list of pesticides which will not be used in agricultural products intended for use in the manufacture of infant formulae and baby foods respectively. They would extend existing controls laid down in these directives which already limit the maximum level of individual pesticides permitted in these foods to 0.01 mg/kg as consumed. The proposals would amend the Commission's directives on the labelling and composition of infant formula and follow-on formula.

As stated above, both Directives have a maximum residue limit for any individual pesticide of 0.01 mg/kg. Following a review by the Scientific Committee on Food of the acceptable daily intake (ADI) of pesticides, the Commission proposed that the use of pesticides with an ADI of below 0.0005 mg/kg body weight should be prohibited in agricultural products for use in the production of processed cereal-based foods and baby foods, infant formulae and follow-on formulae. The proposal listed 27 pesticides with a recommended ADI of below 0.0005 mg/kg and which it is therefore proposed to ban.[8]

---

8 The following is the list of pesticides which, it is proposed, shall not be used in agricultural products intended for the production of processed cereal-based foods and baby foods and gives the JMPR ADI (mg/kg bw) for information only:

Aldrin 0.0001
Cadusafos 0.0003
Carbophenothion 0.0005
Chlordane 0.0005

Food for weight reduction

Directive 96/8[9] covers foods intended for use in energy restricted diets for weight reduction. These are products which, when used as instructed by the manufacturer, replace all or part of the normal daily diet. There are two categories of such products:

(a) food products presented as a replacement for the whole of the daily diet and sold as 'total diet replacement for weight control';

(b) food products intended as replacements for one or more meals of the daily diet and sold as 'meal replacement for weight control'.

Annex 1 lists the compositional criteria as regards energy value, protein, fat, dietary fibre, vitamins and minerals, with which these products must comply.

As far as labelling is concerned, the products must comply with the requirements of the framework Directive 79/112 and there are also further requirements contained in Directive 96/8. The product label must include the following information:

(a) the available energy value;

(b) the amount of every vitamin and mineral;

(c) instructions for correct preparation;

Chlorfenvinphos 0.0005
Demeton-S-methyl 0.0003
Demeton-S-methylsulphoxide 0.0003
Dieldrin 0.0001
Disulfoton 0.0003
Endrin 0.0002
Ethoprophos 0.0004
Fensulfothion 0.0003
Fentin acetate 0.0005
Fentin chloride 0.0005
Fentin compounds 0.0005
Fentin hydroyde 0.0005
Fipronil 0.0002
Raloxyfop 0.0003
Heptachior 0.0001
Heptachlor epoxide 0.0001
Monocrotophos 0.0006
Oxydemeton-methyl 0.0003
Phorate 0.0005
Phosphamidon 0.0005
Propylenethiourea 0.0003
PTU 0.0003
Terbufos 0.0002

9   Commission Directive 96/8/EC (OJ 1995 L55/22).

(d) a statement on the importance of maintaining an adequate daily intake of fluids.

Products replacing the whole of the daily diet must also state that they contain an adequate amount of all essential daily nutrients and a statement that the product should not be used for more than three weeks without medical advice.

The labelling of foods intended for weight reduction must not include any claim as to the rate or amount of weight loss which could result from the use of such products or any other related claims.

In the UK, the relevant Regulations are the Foods Intended for Use in Energy Restricted Diets for Weight Reduction Regulations 1997.[10]

These Regulations came into force on 31 March 1999.

Definitions

Relevant food is specially formulated food intended for use in energy restricted diets for weight reduction, being food which complies with the specified compositional given below and which, when used as instructed by the manufacturer, replaces: (a) the whole of the total daily diet; or (b) one or more meals of the daily diet.

Compositional requirements

The following specifications refer to the products ready for use, sold as such or reconstituted as instructed by the manufacturer.

Name of the food

(1) No person shall sell any relevant food under any name other than:

   (a) 'total diet replacement for weight control' in the case of products intended as a replacement for the whole of the daily diet; or

   (b) 'meal replacement for weight control' in the case of products intended as a replacement for one or more meals of the daily diet.

(2) No person shall sell any food in the labelling of which the name 'total diet replacement for weight control' or 'meal replacement for weight control' is used unless that food is relevant food.

Labelling, advertising and presentation

(1) No person shall sell any relevant food unless it is labelled with the following particulars:

   (a) the available energy value expressed in kJ and kcal, and the content of proteins, carbohydrates and fat, expressed in numerical form, per specified quantity of the product ready for use as proposed for consumption;

---

10   SI 1997/2182.

(b) the average quantity of each mineral and each vitamin for which compositional requirements are specified in the table, expressed in numerical form, per specified quantity of the product ready for use as proposed for consumption and, for meal replacements for weight control, that average quantity expressed as a percentage of the values as set out in the tables of minerals and vitamins in the Food Labelling Regulations 1996;

(c) instructions for appropriate preparation, where necessary, and a statement as to the importance of following those instructions;

(d) where a product, when used as instructed by the manufacturer, provides a daily intake of polyols in excess of 20 g per day, a statement to the effect that the food may have a laxative effect;

(e) a statement on the importance of maintaining an adequate daily fluid intake;

(f) for total diet replacements for weight control, a statement that the product provides adequate amounts of all essential nutrients for the day and a statement that the product should not be used for more than three weeks without medical advice; and

(g) for meal replacements for weight control, a statement to the effect that the product is useful for the intended use only as part of an energy-restricted diet and that other food should be a necessary part of such diet.

(2) No person shall sell any relevant food the labelling, advertising or presentation of which refers to the rate or amount of weight loss which may result from its use or to a reduction in the sense of hunger or an increase in the sense of satiety.

Packaging

No person shall sell any total diet replacements for weight control unless all individual components making up the product are contained in the same package.

Defence in relation to exports

It is a defence to prove:

(a) that the food is intended for export to a country which has legislation analogous to these Regulations and that such food complies with that legislation; and

(b) that the legislation complies with the provisions of Commission Directive 96/8 on foods intended for use in energy-restricted diets for weight reduction, in the case of export to an EEA State.

Food supplements

As early as 1991, the Commission indicated that it was of the view that there was a need to establish a single market for food supplements. At the Summit meeting in 1992, it was decided by the Government representatives of the

Member States not to take any action on this issue as it was not felt to be necessary. In 1997, however, following a huge increase in the use of food supplements, the Commission issued a discussion paper on the subject,[11] in which it reconsidered the need for the harmonisation of standards in this largely unregulated market.

In May 2000, the European Commission adopted a proposal for a Directive on Food Supplements setting out harmonised rules for the sale of vitamins and minerals as dietary supplements. The proposal is a response to an increase in the use of pills and capsules as dietary supplements and to varying national rules and attitudes to these products. The objective of the proposal is twofold: first, to set out a general framework and safety rules for vitamins and minerals in the European Union; and secondly, to give the consumer detailed information such as recommended daily consumption, a warning about exceeding this limit or a breakdown of contents of minerals and vitamins to enable them to make informed choices. David Byrne, the EU Commissioner for Health and Consumer Protection, said:

> These food supplements mainly serve to compensate for inadequate intake of essential nutrients by certain people or specific population groups, or, for some, to increase their intake of such nutrients. Labels on these products must give consumers adequate and clear information about how to use and how not to use them. For those who find they require supplements, we must make sure that the chemical substances used to produce vitamins and mineral supplements are safe and subject to independent scientific assessment. These principles of food safety and transparent information as outlined in the White Paper on Food Safety apply here as they do to all other food products.

Under the new proposed rules, labels on, for example, bottles of vitamin pills will have to include a recommendation for a daily dose, a warning about possible health risk in case of excess use, and a statement that the pills should not be used as a substitute for a varied diet. Claims that the product can prevent, treat or cure illness are prohibited. Any language suggesting that a varied diet does not provide the necessary amounts of essential nutrients is also prohibited. Pills sold in packaging which resembles that of pharmaceutical products must carry the statement 'This is not a medicinal product'.

The proposed Directive includes a list of chemical substances that are authorised for the production of vitamins and minerals following their scientific assessment by the Scientific Committee for Food. The proposal also foresees that maximum and minimum levels of vitamin and mineral content in the daily dose of food supplements will be set.

The proposal for a Directive on Food Supplements is part of the package of measures announced in the Commission's White Paper on Food Safety. It is

---

11 Commission Discussion Paper on Addition of Vitamins and Minerals to Foods and Food Supplements III/59349?.

based on Art 95 and has to be agreed by the European Parliament and the Council of Ministers in co-decision. It is intended to enter into force on 31 May 2002, allowing the marketing of products complying with the directive as of June 2002 and prohibiting the marketing of products which do not respect its rules by June 2004 at the latest.

The Directive lays down certain definitions:

(a) 'food supplements' means foodstuffs that are concentrated sources of nutrients as specified in (b), alone or in combination, marketed in dose form, whose purpose is to supplement the intake of those nutrients in the normal diet;

(b) 'nutrients' means the following substances: (i) vitamins listed in point 1 of Annex I; (ii) minerals listed in point 2 of Annex I;

(c) 'dose form' means forms such as capsules, tablets, pills and other similar forms, sachets of powder, ampoules of liquids and drop dispensing bottles.

Annex I contains a list of vitamins and minerals which may be used in the manufacture of food supplements.

CHAPTER 9

FOOD HYGIENE

GENERAL ISSUES

Poor hygiene in the production and preparation of food can lead to food poisoning and can have serious and immediate consequences for the public. There is a great deal of concern among consumers about food hygiene and an increasing awareness on the part of politicians and their advisers that strict and effective food hygiene legislation is essential in order to increase and maintain consumer confidence in the food they buy and eat. Because a breach of food hygiene rules and a failure to maintain adequate standards of hygiene can have immediate effects on the consumer, by making them ill very soon after consuming the food, hygiene is often regarded as a more obvious concern than, for example, the potential dangers of food additives, chemical contaminants, hormone and drug residues and genetic modification.

In recent years, there seems to have been a marked increase in the number and frequency of food poisoning outbreaks which has led to growing public concern about the safety of food.

At present, Directive 93/43/EEC EEC on the hygiene of foodstuffs[1] lays down general rules on hygiene and procedures for verification of compliance with these rules. The Directive covers the preparation, processing, manufacturing, packaging, storage, transportation, distribution, handling and offering for sale or supply of foodstuffs not covered elsewhere by product-specific hygiene directives. It also covers gaps in the product-specific directives. For example, few of the product-specific directives cover the sale and supply of their products and where this is the case, Directive 93/43 will apply.

In the UK, Directive 93/43/EEC has been implemented by the Food Safety (General Food Hygiene) Regulations 1995.[2] The Regulations place obligations on the proprietors of food businesses to ensure that their activities are carried out in a hygienic way.

Directive 96/3/EC grants a derogation from certain dedicated transport provisions contained in Directive 93/43 as regards the transport of bulk liquid

---

1   Council Directive 93/43/EEC (OJ L175, 19.7.93), p 1.
2   SI 1995/1763. These Regulations also implement Council Directive 80/778/EEC (OJ 1980 L229) on the quality of water for human consumption where it relates to water used in food production.

oils and fats by sea.[3] Commission Directive 98/28/EC grants a derogation from certain dedicated transport provisions regarding the bulk transport of raw sugar by sea.[4]

In July 2000, the European Commission introduced proposals for new food safety hygiene rules, described as 'The most radical shake up for 25 years of the Community's food safety hygiene rules'.[5] Under the proposals, contained in four Regulations, food operators right through the food chain will have primary responsibility for food safety. The new regulations are intended to merge, harmonise and simplify very detailed and complex hygiene requirements that are, at present, contained in more than 17 existing directives. The aim of the new legislation is to make a single, transparent hygiene policy applicable to all food and all food operators, 'from the farm to the table', together with effective instruments to manage food safety and any future food crises throughout the whole of the food chain.

The legislative proposals will take the form of Council and European Parliament Regulations, rather than Directives. This will ensure uniform application throughout the EU. It is also hoped that, by using Regulations, this will lead to greater transparency and will make it easier to update the Regulations in the light of new technical and scientific developments. The Regulations are to be adopted jointly by the Council and the EP, using the co-decision procedure. They will replace Directive 9/43 and 16 product-specific Council Directives.[6]

---

3   Implemented in the UK by the Imported Food Regulations 1997 (SI 1997/2537), reg 10 (Sched 2) of which amends the General Food Hygiene Regulations of 1995.

4   Implemented in the UK by the Food Safety (General Food Hygiene) (Amendment) Regulations 1999 (SI 1999/1360).

5   Health and Consumer Protection Directorate, General Press Release, Brussels, 17 July 2000.

6   The following Directives will be withdrawn:
    Directive 64/433/EEC (fresh meat)
    Directive 71/118/EEC (poultry meat)
    Directive 72/461/EEC (fresh meat)
    Directive 77/96/EEC (trichina examination)
    Directive 77/99/EEC (meat products)
    Directive 80/215/EEC (meat products)
    Directive 89/362/EEC (milking hygiene)
    Directive 89/437EEC (egg products)
    Directive 91/492/EEC (live bivalve molluscs)
    Directive 91/493/EEC (fishery products)
    Directive 91/494/EEC (poultry meat)
    Directive 91/495/EEC (rabbit meat and farmed game meat)
    Directive 92/45/EEC (game meat)
    Directive 92/46/EEC (milk and milk products)
    Directive 92/48/EEC (fishing vessels)
    Directive 93/43/EC (foodstuffs)
    Directive 94/65/EC (minced meat).

The press release makes it clear that the Regulations will set down objectives, rather than prescribing specific safety measures in great detail. This is to allow businesses the flexibility to decide what safety measures to take.

The basic principles underlying the new hygiene rules are, first, the introduction of the 'farm to the table' principle to hygiene policy. Currently, there is no systematic hygiene regime covering all food in all sectors, but rather a 'patchwork' of rules for specific sectors and types of produce with gaps notably at primary production level, namely farms.

A second important principle is to give food producers the primary responsibility for the safety of food through the use of programmes for self-checking and modern hazard control techniques. The implementation of a harmonised Hazard Analysis Critical Control Point (HACCP) system will become obligatory for all non-primary food operators. This type of self-checking programme is already in place in parts of the food industry, such as the larger food factories, but is not yet required in, for example, slaughterhouses. HACCP prescribes a logical series of steps to identify throughout the production chain points where control is critical to food safety and to focus on the specific hazards particular to the business concerned.

In most food businesses, checking the quality of raw materials, avoiding bacterial contamination, maintaining the cold chain during storage and transport and appropriate anti-bacterial heat treatment are critical in controlling safety. Companies will be obliged to keep records of safety checks carried out under HACCP for surveillance purposes. On farms, Codes of Good Practice will be used as the safety management instrument rather than full HACCP implementation, which is considered to be somewhat over-ambitious in the farming context at present.

A third important principle is to ensure the traceability of all food and food ingredients. To achieve this, compulsory registration of all food businesses will be introduced. Record keeping to enable the identification of suppliers of ingredients and foods will be made obligatory. Producers must also put in place procedures for the withdrawal from the market of products presenting a serious risk to consumer health.

The basic hygiene rules that are part of standard operating procedures of food businesses – cleanliness of premises, washing hands before handling food, etc – will remain as before.

The Commission has acknowledged that the implementation of harmonised hygiene rules has, in the past, proved difficult in traditional food production and in food businesses in geographically isolated regions. In order to ensure flexibility, the responsibility for adapting the rules to such local situations is left to Member States, since they are better placed to judge and find appropriate solutions, provided the basic principle of food safety is not compromised.

Implementation of an HACCP system implies the involvement of staff with specialised skills, which small and medium enterprises (SMEs) may not have. It is therefore envisaged that special arrangements to facilitate HACCP implementation in SMEs will be introduced, such as the development of sector-specific codes of good hygiene practice.

There is a second proposal for a regulation on additional hygiene rules for food of animal origin, such as meat and processed meat products, fishery products and dairy products. The existing legislation is, in many respects, very detailed and prescriptive, but the new text will introduce greater flexibility. The intention is that, in the longer term, with the implementation of the HACCP framework, further simplification will be possible. At the same time, new rules to reduce contamination of carcasses at slaughter will be introduced, and a certain level of detail will be maintained in view of the special risks in this area. The Commission will evaluate the experience with this more flexible approach to find the right balance between streamlining and the need for detailed rules.

Controls by national authorities

The third proposal deals with the obligations of the veterinary authorities in the Member States, and begins the process of separating responsibilities and introducing the 'farm to fork' principle. More updated inspection and control procedures for ante and post mortem inspection of animals at slaughter are to be put forward within this framework on a solid scientific basis – as envisaged in the White Paper on Food Safety for September 2001. The current proposal allows the Member States more flexibility in setting up veterinary controls. For example, in meat cutting plants, controls by trained meat inspectors acting under the responsibility of a qualified vet will be sufficient.

The fourth proposal consolidates, updates and improves the transparency of animal health measures that are at present contained in seven different directives. Finally, there is a proposal for a directive to repeal 17 existing directives, while leaving the implementing decisions in force.

ZOONOSES

Zoonoses are diseases and infections that can be transmitted naturally between humans and other vertebrates. One of the best known examples of a zoonosis is the Salmonella bacterium which is able to survive and multiply in animals. Humans can become ill if they eat animal products that are contaminated with Salmonella. All EC legislation that deals with the hygiene of products from animal origins contains provisions to control zoonoses. There is also Council Directive 92/117/EEC,[7] which deals with the protection of human health from specified zoonoses. The Directive contains rules for the collection of information, at both national and Community level, on zoonoses and zoonotic diseases. The competent authorities in all Member States must evaluate information on the prevalence of zoonoses and zoonotic agents in food establishments such as slaughterhouses and food manufacturing plants and report every year to the Commission on trends and sources of zoonotic infections.

The Commission White Paper on Food Safety indicates in the action plan that there is to be a proposal for amendments to Directive 82/117/EEC with the aim of improving the monitoring and reporting of zoonotic diseases.

---

7   Council Directive 92/117/EEC (OJ 1993 L62/38).

CHAPTER 10

RISK ANALYSIS

Risk analysis is an increasingly important issue in relation to food. Manufacturers and producers of food products are required to undertake risk analysis to ensure that their processes are safe. Governments and international organisations undertake risk analysis to help them to develop policies and practices on food safety. There are three elements to risk analysis: risk assessment, risk management and risk communication. These are the accepted elements, although they overlap and, to deal with the issue of risk analysis in a coherent way, it is necessary to consider them as a whole rather than attempt to deal with them separately.

Risk assessment involves identifying and characterising the hazard, assessing the exposure to the risk and characterising the nature of the risk. Risk management involves evaluating the risk, assessing the available options for managing the risk, implementing the decision on how to manage the risk and monitoring and reviewing the management of the risk. Risk communication involves decisions as to what information should be communicated to whom, and when it should be communicated.

The importance now given to the issue of risk analysis is evident from the flurry of activity at international, European and national level in recent years. The issue of risk analysis with regard to food has become particularly important following the adoption of the WTO Sanitary and Phytosanitary Agreement. The agreement specifies that countries should base their SPS measures on 'international standards, guidelines and recommendations'. However, there is a clause which allows for the use of risk assessment techniques and the setting of 'an appropriate level of protection'. These are set out in Art 5:

Article 5 – Assessment of Risk and Determination of the Appropriate Level of Sanitary or Phytosanitary Protection

5(1) Members shall ensure that their sanitary or phytosanitary measures are based on an assessment, as appropriate to the circumstances, of the risks to human, animal or plant life or health, taking into account risk assessment techniques developed by the relevant international organizations.

Under 5(1), SPS measures must be based on a risk assessment. The article refers to 'risk assessment techniques developed by the relevant international organisations'. For food, this is the Codex Alimentarius Commission. This is the basis for much of the present focus within the Codex Committee on risk analysis and risk assessment.

5(2) In the assessment of risks, Members shall take into account available scientific evidence; relevant processes and production methods; relevant inspection, sampling and testing methods; prevalence of specific diseases or pests; existence of pest- or disease-free areas; relevant ecological and environmental conditions; and quarantine or other treatment.

5(3) In assessing the risk to animal or plant life or health and determining the measure to be applied for achieving the appropriate level of sanitary or phytosanitary protection from such risk, Members shall take into account as relevant economic factors: the potential damage in terms of loss of production or sales in the event of the entry, establishment or spread of a pest or disease; the costs of control or eradication in the territory of the importing Member; and the relative cost-effectiveness of alternative approaches to limiting risks.

5(4) Members should, when determining the appropriate level of sanitary or phytosanitary protection, take into account the objective of minimizing negative trade effects

5(5) With the objective of achieving consistency in the application of the concept of appropriate level of sanitary or phytosanitary protection against risks to human life or health, or to animal and plant life or health, each Member shall avoid arbitrary or unjustifiable distinctions in the levels it considers to be appropriate in different situations, if such distinctions result in discrimination or a disguised restriction on international trade. Members shall cooperate in the Committee, in accordance with paras 1, 2 and 3 of Art 12, to develop guidelines to further the practical implementation of this provision. In developing the guidelines, the Committee shall take into account all relevant factors, including the exceptional character of human health risks to which people voluntarily expose themselves.

5(6) Without prejudice to para 2 of Art 3, when establishing or maintaining sanitary or phytosanitary measures to achieve the appropriate level of sanitary or phytosanitary protection, Members shall ensure that such measures are not more trade-restrictive than required to achieve their appropriate level of sanitary or phytosanitary protection, taking into account technical and economic feasibility.

5(7) In cases where relevant scientific evidence is insufficient, a Member may provisionally adopt sanitary or phytosanitary measures on the basis of available pertinent information, including that from the relevant international organizations as well as from sanitary or phytosanitary measures applied by other Members. In such circumstances, Members shall seek to obtain the additional information necessary for a more objective assessment of risk and review the sanitary or phytosanitary measure accordingly within a reasonable period of time.

Art 5(7) refers to cases where insufficient scientific evidence is available when members follow a precautionary approach (the 'precautionary principle'). It is clear, however, that these precautionary measures must only be 'provisional' and reviewed 'within a reasonable period of time'. The use of this article is supposed to be limited in time, although this is not precisely defined.

5(8) When a Member has reason to believe that a specific sanitary or phytosanitary measure introduced or maintained by another Member is constraining, or has the potential to constrain, its exports and the measure is not based on the relevant international standards, guidelines or recommendations, or such standards, guidelines or recommendations do not exist, an explanation of the reasons for such sanitary or phytosanitary measure may be requested and shall be provided by the Member maintaining the measure.

The Codex Alimentarius Commission (CAC) is also involved in the development of principles to govern the issue of risk analysis. In 1999, the CAC sent a request[1] to Codex contact points and interested international parties for comments on the 'working principles for risk analysis developed by the Codex Committee on General Principle (CCGP). In the proposed draft working principles, the purpose of risk analysis is stated to be 'the protection of public health'. The draft goes on to state that the three components of risk analysis (risk assessment, risk management and risk communication) should be documented separately and systematically with the documentation accessible to interested parties. To use the risk analysis process in an effective way, there is a need for 'communication and interaction where appropriate between the parties involved in these three components' (para 1). The proposal continues:

2 The risk analysis procedures used by the Codex and those used by other relevant international intergovernmental [and non-governmental] bodies should be harmonised where appropriate.

3 The needs of developing countries should be specifically identified and addressed in the different stages of the risk analysis process.

4 The risk analysis process used in the Codex should be seen as consistent, open and transparent.

In the proposed draft it is stated that:

The principles for risk analysis are intended for application in the framework of Codex and are also intended to provide advice to governments where applicable [para 1] and that the primary purpose of risk analysis in Codex is the protection of the health of consumers [para 2].

The proposal goes on to state:

(3) The objective of the Working Principles is to ensure that Codex standards and related texts intended to protect the health of consumers are consistently based on a thorough risk analysis.

(4) Within the framework of Codex, the responsibility for risk management lies with the Commission and its subsidiary bodies, while the responsibility for risk assessment normally lies with the Joint FAO/WHO Expert Committees and Consultations.

The draft proposals identify the principles on which Risk Analysis within the Codex is to be based.

---

1   Codex Alimentarius Commission, Request for Comments on Working Principles For Risk Analysis, CL 1999/16-GP, July 1999.

Risk Analysis – General Aspects

1 The risk analysis process used in Codex should be consistent, open and transparent and follow a structured approach including three components of risk analysis (risk assessment, risk management and risk communication), each component being integral to the overall risk analysis process.

2 The three components of risk analysis should be documented fully and systematically in a transparent manner, with the documentation accessible to interested parties.

3 Effective communication and consultation with interested parties should be ensured throughout the risk analysis process as appropriate.

4 There should be a functional separation of risk assessment and risk management, in order to ensure the scientific integrity of the risk assessment and reduce any conflict of interest between risk assessment and risk management. However it is recognized that risk analysis is an iterative process, and interaction between risk managers and risk assessors are essential for practical application.

5 The situations where scientific evidence is insufficient or negative effects are difficult to evaluate should be clearly identified, in order to ensure that adequate precaution is integrated in the risk analysis process.

6 The needs of developing countries should be specifically identified and addressed in the different stages of the risk analysis process.

The Codex Alimentarius Commission has adopted Statements of Principle that lay down the standards which should govern all decisions taken at Codex Meetings. These principles will therefore also govern decisions on risk analysis.

Statements of Principle Concerning the Role of Science in the Codex Decision-Making Process and the Extent to Which Other Factors Are Taken into Account[2]

1 The food standards, guidelines and other recommendations of Codex Alimentarius shall be based on the principle of sound scientific analysis and evidence, involving a thorough review of all relevant information, in order that the standards assure the quality and safety of the food supply.

2 When elaborating and deciding upon food standards Codex Alimentarius will have regard, where appropriate, to other legitimate factors relevant for the health protection of consumers and for the promotion of fair practices in food trade.

3 In this regard it is noted that food labelling plays an important role in furthering both of these objectives.

4 When the situation arises that members of Codex agree on the necessary level of protection of public health but hold differing views about other considerations, members may abstain from acceptance of the relevant standard without necessarily preventing the decision by Codex.

Statements of Principle Relating to the Role of Food Safety Risk Assessment[3]

---

2   Decision of the 21st Session of the Commission, 1995.

1 Health and safety aspects of Codex decisions and recommendations should be based on a risk assessment, as appropriate to the circumstances.

2 Food safety risk assessment should be soundly based on science, should incorporate the four steps of the risk assessment process, and should be documented in a transparent manner.

3 There should be a functional separation of risk assessment and risk management, while recognizing that some interactions are essential for a pragmatic approach.

Risk analysis in the European Union

On 2 February 2000, the European Commission adopted a Communication on the use of the precautionary principle. The objective of the Communication was to inform all interested parties how the Commission intends to apply the principle and to establish guidelines for its application. The aim was also to provide input to the ongoing debate on this issue both at EU and international level. The Communication underlines that the precautionary principle forms part of a structured approach to the analysis of risk, as well as being relevant to risk management. It covers cases where scientific evidence is insufficient, inconclusive or uncertain, and preliminary scientific evaluation indicates that there are reasonable grounds for concern that the potentially dangerous effects on the environment, human, animal or plant health may be inconsistent with the high level of protection chosen by the EU. The Communication can be seen as complementing the Commission's White Paper on Food Safety and the agreement reached in Montreal on the Cartagena Protocol on Bio-safety.

The Communication also qualifies the measures that may be taken under the precautionary principle. Where action is deemed necessary, measures should be proportionate to the chosen level of protection, non-discriminatory in their application and consistent with similar measures already taken. The measures taken should also be based on an examination of the potential benefits and costs of action or lack of action and subject to review in the light of new scientific data and should thus be maintained as long as the scientific data remain incomplete, imprecise or inconclusive and as long as the risk is considered too high to be imposed on society. Finally, they may assign responsibility or the burden of proof for producing the scientific evidence necessary for a comprehensive risk assessment. These guidelines guard against unwarranted recourse to the precautionary principle as a disguised form of protectionism.

The Communication acknowledged that a number of recent events had undermined the confidence of public opinion and consumers because decisions or absence of decisions were not supported by full scientific evidence and the legitimacy of such decisions was questionable. It

---

3   Decision of the 22nd Session of the Commission, 1997.

emphasised that the Commission had consistently tried to achieve a high level of protection in areas such as the environmental and human, animal and plant health fields. It is the Commission's policy to take decisions aimed to achieve this high level of protection on a sound and sufficient scientific basis. Where there are reasonable grounds for concern that potential hazards may affect the environment or human, animal or plant health, and when at the same time the lack of scientific information precludes a detailed scientific evaluation, the Communication recognises that the precautionary principle is the politically accepted risk management strategy in several fields.

Although the precautionary principle is not explicitly mentioned in the EC Treaty except in relation to the environment, the Commission considers that this principle has a scope far wider than the environment field and that it also covers the protection of human, animal and plant health.

The Communication makes it clear that the precautionary principle is neither a politicisation of science nor the acceptance of zero-risk, but that it provides a basis for action when science is unable to give a clear answer. The Communication also made clear that determining what is an acceptable level of risk for the EU is a political responsibility. The precautionary principle provides a reasoned and structured framework for action in the face of scientific uncertainty and is not a justification for ignoring scientific evidence and taking protectionist decisions.

It was anticipated that the horizontal guidelines established in this Communication would provide a useful tool in the future for taking political decisions and would contribute to legitimate decisions taken when science proved unable to assess completely the risk rather than decisions based on irrational fears or perceptions.

Thus, one of the objectives of the Communication was to describe the situations in which the precautionary principle could be applied and to determine the scope of measures taken in this respect to ensure the proper functioning of the internal market as well as a high level of protection and predictability for consumers and economic operators located in the EU and elsewhere.

Communication from the Commission on the precautionary principle

Summary

1 The issue of when and how to use the precautionary principle, both within the European Union and internationally, is giving rise to much debate, and to mixed, and sometimes contradictory views. Thus, decision-makers are constantly faced with the dilemma of balancing the freedom and rights of individuals, industry and organisations with the need to reduce the risk of adverse effects to the environment, human, animal or plant health. Therefore, finding the correct balance so that the proportionate, non-discriminatory, transparent and coherent actions can be taken, requires a structured decision-making process with detailed scientific and other objective information.

2 The Communication's fourfold aim is to:

– outline the Commission's approach to using the precautionary principle,

– establish Commission guidelines for applying it,

– build a common understanding of how to assess, appraise, manage, and communicate risks that science is not yet able to evaluate fully, and

– avoid unwarranted recourse to the precautionary principle, as a disguised form of protectionism.

It also seeks to provide an input to the ongoing debate on this issue, both within the Community and internationally.

3 The precautionary principle is not defined in the Treaty, which prescribes it only once – to protect the environment. But in practice, its scope is much wider, and specifically where preliminary objective scientific evaluation indicates that there are reasonable grounds for concern that the potentially dangerous effects on the environment, human, animal or plant health may be inconsistent with the high level of protection chosen for the Community.

The Commission considers that the Community, like other WTO members, has the right to establish the level of protection – particularly of the environment, human, animal and plant health – that it deems appropriate. Applying the precautionary principle is a key tenet of its policy, and the choices it makes to this end will continue to affect the views it defends internationally, on how this principle should be applied.

4 The precautionary principle should be considered within a structured approach to the analysis of risk which comprises three elements: risk assessment, risk management, risk communication. The precautionary principle is particularly relevant to the management of risk.

The precautionary principle, which is essentially used by decision-makers in the management of risk, should not be confused with the element of caution that scientists apply in their assessment of scientific data. Recourse to the precautionary principle presupposes that potentially dangerous effects deriving from a phenomenon, product or process have been identified, and that scientific evaluation does not allow the risk to be determined with sufficient certainty. The implementation of an approach based on the precautionary principle should start with a scientific evaluation, as complete as possible, and where possible, identifying at each stage the degree of scientific uncertainty.

5 Decision-makers need to be aware of the degree of uncertainty attached to the results of the evaluation of the available scientific information. Judging what is an 'acceptable' level of risk for society is an eminently political responsibility. Decision-makers faced with an unacceptable risk, scientific uncertainty and public concerns have a duty to find answers. Therefore, all these factors have to be taken into consideration. In some cases, the right answer may be not to act or at least not to introduce a binding legal measure. A wide range of initiatives is available in the case of action, going from a legally binding measure to a research project or a recommendation. The decision-making procedure should be transparent and should involve as early as possible and to the extent reasonably possible all interested parties.

6 Where action is deemed necessary, measures based on the precautionary principle should be, *inter alia*:

– proportional to the chosen level of protection,

– non-discriminatory in their application,

– consistent with similar measures already taken,

– based on an examination of the potential benefits and costs of action or lack of action (including, where appropriate and feasible, an economic cost/benefit analysis),

– subject to review, in the light of new scientific data, and

– capable of assigning responsibility for producing the scientific evidence necessary for a more comprehensive risk assessment.

Proportionality means tailoring measures to the chosen level of protection. Risk can rarely be reduced to zero, but incomplete risk assessments may greatly reduce the range of options open to risk managers. A total ban may not be a proportional response to a potential risk in all cases. However, in certain cases, it is the sole possible response to a given risk.

Non-discrimination means that comparable situations should not be treated differently, and that different situations should not be treated in the same way, unless there are objective grounds for doing so. Consistency means that measures should be of comparable scope and nature to those already taken in equivalent areas in which all scientific data are available. Examining costs and benefits entails comparing the overall cost to the Community of action and lack of action, in both the short and long term. This is not simply an economic cost-benefit analysis: its scope is much broader, and includes non-economic considerations, such as the efficacy of possible options and their acceptability to the public. In the conduct of such an examination, account should be taken of the general principle and the case law of the Court that the protection of health takes precedence over economic considerations.

Subject to review in the light of new scientific data, means measures based on the precautionary principle should be maintained so long as scientific information is incomplete or inconclusive, and the risk is still considered too high to be imposed on society, in view of chosen level of protection. Measures should be periodically reviewed in the light of scientific progress, and amended as necessary. Assigning responsibility for producing scientific evidence is already a common consequence of these measures. Countries that impose a prior approval (marketing authorisation) requirement on products that they deem dangerous *a priori* reverse the burden of proving injury, by treating them as dangerous unless and until businesses do the scientific work necessary to demonstrate that they are safe. The precautionary measure might be taken to place the burden of proof upon the producer, manufacturer or importer, but this cannot be made a general rule.

Risk analysis in the UK

In July 2000, a group led by Sir Robert May, the Chief Scientific Adviser, issued a report on the way in which risk is handled by the Government's scientific advisory committees dealing with food safety.[4] The report was requested by the Prime Minister. The group[5] asked the chairmen of the relevant scientific advisory committees to give details on the way in which their committee approaches risk assessment; how information about risk is communicated and the role of their committee in risk management. The review group also met the committee chairmen to discuss how their committee used risk assessment and 'tested out on them' the review group's own ideas about 'the robustness of the ways in which risk is currently assessed, managed and communicated'.

The report described the nature of the issue as follows:

5 Risk and food safety are complex and emotive issues. Hard evidence of the risks involved can often be incomplete or even absent. The scientific committees that advise Government on food safety have a key and valued role to play through their consideration of evidence and assessment of risks. Their work may involve a study with no direct precedent, or be part of a routine approval process, or be in response to departments faced with an emergency situation and needing urgent advice. Our key findings were:

- Committees' risk practices vary considerably, largely reflecting differences in their tasks.

- The stages of the risk analysis process (risk assessment, risk communication and risk management) are closely linked and cannot be neatly separated.

- Advisory committees' openness has increased, but communication could still be better.

In its conclusions, the report acknowledges that the work of the many committees that advise the Government on food safety is 'complex and diverse'. The group believes that in general, the system is working well, but that there are a number of areas where clearer responsibilities and processes and greater openness 'would help to strengthen it further'.[6] They divide their conclusions into two categories: the relationship between the Government and committees and best practice for committees:

The relationship between the Government and committees

Departments and agencies should ensure that the right questions are asked of their advisory committees when seeking advice on the assessment of a particular risk.

Departments and agencies should set out any constraints when asking committees to advise on risk management options.

Government, and not its advisory committees, is responsible for taking decisions on the management of risk, and needs to take an abiding interest in

---

4   *Review of Risk Procedures Used by the Government's Advisory Committees Dealing With Food Safety*, July 2000.

5   Sir Robert May, Chief Scientific Adviser, Professor Liam Donaldson, Chief Medical Officer and Sir John Krebs, Chairman of the Food Standards Agency.

6   Paragraph 17.

matters of risk, although committees may be best placed to advise on management options.

The distinction between voluntary and involuntary risks, the needs of vulnerable groups, as well as the implications for risk management standards need to be fully recognised by both Government and advisory committees.

Best practice for committees

Advisory committees will usually be helped by following a formal structure for the process of risk assessment, even when the scientific facts are cloudy, disputed or even unknown.

Advisory committees should be open at all stages of the risk assessment process and in their consideration of options for risk management, and find ways of being as open as possible when there are commercial confidentiality constraints.

Training should be made generally available to the members and secretariats of advisory committees to enable them to convey the complexities and uncertainties surrounding some food safety issues. We are asking the Cabinet Office to facilitate this.

Advisory committees dealing with food safety issues should establish better links and lines of communication with each other in order to ensure a coherent and consistent approach to risk. These might be achieved through cross-membership, occasional joint meetings, circulation of papers or discussions between the secretariats.

Advisory committees should, when appropriate, set out a range of risk management options for policy makers, together with their implications, to avoid placing unnecessary constraints upon the decision making process.

CONCLUSION

It is often said that people are becoming increasingly 'risk averse' and less likely to accept that almost everything one does in life entails some element of risk. This is particularly true with regard to food. While consumers have every right to expect that food will be manufactured, packaged, distributed and sold in a safe and hygienic manner and that at every stage in the process potential risks will have been identified and, as far as possible, eliminated, consumers themselves must also take responsibility for their own safety.

With the increasing use of pre-prepared 'ready meals' there is concern that people no longer have the knowledge previous generations had about how to store, prepare and cook food. While home economics classes in school concentrate on how to design suitable packaging for a food product rather than how to cook it, there is a real danger that future generations will have very little idea about how to handle food and a very limited understanding and awareness of where their food comes from and how it it is grown or reared.

The never ending demand for cheaper food has in the recent past led to some highly dubious farming and production practices that have resulted in tragic consequences for both humans and animals.

International and national bodies are very active in developing legislation and regulations governing the assessment, management and communication of risk. Prevention of further catastrophes such as BSE also depends on people showing some respect for the way in which animals are treated and fed and for the environment in the way in which crops are grown.

There is a clear connection between what we feed our animals and spray on our crops and the safety of the food we eat.

CHAPTER 11

BIBLIOGRAPHY

Advisory Committee on the Microbiological Safety of Food, *Report on Microbial Antibiotic Resistance in Relation to Food Safety*, 1999, London: HMSO

Advisory Committee on Novel Foods and Processes, *Guidelines on the Assessment of Novel Foods and Processes*, 1991, Department of Health Report on Health and Social Subjects 38

Advisory Committee on Novel Foods and Processes, *Report on the Use of Antibiotic Resistance Markers in Genetically Modified Food Organisms*, July 1994

Advisory Committee on Novel Foods and Processes, *Report of the Use of Antibiotic Resistance Marker in Genetically Modified Plants for Human Food: Clarification of Principles for Decision Making*, July 1996

Advisory Committee on Novel Foods and Processes, paper on the toxicological assessment of novel foods, 1998, available from the ACNFP website at www.maff.gov.uk/food/novel/nfrregn.htm

Bradgate, R, and Howells, G, *The Food Safety Act 1980*, 1980, London: Blackstone

Bradgate, R and Howells, G, 'Food safety – an appraisal of the new law', [1991] J Bus Law 320

Codex Alimentarius Commission, Joint FAO/WHO Food Standards Programme, *Report of the 21st Session of the Codex Committee on Food Labelling* (draft) ALINORM 99/22A, 1999, Rome: FAO/WHO

Codex Alimentarius Commission, Joint FAO/WHO Food Standards Programme, *Report of the 21st Session of the Codex Committee on Nutrition and Foods for Special Dietary Uses*, ALINORM 99/26, 1999, Rome: FAO/WHO

Codex Alimentarius Commission, Joint FAO/WHO Food Standards Programme, *Report of the First Session of the Codex Ad Hoc International Task Force on Foods Derived from Biotechnology*, 2000, Rome: FAO/WHO

Donaldson, L and May, R, *Health Implications of Genetically Modified Foods*, 1999, London: HMSO

FAO/WHO, *Joint FAO/WHO Expert Consultation on Biotechnology and Food Safety*, 1995, Rome: FAO/WHO

FAO/WHO Consultation: *Strategies for Assessing the Safety of Foods Produced by Biotechnology*, 1991

Food Standards Agency, *Food Law Guide*, August 2000

Gold, HS and Moellering, Jr (MD), 'Anti-microbial drug resistance' (1996) 35 New England Journal of Medicine 1445

Gourlie, K, 'Food labelling: a Canadian and international perspective' (1995) 53 Nutrition Review 103

Harvey, J and Mason, L, 'The use and misuse of antibiotics in UK agriculture' Part 1: Current Usage, 1998, The Soil Association

Horton, LR, 'International harmonization and compliance', in *Nutrition Labeling Handbook*, 1995, New York: Marcel Dekker

Howells, G, Bradgate, D and Griffiths, J, *Blackstone's Guide to the Food Safety Act 1990*, 1990, London: Blackstone

Howie, J, 'The situation in the UK – then and now', in *Ten Years on from Swann*, 1981, London: Association of Veterinarians in Industry, Royal College of Physicians pp 3–7

House of Lords, *Resistance to Antibiotics and Other Antimicrobial Agents*, 1998, London: HMSO

House of Lords, 'Lords lead fight against killer bugs', press information, London, 23 April 1998

House of Lords Select Committee on Science and Technology (Sub-Committee 1), *Inquiry into Resistance to Antimicrobial Agents*, April 1998

Jones, P, Clark Hill, C, Hillier, D and Shears, P, 'Food retailers' responses to the GM controversy within the UK' (2000) 102(5/6) British Food Journal 441 (MCB UP, Bradford)

Jukes, D, *Review of the Statements of Principle on the Role of Science and the Extent to which Other Factors should be Taken into Account*, (1) 'Role of science in relation to risk analysis' and (2) 'Application in the case of BST', 1999, papers prepared for Codex Committee on General Principles, Reading, available at www.fst.rdg.ac.uk/foodlaw/codex

Jukes, D, 'The Codex Alimentarius Commission – current status', 1998, Food Science and Technology Today, reproduced at www.fst.rdg.ac.uk/foodlaw/codex

Jukes, D, *Food Legislation of the UK – A Concise Guide*, 4th edn, 1997, London: Butterworths

Lewis, CJ, 'Harmonisation, mutual recognition and equivalence: labelling and nutritional requirements – how much information is necessary', paper delivered at FAO Conference on International Food Trade Beyond 2000: Science Based Decisions, Harmonisation, Equivalence and Mutual Recognition, 1999, Melbourne

Lewis, CJ, Randell, A and Scarborough, FE, 'Nutrition labelling of foods: comparisons between US Regulations and Codex guidelines' (1996) 7 Food Control 285

MAFF, *Report of the Committee on the Ethics of Genetic Modification and Food Use*, 1993, London: HMSO

Miles, S, Blaxton, D and Frewer, L, 'Public perceptions about microbiological hazards in food' (1999) 101(10) British Food Journal 744 (MCB UP, Bradford)

OECD, *Briefing on Activities in the OECD on Sustainable Development*, Agriculture and Natural Resource issue prepared by Wilfrid Legg, Head of Policies and Environment Division, April 2000, Paris: OECD

O'Rourke, R, *European Food Law*, 1998, Benbridge: Palladian Law

Painter, A (ed), *Butterworths' Law of Food and Drugs*, London: Butterworths

Royal Society, *Statement on Genetically Modified Plants for Food Use*, 3 September 1998

Royal Society, *Review of Data on Possible Toxicity of GM Potatoes*, 18 May 1999

Stapleton, J, *Product Liability*, 1994, London: Butterworths

Steinbrecher R and Ho, M, *Fatal Flaws in Food Safety Assessment: Critique of the Joint FAO/WHO Biotechnology and Food Safety Report*, 1996; *Safety Evaluation of Foods Derived Through Modern Biotechnology: Concepts and Principles*, 1993, Paris: OECD

Swann, MM, Blaxler, KL, Field, HI, Howie, JW, Lucas, AIM, Miller, ELM, Murdock, JC, Parsons, JH and White, EG, *Report of the Joint Committee on the Use of Antibiotics in Animal Husbandry and Veterinary Medicine*, Cmnd 4190, 1969, London: HMSO

Thompson, K, *The Law of Food and Drink*, 1996, Crayford: Shaw

WHO, *The Medical Impact of the Use of Antibiotics in Food Animals: Report of a WHO Meeting*, Berlin, 13–17 October 1997

Young, R, Cowe, A, Nunan, C, Harvey, J and Mason, L, *The Use and Misuse of Antibiotics in UK Agriculture'*, Part 2: 'Antibiotic resistance and human health', 1999, The Soil Association (amended)

INDEX